Richard Whately

The Kingdom of Christ

Delineated in two essays on our Lord's own account of His person and of the nature of His kingdom, and on the constitution, powers, and ministry of a Christian church as appointed by Himself. Sixth Edition

Richard Whately

The Kingdom of Christ

Delineated in two essays on our Lord's own account of His person and of the nature of His kingdom, and on the constitution, powers, and ministry of a Christian church as appointed by Himself. Sixth Edition

ISBN/EAN: 9783337164430

Printed in Europe, USA, Canada, Australia, Japan

Cover: Foto ©Lupo / pixelio.de

More available books at **www.hansebooks.com**

THE KINGDOM OF CHRIST

DELINEATED,

IN TWO ESSAYS

ON

OUR LORD'S OWN ACCOUNT OF HIMSELF,

AND ON THE

CHARACTER OF A CHRISTIAN CHURCH.

BY

RICHARD WHATELY, D.D.,

ARCHBISHOP OF DUBLIN.

THE SIXTH EDITION.

LONDON:
JOHN W. PARKER AND SON, WEST STRAND.
MDCCCLX.

TO THE CANDIDATES WHO RECEIVED

ORDINATION

AT CHRIST CHURCH, DUBLIN, NOVEMBER, MDCCCXL.

TO THE MOST REV. CHARLES DICKINSON, D.D., LORD BISHOP OF MEATH,*

WHOSE

CONSECRATION

TOOK PLACE IN THE SAME CHURCH,

DECEMBER, MDCCCXL.

AND TO THE BISHOPS AND CLERGY OF THE PROVINCE OF DUBLIN,

WHO ATTENDED THE TRIENNIAL

VISITATION

HELD IN AUGUST AND SEPTEMBER, MDCCCXLI.

This Volume,

CONTAINING THE SUBSTANCE OF THE DISCOURSES DELIVERED

ON THOSE OCCASIONS, RESPECTIVELY,

IS INSCRIBED,

WITH EARNEST WISHES FOR THEIR PRESENT AND ETERNAL WELFARE,

BY THEIR SINCERE FRIEND AND FELLOW LABOURER,

THE AUTHOR.

---

* Of this inestimable Prelate the Church was deprived by death, in July, 1842, subsequently to the first publication of this Volume. May those who were so happy as to know and to appreciate him, have the grace to profit by the rich legacy he has left them in his bright example!

PREFACE.

THE following Essays contain the substance of some Discourses not originally designed for the Press, but which I was strongly urged to publish by several of the persons to whom the Volume is inscribed.[1]

I have endeavoured to throw the materials into a form more suited for private perusal than that of the Discourses originally delivered. I fear, however, that in consequence of frequent interruptions during the preparation of the work for the Press,

---

[1] In the earlier part of the first Essay, I have been much indebted to a valuable Work which, for several years, I have been in the habit of recommending to divinity-students, —*Wilson on the Interpretation of the New Testament.* In the first edition this notice, though referred to in a foot-note to § 6, (as if inserted,) was accidentally omitted in this place.

In the second Essay I am indebted for some useful hints, to the valuable work of *Vitringa* (now rendered much more accessible by Mr. Bernard's abridged translation) on *The Synagogue and the Church*. The most important points, however, of coincidence of views between this writer and myself, are to be found, in substance, in works published before I was at all acquainted with Vitringa's.

some defects may be found in the arrangement and comparative development of the several topics, and other such imperfections in the composition, which can only be effectually guarded against by means of a period of unbroken leisure beyond what I can ever reasonably expect.

But whatever may be thought of the Work as a Composition, I trust that, in respect of the *matter* of it, the reader will give me credit for being incapable of putting forth, on subjects so important, any views that have not been carefully considered.

In fact, among the subjects here treated of are some on which I have not only reflected much, but have written and published, from time to time, for above twelve years past.

And it may not be impertinent here to remark, that in respect of some most important points now maintained, I may appeal (besides the arguments contained in the following pages) to the strongest of all external confirmations, the testimony of opponents. Not that I have ever written in a polemical form, or sought to provoke controversy; but by opponents, I mean, those who have maintained, and who still maintain, opinions opposite to those I have put forth; but who have never, to the best of my knowledge, even attempted any refutation of the reasons I have adduced.

For instance, that the introduction into the christian Religion of Sacrifices and Sacrificing-Priests is utterly at variance with the whole System of the Gospel, and destructive of one of its most important characteristics; and, again, that the implicit deference due to the declarations and precepts of Holy Scripture, is due to *nothing else*, and that it is not humble piety, but profane presumption, either to attribute infallibility to the traditions or decision of any uninspired Man or Body of men, (whether Church, Council, Fathers, or by whatever other title designated,) or, still more, to acknowledge in these, *although fallible*, a right to fix absolutely the interpretation of Scripture, to be blended therewith, and to supersede all private judgment,—these are positions which I have put forth, from time to time, for many years past, in various forms of expression, and supported by a variety of arguments, in several different works,[1] some of which have appeared in more than one edition. And though opposite views are maintained by many writers of the present day, several of them professed members of the Church of England, I have never seen even an attempted refutation of any of those arguments.

It cannot be alleged that they are not worth

---

[1] See *Essays*, (3rd Series,) Third Edition.

noticing: since, whether intrinsically weak or strong, the reception they have met with from the Public indicates their having had some influence.

And again, if any one is averse to entering into controversy, and especially personal controversy (a feeling with which I cordially sympathize,) this would not compel him to leave wholly unnoticed all the arguments that can be urged against his views.[1] It would be absurd to speak as if there were no medium between, on the one hand, engaging in a controversy, and on the other hand, passing over without any notice at all, everything that ever has been, or may be, urged on the opposite side. Nothing is easier, or more common, and I should add, nothing more advisable, than to notice in *general* terms the opinions or arguments opposed to one's own, and without reference to any particular book or author: as by saying, for instance, "Such and such a doctrine has been held:"—"this or that may be alleged;"—"some persons may object so and so," &c. In this way, not only personal controversy may be avoided, without undue neglect of what may be said on the opposite side, but also the advantage is gained (to the cause of truth, I mean) of confining the reader's attention to the real

---

[1] See *Essays*, (1st Series,) Preface.

merits of the case, independently of the extraneous circumstances,[1] which ought not to influence the decision.

It is true, no one should be required to notice every minor objection,—every difficulty relative to points of detail,—that may be alleged against any principle or system he is contending for; since there may be even valid objections against each of two opposite conclusions.[2] But this does not affect the present case; the arguments I am alluding to having relation to *fundamental principles*. Whatever any one may think of the soundness of those arguments, no one can doubt that, if admitted, they go to prove that the system contended against is (not merely open to objections, but) radically wrong throughout; based on false assumptions, supported by none but utterly fallacious reasoning, and leading to the most pernicious consequences.

And these arguments, though it is not for me to say that they are unanswerable, have certainly been hitherto, as far as I know, wholly unanswered, even by those who continue to advocate opposite conclusions.

Should it be asked why they do not either

---

[1] Ἔξω τοῦ πράγματος, Arist. *Rhet.*
[2] See *Logic*, b. iii. § 17.

abandon those conclusions, or else attempt a refutation of the reasons urged against them, *that* is evidently not a question for me, but for them, to answer. Else, an answer is not unlikely to occur to some minds, in the words of the homely proverb, "he that's convinced against his will, is of his own opinion still."

It is only, however, in reference to the subject-matter itself of the question under discussion—to the intrinsic soundness of the conclusions advocated—that the opinions and procedure of individuals can be worth the attention of the general reader. All that I wish to invite notice to, is, the confirmation that is afforded to the conclusiveness of arguments to which no answer is attempted, even by those who continue to maintain doctrines at variance with them.

All that has been said in reference to the positions above alluded to (which are among those maintained in the second of these Essays) will apply equally to some of those maintained in the first Essay: for instance, that Jesus knew He was understood to be claiming a *divine* character,—that to attempt the propagation or support of Gospel-truth by secular force, or by establishing in behalf of Christians, as such, a monopoly of civil rights, is utterly at variance with the true character of

Christ's Kingdom, and with the teaching and practice of Himself and his Apostles;[1] and that to attribute to them any such design, is to impugn their character, not merely as inspired Messengers from Heaven, but even as sincere and upright men.

These conclusions have been maintained by arguments which have been as long before the Public[2] as the others above alluded to, and have remained equally unanswered.

In respect of the greater part of the arguments alluded to, the above remark is as applicable as ever; but to a portion of them, objections have since appeared; most of which however had been answered by anticipation, in the second edition of this Volume, or in former Works. In a few places I have judged it advisable to insert some additional remarks and explanations, in further illustration of the principles maintained, and with a view to guard, as far as lies in myself, against all danger of misapprehension.

Independently however of these additions, I am well content to leave the questions at issue to

---

[1] See a very interesting pamphlet on the present condition of the Vaudois. (Murray, Albemarle Street.)

[2] Particularly in the Essay *On Persecution*, (Third Series,) and in Appendix E. and F. to the Essays *On the Dangers*, &c. (Fourth Series).

the judgment of intelligent and unbiassed readers who may think it worth while carefully to examine and compare the reasons on both sides.

Some elaborate criticisms have also appeared, of arguments and tenets that have been represented as mine, but so remote from any thing I have ever maintained, that I am left to suppose those criticisms must have been designed to meet the eyes of such persons only as have never read, nor are likely to read, the Works referred to, but are content to judge from report. I need only remark, that this affords some degree of presumption that what I really have said, is not—at least in the opinion of those opponents—open to refutation.

If in these, or in any other points, I am in error, I trust I shall be found open to conviction whenever my errors shall be pointed out. In the meantime, I trust I shall not be thought to have been unprofitably employed, in endeavouring more fully to elucidate, and to confirm by additional arguments, what appear to me to be momentous truths, and in developing some of the most important of the practical conclusions which result from them.

CONTENTS.

ESSAY I.

		PAGE
§ 1	Christ's own Account of Himself and of his Kingdom, at his two Trials	3
2	His Trial and Condemnation by the Jewish Council .	5
3	Jesus, the Son of God, in a peculiar sense . . .	8
4	Christ charged with *blasphemy*, as claiming to be the Son of God, in a sense authorizing *adoration* . .	9
5	Proofs that He was so understood	14
6	A *divine* Messiah not expected by the Jews . . .	17
7	Proofs that the sense in which He was understood, was that which He *designed*	19
8	His Testimony concerning Himself at his Trial, must have been *true*	21
9	His declarations concerning Himself, at his Second Trial,—that before Pilate	22
10	Sense in which his disclaimer of a Kingdom of this World is to be understood	27
11	Impiety of attributing to Him a *hidden* meaning . .	34
12	Spiritual Societies, and Secular, not to be confounded .	38
13	Intolerance, a natural accompaniment of Insincerity; Tolerance the Fruit of christian Faith and Knowledge	45

APPENDIX TO ESSAY I.

In what sense the *Political* Community is the *highest* . . 49

ESSAY II.

		PAGE
§ 1	CHRISTIANITY designed to be a social Religion	75
2	Properties of a Community	78
3	Rights divinely conferred on a christian Community	81
4	Constitution of the Jewish Church	83
5	How the Disciples would understand the commission given them	85
6	Penalties for ecclesiastical Offences	87
7	Power of the Keys	89
8	Procedure of the Disciples in conformity with their Master's directions	91
9	Christian Churches derived from Synagogues	94
10	Scanty Records of what relates to Church-government, and copious, of moral and doctrinal instructions	99
11	Remarkable circumstances in the matters of detail which they do record	101
12	Internal Evidence of the Gospel resulting from the above views	107
13	Things enjoined, things excluded, and things left at large	109
14	Christianity a Religion without Sacrifice, Altar, Priest, or Temple	111
15	The christian Church Universal has no one Spiritual Head on Earth	115
16	Importance of Points *excluded*	121
17	Contrary Errors opposed to the above Principles	122
18	Church Ordinances removed from a firm foundation and placed on one of sand	126
19	The English Reformers chose the true Foundation	128
20	Pretended Church-principles fatal to the christian hopes and privileges, even of their advocates	137
21	Appeal to the practice of the early Churches, an argument inaccessible to the great Mass of Christians	141

			PAGE
§ 22	Pretended decisions of the Catholic Church	. .	144
23	Appeals to supposed decisions, &c. of the Catholic Church, as superfluous as they are unsound	. .	152
24	The Articles, the Symbol embodying the deliberate decisions of our Church		156
25	Pretended distinction between co-ordinate and subordinate tradition		162
26	Alleged importance of human teaching	. . .	167
27	Use and abuse of human instruction .	. . .	171
28	The System of Reserve		173
29	Unsound Reasons brought in aid of sound ones .	.	176
30	Difficulty of ascertaining unbroken succession in the case of individuals		180
31	Increased Danger of Schism		189
32	Irregular formations of christian Communities .	.	191
33	Presumption in favour of the Church to which one actually belongs		197
34	Apprehension of what is called unsettling men's minds		199
35	Supposed case neither an impossible one, nor useless even if it were		202
36	Cases of a moral necessity for Separation .	. .	203
37	Mistakes to be guarded against by reformers when compelled to separation		206
38	Certain views seductive to the Feelings and Imagination		211
39	Case of *deposed* Bishops and Presbyters	. . .	216
40	System of traditionists incapable of being supported by clear argument		219
41	Fallacies resorted to on religious subjects .	. .	222
42	False views of what is christian Faith and Humility .		224
43	Principles of the Anglican Reformers	. . .	226

NOTES TO ESSAY II.

A. Enforcement of the Rules of an Ecclesiastical Society 230

		PAGE
B.	Extract from Lightfoot	234
C. D.	Extracts from *Essay on Omissions*	240 245
E.	Extract from *Encyclopædia Metropolitana*	247
F.	Extract from *Essay on Omissions*	251
G.	*Scripture* the interpreter of *Tradition*	252
H.	Extract from *Lesson on Evidences*	253
I.	Ambiguity of the phrase, *Authority of the Church*	257
K.	Extract from Dr. Hawkins on the *Ministry of Men*	260
L.	Extract from *Essay on Omissions*	262
M.	Extract from Luther	264
N.	Church-Government	266
O.	Apparent hostility and real coincidence, between *Rationalists* and advocates of *Reserve*	283
INDEX		287

ESSAY I.

ON

CHRIST'S OWN ACCOUNT

OF

HIS PERSON,

AND OF

THE NATURE OF HIS KINGDOM,

AS SET FORTH AT HIS TWO TRIALS.

Οὐδὲ εὑρέθη ΔΟΛΟΣ ἐν τῷ στόματι αὐτοῦ.

ESSAY I.

§ 1. TO any one who is convinced of the divine origin of the christian Religion,—who is satisfied that what is called in Scripture "The Kingdom of Heaven" does really deserve that title,—and who is inquiring into the personal character of its Founder, *Christ's own account of Himself and his kingdom, the first inquiry.* and into the nature of the Kingdom which He proclaimed and established, the most obvious and natural course would seem to be, to appeal, in the first instance, to that Founder Himself, and to consider what account He gave of his own character and that of his kingdom. For to believe Him sent from God, is to believe Him incapable of either deceiving or being deceived, as to these points. He must have understood both his own personal nature, and the principles of the religion He was divinely commissioned to introduce. Having a full reliance therefore both on his unerring knowledge, and his perfect veracity, our first inquiry should be, as I have said (without any disparagement of other sources of instruction) into the accounts He gave of Himself and his religion; both in the various discourses which He delivered and declarations which He made, on sundry occasions, and, most especially, on the great and final occasion of his being tried and condemned to death.

We collect from the sacred historians that He underwent *two* trials, before two distinct *Christ tried twice.*

tribunals, and on charges totally different; that on the one occasion He was found guilty, and on the other, acquitted; and that ultimately He was put to death under the one Authority in compliance with the condemnation which had been pronounced by the other.

Trial before the Sanhedrim first, and then before Pilate.

He was tried first before the Sanhedrim, (the Jewish Council,) "for blasphemy," and pronounced "guilty of death." Before the Roman governor, Pilate, (and probably before Herod[1] also) He was tried for rebellion, in setting up pretensions subversive of the existing Government; and was pronounced not guilty. The Jewish rulers had the will, but not the power, to inflict capital punishment on Him; Pilate had the power, and not the will. But though he "found no fault in Him," he was ultimately prevailed on by the Jews to inflict *their* sentence of death. "We[2] have a law," they urged, "and by our law He ought to die, because He made Himself the Son of God."

Of this most interesting and important portion of the sacred narrative, many persons, I believe, have a somewhat indistinct and confused notion; partly from the brevity, scantiness, and indeed incompleteness, of each of the four narratives, when taken alone; each evangelist recording, it may be supposed, such circumstances, as he was the most struck with, and had seen or heard the most of: and partly, again, from the commonly prevailing practice of reading the Scripture-histories irregularly, and in detached fragments, taken indiscriminately and without any fixed object, out of different books.[3]

---

[1] "No, nor yet Herod," &c. Luke, xxiii. 15.

[2] 'Ημεῖς is expressed in the original.

[3] The whole of the *New* Testament is read in this irregular mode, in the Second Lessons appointed in our Service; as these are appointed in reference to the day of the month only; and it is consequently a matter

This indistinctness a reader of ordinary intelligence may I think very easily clear away, by attentively studying and *comparing together* all the four accounts that have come down to us: and he will then find that this portion of the history, so examined, will throw great light on some of the most important points of Gospel-truth;—on those two great questions especially which were alluded to in the outset, as to the fundamental character of "the kingdom of Heaven," and the person of its Founder.

§ 2. When the Jewish Rulers and People were clamorously demanding the death of Jesus under sentence of the Roman Authorities, and Pilate in answer declared, that before his—the Roman—tribunal, no crime had been proved, saying, "Take ye Him and judge Him according to your law," his intention evidently was that no heavier penalty should be inflicted than the scourging, which was the utmost that the Jewish Authorities were permitted to inflict. But they replied that the crime of which they had convicted Him, was, by their law, *capital*, while yet they were restricted by the Romans from inflicting capital punishment; ("it is not lawful for *us* to put any man to death;") on which ground accordingly they called on the Governor to execute the capital sentence of *their* Court.

Application of the Jews to Pilate for infliction of capital punishment.

Their clamours prevailed, through Pilate's apprehension of a tumult,[1] and of himself incurring suspicions of disloyalty towards the

Pilate's motives for yielding.

---

of chance which of them shall fall on Sunday. This is one of the imperfections which a Church-government, if we had one, would not fail to remedy. See *Notes* to the Second Essay; and also *Charge*, 1844, and "Appeal," &c. in Bishop Dickinson's *Remains*.

[1] It seems to have been not unusual for the Roman Governors of Provinces to endeavour thus to prevent, or mitigate, or cut short, any

Emperor; which they had endeavoured to awaken by crying out that "if he let this man go, he was not Cæsar's friend: whosoever maketh himself a king, speaketh against Cæsar." But this was only brought forward as a plea to influence Pilate. The trial before the Jewish Council had nothing to do with the Roman Emperor, but was for "blasphemy," because "He made Himself the SON OF GOD."

Meanings of the expression, Son of God.

It is important, therefore, to inquire,—since this phrase may conceivably bear more than one meaning,—in what sense it was understood by those who founded on it the sentence of death.

God's Elect People called Sons.

In a certain sense all mankind may be called children of God.[1] In a more especial manner,—in a higher sense,—those are often called his children whom He has from time to time chosen to be his "peculiar People,"—to have his will revealed to them, and his offers of especial favour set before them. Such were the Israelites of old (to whom the title of Son is accordingly assigned by the Lord Himself, Exod. iv. 22,) as being the chosen [or "Elect"] People of God, called from among all the nations of the world to receive direct communications, and especial blessings from their Heavenly

---

tumult *not directed against the Roman power itself*, by yielding to the wishes of the populace, however unreasonable, or conniving at their disorders. A sort of compromise was thus made with the most turbulent and violent among them; who, provided they made no attempt to throw off the yoke of a foreign Power, were permitted to sacrifice a fellow-citizen to their lawless fury. Thus Gallio at Corinth left the rioters to settle their own disputes as they would; (Acts, xviii.) and the magistrates at Philippi, readily and spontaneously, gratified the populace by seconding and sanctioning their unjust violence. Pilate on this occasion did so, tardily and reluctantly.

[1] (Acts, xvii.) . . . . . "for we are also his children."

Father. And the like privilege of peculiar "Sonship," (only in a far higher degree,) was extended afterwards to all nations who should embrace the Gospel; "who aforetime" (says the Apostle Peter) "were not a People, but now are the People of God." And Paul uses like expressions continually in addressing his converts, whether they walked worthy of their high calling or not. We find the Evangelist John, also, in the opening of his Gospel, saying, in like manner, "as many as received Him, to them gave He power to become sons of God."

Yet again, still more especially, those who do avail themselves of the privileges offered to them, and "walk as Children of the light," are spoken of as, in another and a superior way, the "Sons" of Him whom they love and submit to as a Father: "as many," says Paul, "as are led by the Spirit of God, they are the Sons of God."

Those Patriarchs and Prophets again, to whom, of old, God revealed Himself immediately, and made them the means of communication between Himself and other men, —his messengers to his People,—and endowed with miraculous powers as the credentials of a heavenly embassy,— to such men, as having a peculiar kind of divine presence with them, we might conceive the title of Children of God to be applicable in a different sense, as distinguishing them from uninspired men. *Prophets and others supernaturally endowed.*

Now it is a most important practical question whether Jesus, the Author and Finisher of our faith,—He| to whom we are accustomed emphatically to apply the title of "*the* Son of God,"—was so designated, in the Angel's first announcement, and on so many occasions afterwards, merely as being an inspired messenger from heaven, or in some different and higher sense; and what that higher sense is?

Jesus, the Son of God in a peculiar sense.

§ 3. And first, that Jesus is spoken of in Scripture as the Son of God, in some different sense from any other person, is evident at once from the very circumstance of his being styled "the only-begotten Son;" which title is particularly dwelt on when He is speaking of Himself, (John, iii.) This is a further stage in the revelation given; for the Angel had not told Mary that He should be "*the* Son of God," (though it is so rendered in our version) but only "*a* Son of God," υἱὸς θεοῦ.

Revelations made on the occasion of the Transfiguration.

I need not multiply the citations of passages of which so many must be familiar to every one even tolerably well-read in the New Testament. But there is one that is peculiarly worthy of attention, on account of the care which divine Providence then displayed in guarding the disciples against the mistake of supposing Jesus to be merely one—though the most eminent one—of the prophets. In the transfiguration "on the Mount," three favoured Apostles beheld their Master surrounded with that dazzling supernatural light which had always been, to the Israelites, the sign of a divine manifestation, and which we find so often mentioned in the Old Testament as the glory of the Lord—the Shechinah;—which appeared on Mount Sinai,—on the Tabernacle in the Wilderness,—in Solomon's Temple, &c.: and they beheld at the same time, in company with Him, two persons, each of whom had been seen in their lifetime accompanied by this outward mark of supernatural light; Moses, their great lawgiver, whose "face shone when he came down from Mount Sinai," so that the Israelites could not fix their eyes on it, and Elias (Elijah), their most illustrious Prophet, who was seen borne away from the earth in that Shechinah appearing as a "chariot and horses of fire:" and now, these same two persons were seen along with Jesus. It might naturally have occurred to the three disciples (perhaps some such idea was indicated by the incoherent words which dropped from them)—the thought might have occurred to them,—were Moses and Elias also Emmanuels?—were all three, manifestations of "God dwelling with his People?" and was Jesus merely the greatest of the three? To correct, as it should seem, any such notion, it was solemnly announced to them that their Master was a Being of a different character from the others: "there came a voice out of the cloud, saying, This is *my beloved* SON: hear *Him*." And on two other occasions we read of the same signs being given.

§ 4. No one can doubt then, that those who believed in Jesus at all, must have believed Him to be the Son of God in a far different and superior sense from that in which any other could be so called. But what *was* the sense, it may be asked, in which they did understand the title? *Whether Jesus was the Son of God in a sense authorizing adoration.* Did the people of that time and Country understand that God was with Him, not only in some such way as He never was with any other man, but so as to permit and require *divine worship* to be addressed to God in Christ? Many passages by which this tenet is supported are commonly cited from the Evangelists and Apostles; but I wish at present to confine myself to the expression " the Son of God," and to inquire in what sense *that* was understood at the time.

Waiving then all abstruse disquisition on the notions conveyed by such terms as "consubstantiality,"—"personality,"—"hypostatic-union,"—" eternal filiation," and the like, (oftener I conceive debated about with eagerness than clearly understood,) let us *Metaphysical disquisitions on abstruse scholastic terms, unnecessary.*

confine ourselves to such views as we may presume the Apostles to have laid before the converts they were instructing; who were most of them plain unlearned persons, to whom such abstruse disquisitions as I have been alluding to, must have been utterly unintelligible; but who, nevertheless, were called on,—all of them, of whatever age, sex, station, and degree of intellectual education,—to receive the Gospel, and to believe, and feel, and act, as that Gospel enjoined.[1]

There is one great practical point clearly intelligible to all, thus far, at least, that they can understand what the question is that is under discussion, and which it is, and ever must have been, needful to bring before all Christians without exception: viz. whether there is that divine character in the Lord Jesus which entitles Him to our *adoration:*—whether He is the Son of God in such a sense as to authorize those who will worship none but the one God, to worship Jesus Christ; so that "all men[2] should honour the Son even as they honour the Father."

Christ's words to be taken in the sense understood at the time.

Now there is a maxim relative to the right interpretation of any passage of Scripture, so obvious when stated, that it seems strange it should be so often overlooked; viz., to consider *in what sense the words were understood by the generality of the persons they were addressed to;* and to keep in mind that the *presumption* is in favour of that, as the true sense, unless reasons to the contrary shall appear.

Some are accustomed to consider, what sense such and such words can be *brought* to *bear;* or how *we* should be most naturally inclined to understand them. But it is evident that the point we have to consider—if we would

---

[1] See Discourse on *The Shepherds at Bethlehem.*   [2] John, v. 23.

understand aright what it is that God did design to reveal,—is, the sense (as far as we can ascertain it) which the very hearers of Christ and his Apostles did *actually* attach to their words. For we may be sure that if this was, in any case, a *mistaken* sense, a correction of the mistake (if it relate to any important practical point) will be found in some part of the Sacred Writings.

However strange therefore it may seem to any one that the phrase "Son of God" should have been so understood as it was at the time, and however capable of another sense it may appear to us, still, the sense which Jesus and his Apostles meant to convey, must have been that,—whatever it was, in which they *knew that their hearers understood them*.

And what this meaning was, may, I think, be settled even by the testimony of his adversaries alone, as to the sense in which *they* understood Him. They charged Him, not only on his trial, but on many other occasions also, with "blasphemy," as "making Himself God,"—"making Himself equal with God;" and threatened to "stone Him," according to the law of Moses against blasphemers; understanding blasphemy to comprehend the crime of enticing the People to worship any besides the one true God, Jehovah.[1]

Now if they had *mis*understood his words, and had supposed his language to imply a claim to such divine honour as He did *not* really mean to claim, we may be sure that any one—I do not say merely, any inspired messenger from heaven, but—any man of *[margin: Christ would have warned his hearers against a mistake as to his meaning.]* common integrity, would at once have disavowed the imputation, and explained his real meaning. If any christian

---

[1] See Deut. xiii.

ministers, in these days, or at any time, were to have used some expression which they found was understood,—either by friends or foes,—as implying a claim to divine worship, what would they not deserve, if they did not hasten to disclaim such a meaning?

Christ must have foreseen that his followers would pay Him divine honours.

And much more would this be requisite in the case of a person who foresaw (as Jesus must have done) that his followers *would* regard Him as divine,—*would* worship Him—if He did not expressly warn them against it. Such a one would be doubly bound to make such explanations and such disavowals as should effectually guard his disciples against falling into the error —through anything said or done by Himself—of paying adoration to a Being not divine: even as the Apostle Peter warns the Centurion Cornelius against the adoration which he suspected that Cornelius designed to offer him; saying, " Stand up, I myself also am a man." Jesus of course would have taken care to give a like warning, if He had been conscious of not having a claim to be considered as divine, and had at the same time been aware that the title of Son of God would be understood as implying that claim.

Cases in which an explanation of his meaning may or may not be expected.

Many of our Lord's sayings, it is true, were not understood, or were but imperfectly understood, at the time; and some were even understood in a somewhat different sense from what was afterwards explained to the disciples. For instance, when He said "Destroy this temple, and in three days I will build it up," no one, at the time, could be supposed to understand that "He was speaking of the temple of his body:" most would probably suppose Him to be speaking of the literal temple at Jerusalem; though it is not likely any one would understand Him as expecting that the Jews would themselves destroy their own much-venerated temple. But it is evident (and this is the point that is to the present purpose), that every one is *responsible* for any practical *results* of the sense in which he knows his words to be understood. Suppose for instance that there had been a law in the Mosaic code, making it a capital crime to speak of such a thing as the destruction of the temple, and that Jesus had been brought to trial for that crime, on the strength of the above expression: it is plain He would have been bound to explain — and doubtless would have explained — the sense in which He used the words, and that He had not been speaking of the literal temple; else, He would have *borne false witness* against Himself.

But that his words (even literally understood) did *not* constitute any crime, was well known to his accusers; who accordingly suborned " false witnesses," to impute to Him a different expression, and one which *might* imply something criminal; pretending that He had said " *I will* destroy this temple." But the attempt failed; for " even so, their witness did not agree together."

Our Lord then cannot be conceived (indeed no honest man could) to have omitted to give a sufficient explanation of his meaning in any case in which his words in the sense in which He knew them to be understood (when this was *not* the true sense) would have led to the *commission of a sin*. We may be sure therefore that if He had *not* been a divine person, He would have disclaimed the title of Son of God, when He was aware that it was understood in that sense.

That the title *was* so understood, is the point to which I am now calling the reader's attention.

Jesus understood to claim a divine character.

§ 5. On one occasion, when He had healed a cripple on the Sabbath-day, and had commanded him immediately to "take up his bed," (which was a work prohibited by the Jewish law,) He vindicates Himself against his opponents by saying, "My Father worketh hitherto,[1] and I work;" or, as it might be rendered more clearly, according to our modern usage, "My Father has been working up to this time;" (that is, ever since the creation, the operations of God have been going on throughout the Universe, on all days alike;) "and I work;" I claim the right to perform, and to authorize others to perform, whatever and whenever I see fit.[2] "Therefore the Jews" (says the Evangelist) "sought the more to kill Him, because He not only had broken the Sabbath, but said also that God was his [proper] Father; *making himself equal with God.*"[3]

Defence of Jesus when charged with blasphemy by the populace.

On another occasion (John, x. 33) when He had said "I and the Father are one," the Jews were about to stone Him for blasphemy, "because (said they) thou being a man makest thyself God." He defends Himself by alleging a passage of their Scripture in which the title of "God" is applied to those "to whom the word of God came;" implying however at the same time a *distinction* between Himself and those persons, and his own *superiority* to them: "Say ye of Him" (he does not say "to whom the word of God came" but) "whom the Father hath anointed and sent

---

[1] Ἐργάζεται ἕως ἄρτι.

[2] I have treated more fully on this point, in an Essay entitled *Thoughts on the Sabbath.*

[3] Our version, it is important to observe, does not give the full force of the passage as it stands in the Original. It should be rendered, "that God was his *own proper* (or *peculiar*) Father" πατέρα ἴδιον. This it seems was the sense in which (according to the Evangelist) He was understood by his hearers to call God his Father, and Himself "the Son of God." See Wilson *on the New Testament,* referred to in the Preface.

into the world, Thou blasphemest, because I said I am the Son of God?" *This* however did not necessarily imply anything more than *superiority*, and divine *mission;* and accordingly *we find the Jews enduring it;* but when He goes on to say "that ye may know and believe that *the Father is in me, and I in Him*," we find them immediately *seeking again to lay hands on Him;* and He withdraws from them.[1] "We are not, therefore," (as Dr. Hawkins observes in his *Fourth Bampton Lecture,*) "to cite words like these apart from their context. As distinct propositions viewed in their place and with their context, and with their effect upon the hearers considered, and that effect clearly foreseen by our Lord, they become argument of his meaning and intention."

But the most important record by far in respect of the point now before us is that which I originally proposed to notice,—the account of our Lord's trial and condemnation before the Jewish Council. In order to have a clear view of this portion of the history, it is necessary to keep in mind, that

His defence before the Council.

---

[1] Evidently in a *miraculous* manner; as also on a former occasion of a similar tumultuous and irregular outrage, (see Luke, iv. 30,) when the people of Nazareth were about to cast Him down a precipice. For though his miraculously concealing Himself from their sight is not expressly mentioned — which was not necessary, considering how familiar both to the writers and to their readers must have been the supernatural power of Jesus—it is plainly implied by the narrative. A man surrounded by enemies bent on his destruction, and perfectly acquainted with his person, could not, in daylight, have escaped from them in a natural way, by "passing through the midst of them" unobserved. And Judas doubtless expected that on the occasion of his last apprehension also, Jesus would, in some way or other, miraculously deliver Himself. (See Sermon on the Treason of Judas, appended to *Essays*, 4th Series.) But on this last occasion, the act was not — as in the former cases — that of a *lawless multitude,* which no one, however scrupulous, would feel *bound* to submit to, but a regular and *legal* (however unjust) proceeding of the Constituted Authorities, to whose power submission is due.

This is a distinction which has not been sufficiently attended to.

when He was tried before the Roman governor, it was (as I observed at the beginning) not for the same crime He was charged with before the Council of the Jews; but for seditious and treasonable designs against the *Roman* Emperor: "We found this fellow perverting the nation and forbidding to give tribute to Cæsar, saying that He Himself is Christ a King." "Whosoever maketh himself a King, speaketh against Cæsar." Now need I hardly remark that this was no crime under the law of *Moses;* and would in fact have been a merit in the sight of most of the Jews. But what He was charged with before *them*, was blasphemy, according to the Law of Moses;[1] and of this they pronounced Him guilty, and sentenced Him to death; but not having power to inflict capital punishment, they prevailed on Pilate, who had acquitted Him of the charge of treason, to inflict their sentence: "We have a law, and by *our law* He ought to die, because He made Himself the Son of God."

Accounts of the trial, in the four Gospels, to be compared together.

In order to understand clearly the trial and condemnation of our Lord before the Jewish Council (which is in many respects a most important part of Sacred History) we should study, as I have said, the accounts given of it by all four of the Evangelists. Each relates such circumstances as most struck his own mind; where one is abridged, another is more diffuse; each omits some things that are noticed by another; but no one can be supposed to have recorded anything that did *not* occur. All the four, therefore, should be compared together, in order to obtain a clear view of the transaction.

Jesus convicted on his own testimony.

It seems to have been divinely appointed that Jesus should be convicted on no testimony but *his own;* perhaps in order to fulfil the more emphatically his declaration, "No

---

[1] See Deut. xiii. 7.

man taketh away my life, but I lay it down of myself." For the witnesses brought forward to misrepresent and distort his saying " Destroy this temple," into "*I* am able to destroy," could not make their evidence agree.¹

Two questions asked before the Council.

The High Priest then endeavoured, by examining Jesus Himself, to draw from Him an acknowledgment of his supposed guilt. He and the others appear to have asked Him *two* questions; which, in the more abridged narrative of Matthew and Mark, are compressed into one sentence; but which Luke has given distinctly as two. After having asked Him " Art thou *the Christ?*" they proceed to ask further " Art thou then the *Son of God?*"² and as soon as He had answered *this last* question in the affirmative (according to the Hebrew idiom " Ye say," " Thou hast said "), immediately " the High Priest rent his clothes," saying, " He hath spoken blasphemy: ye have heard the blasphemy; what need we any further witnesses? for we ourselves have heard of his own mouth."

Jesus not condemned for professing to be the Christ.

§ 6. Some readers, I believe, from not carefully studying and comparing together the accounts of the different Evangelists, are apt to take for granted that the crime for which our Lord was condemned, was that of falsely pretending to be the Messiah or Christ. But whatever the Jews may have thought of *that* crime, they certainly could not have found it mentioned, and death denounced against it, in the Law of Moses. It could, at any rate, have been no crime, unless *proved* to be a *false*

---

¹ This remarkable circumstance Mr. Wilson, to whose valuable work I am so much indebted, seems to have overlooked.
² See John, xx. 31.

pretension; which was not even attempted. Nor could they have brought that offence (even if proved) under the head of *blasphemy;* unless they had been *accustomed to expect* the Messiah as a divine person. *Then*, indeed, the claim of being the Messiah, and the claim of divine honour, would have amounted to the same thing. But so far were

The Messiah not expected by the Jews to be a divine person.

they from having this expectation that (not to multiply proofs) they were completely at a loss to answer our Lord's question, how David, if the Christ were to be David's son, could speak of Him as a divine Being under the title of LORD. "If David then call Him LORD, how is He his son?" is a question which they would have answered without a moment's hesitation, if they had expected that the Christ should be, though the Son of David after the flesh and as a human Being, yet, the Son of God in such a sense as to make him a divine Being also.

Whatever good reasons then they might have found in prophecy for such expectation, it seems plain that they had it not.

And the same I believe is the case, generally speaking, with the Jews of the present day.[1] A learned modern Jew, who has expressly written that Jesus "falsely demanded faith in Himself as the true God of Israel," adds that "if a prophet, or *even the Messiah Himself*, had offered proof of his divine mission by miracles, but claimed divinity, he ought to be stoned to death;" conformably *i.e.* to the command in Deut. xiii. And the only Jew with whom I ever conversed on the subject appeared to hold the same doctrine; though he was at a loss when I asked him to reconcile it with the application of the title of Emmanuel.

---

[1] See Wilson *On the New Testament*, above referred to.

The Jewish Council then could not, it appears, capitally convict our Lord, merely for professing to be the Christ, even though falsely: and accordingly we may observe that they did not even seek for any proof that his pretension *was* false. But as soon as He acknowledged Himself to be the "Son of the living God" they immediately pronounced Him " guilty of death " for blasphemy; *i. e.* as seeking to lead the People (Deut. xiii.) to pay divine honour to another besides the true God. They convict Him on his own testimony (having " heard of his own mouth ") of the crime which they afterwards describe to Pilate. " We have a law, and by our law He ought to die, because He made Himself the Son of God."

<small>*Pretensions of Jesus to be the Christ not attempted to be disproved.*</small>

§ 7. No candid reader then can doubt, I think, that the Jews understood Him to claim by that title a divine character. And He Himself must have *known* that they so understood Him. As little can it be doubted therefore that they must have *rightly* understood Him. For if He—condemned as He was on the evidence of his own words—had known that those words were understood differently from his real meaning, and yet had not corrected the mistake, He would have been Himself bearing false witness against Himself; since no one can suppose it makes any difference in point of veracity, whether a man says that which is untrue in *every* sense, or that which, though in a certain sense true, yet is false in the sense in which he knows it to be understood.[1] It is a mere waste of labour and learning and ingenuity to inquire what meaning such

<small>*Jesus was rightly understood as claiming to be divine.*</small>

---

[1] See note to § 4.

and such an expression is *capable* of bearing, in a case where we know, as we do here, what was the sense which was actually conveyed by it to the hearers, and which the speaker must have been aware it did convey to them.

Whether Jesus was unjustly or justly condemned, depends on his being or not being a divine person.

Jesus did therefore acknowledge the fact alleged against Him; viz. that of claiming to be the Son of God in such a sense as to incur the penalty (supposing that claim unwarranted) of death for blaspheming, according to the law respecting those who should entice Israel to worship any other than the one true God. The whole question therefore of his being rightly or wrongfully condemned, turns on the justness of that claim:—on his actually having, or not having, that divine character which the Jews understood Him to assume. For if He were *not* such, and yet called Himself the Son of God, knowing in what sense they understood the title, I really am at a loss to see on what ground we can find fault with the sentence they pronounced.

It does appear to me therefore—I say this without presuming to judge those who think differently, but to me it appears—that the whole question of Christ's divine mission, and consequently of the truth of Christianity, turns on the claim which He so plainly appears to have made to divine honour for Himself.

A heaven-sent teacher could not have put forth a false claim.

I am not one of those indeed who profess to understand and explain why it was necessary for man's salvation that God should have visited his People precisely in the way He did. On such points, as I dare not believe less, so I pretend not to understand more, than He has expressly revealed. If I had been taught in Scripture that God had thought fit to save the world, through the agency of some Angel, or some great Prophet, not possessing in himself a divine character, I could not have presumed to maintain the impossibility of that. But *this* does strike me as utterly impossible; that a heaven-sent messenger—the Saviour of the world,—should be a person who claimed a divine character that did *not* belong to Him; and who thus gave rise to, and permitted, and encouraged, a system of idolatry. This is an idea so revolting to all my notions of divine purity, and indeed of common morality, that I could never bring myself to receive as a divine revelation any religious system that contained it.

All the difficulties on the opposite side—and I do not deny that *every* religious persuasion has its difficulties—are as nothing in comparison of the difficulty of believing that Jesus (supposing Him neither an impostor nor a madman) could have made the declaration He did make at his trial, if He were conscious of having no just claim to divine honour.

§ 8. And the conclusion to which we are thus led, arises (it should be observed) out of the mere consideration of the title "Son of God," or "only-begotten Son of God," as applied to Jesus Christ; without taking into account any of the confirmations of the same conclusion (and there are very many) which may be drawn from other parts of the Sacred Writings, both of the Evangelists and Apostles—from many things that were said, and that were done, both by our Lord and by his Apostles. *Declarations of Jesus at his trial, alone sufficient.*

There is indeed no one of these their recorded actions and expressions that may not be explained away by an ingenious critic, who should set himself to do so, and who should proceed like a legal advocate, examining every possible sense in which some law *Unfairness of explaining away the declarations of Christ and the Apostles.*

or precedent that makes against his client, may be interpreted. But again, there is hardly one of these passages which can be thus explained away without violating the maxim above laid down; viz. that we should consider, not *any* interpretation whatever that such and such words can bear, but—what notion they conveyed, and must have been known to convey, to the hearers at the time.[1] For if this were a mistaken notion,—an untrue sense,—it follows inevitably that Christ and his Apostles must have been *teachers* of falsehood, even though their words should be capable of a different and true signification.

Impossibility of the Evangelists and Apostles having encouraged idolatry.

Unless, therefore, we conceive them capable of knowingly promoting idolatry,—unless we can consider Jesus Himself as either an insane fanatic, or a deliberate impostor, —we must assign to Him, the "Author and Finisher of our Faith," the "only-begotten Son of God," who is "one with the Father," that divine character which He and his Apostles so distinctly claimed for Him; and acknowledge that God truly "was in Christ, reconciling the World unto Himself."

Declarations before Pilate to be interpreted on similar principles.

§ 9. Not less important, I conceive, are the lessons to be drawn from the second trial,— that before Pilate,—to which our Lord was subjected; provided this portion also of the sacred narrative be studied on the principle already laid down; that of interpreting his declarations with reference to the meaning they were meant to convey at the time, and to the very persons He was addressing.

The Jewish Council, having found Jesus guilty of a

---

[1] See Sermon on *The Name Emmanuel.*

capital crime, and being not permitted,[1] under the Roman laws, to inflict capital punishment (for the stoning of Stephen appears to have been an irregular and tumultuous outbreak of popular fury), immediately bring Him before Pilate on a new and perfectly different charge. "The whole multitude of them arose and led Him unto Pilate: and they began to accuse Him, saying, We found this fellow perverting the nation, and forbidding to give tribute to Cæsar, saying that He Himself is Christ, a King." For the crime of which He had been convicted before *them*, that of blasphemy, in seeking to draw aside the Jews to the worship of another besides the LORD Jehovah, though a capital crime under the Mosaic law, was none at all in the court of the Roman Governor; and again, the crime alleged in this latter court,—treason against the Roman emperor,—was no crime at all under the law of Moses.

Now, in studying the circumstances of this second trial, we ought, as has been above observed, to proceed by the same rule of interpretation as in respect of the former trial; viz. to understand our Lord's expressions, not in any sense whatever that they can be brought to bear, nor, necessarily, in the sense which to *us* may seem the most suitable, but in the sense, as far as we can ascertain it, in which He must have *known that He was understood* at the time.[2]

When then He was charged before Pilate with "speaking against Cæsar" and "making Himself a King," how does He defend Himself? In exact conformity with the principle He had laid down on a former occasion. On that occasion, when his adversaries had tried to *make* Him commit the offence with which they now charged Him, of interfering with the secular government of Cæsar, He, so far from

Defence of Jesus against the charge of treason.

---

[1] οὐκ ἔξεστιν.   [2] See note to § 4.

"forbidding to give tribute," drew the line between secular and spiritual government, saying, "Render unto Cæsar the things which be Cæsar's, and unto God the things which be God's." So, now, before Pilate, He asserts his claim to be a King, but declares that "his kingdom is not of this world," and that, accordingly, his servants were not allowed to fight for Him; and He further describes his kingly office to consist in "bearing witness of the truth." "Every one that is of the truth," said He, "heareth (*i. e.* obeyeth) my voice." He does not, it should be observed, merely set up the claim of being a teacher of what is true: He does not say, "Every one that heareth my voice is of the truth;" but "Every one that is of the truth heareth my voice." Having acknowledged Himself a *King*, He immediately proceeds to prevent the misapprehension that was likely to arise, as to the character of his Kingdom, by pointing out *what description of persons* He was to *reign* over.

What is meant by a Kingdom of Truth.
He came to establish a Kingdom of Truth: that is, not a kingdom whose subjects should embrace on compulsion what is in itself true, and consequently should be adherents of truth by accident; but, a kingdom whose subjects should have been *admitted as such* in consequence of their being "of the truth;" that is, votaries of truth,—men honestly disposed to embrace and "obey the truth," whatever it might be, that God should reveal: agreeably to what our Lord has elsewhere declared, that "if any man will do (θέλει, is willing to do) the will of my Father, he shall know of the doctrine," &c.

To any persons who are not "of the truth," in the above sense,—that is, who, though they believe (as every one does) many things that are true, yet have not heartily set themselves, with perfect candour and self-devotion, to ascertain, as far as possible, and to obey, at all hazards, God's truth,—

to such persons, these views will of course be likely to appear strange and fanciful, perplexing, and perhaps offensive; and they will accordingly seek for some different interpretation.

But when they explain Christ's declaration of his having "come into the world to bear witness of the truth," in some sense in itself intelligible, but quite *unconnected* with the inquiry He was answering, as to his being "a King," they forget that what He said must have had not only *some* meaning, but some meaning *pertinent* to the occasion: and this they seem as much at a loss for, as Pilate himself; who exclaimed, "What is truth?" not from being ignorant of the meaning of the word, but from perceiving no connexion between "truth" and the inquiry respecting the claim to regal office.[1]

The result was that Pilate acquitted Him: declaring publicly that he "found no fault at all in Him." It is plain, therefore, that he must have believed—or at least professed to believe—both that the declarations of Jesus were true, and that they amounted to a total disavowal of all interference with the secular government, by Himself, or his followers, as such. *Acquitted by Pilate.*

Much ingenuity has been expended,—I must needs say, has been *wasted*,—in drawing out from our Lord's expressions before Pilate, every sense that his words can be found capable of bearing; while a man of little or no ingenuity, but of plain good sense and sincerity of purpose, seeking in simplicity to learn what Jesus really did mean, can hardly, I should think, fail of that meaning, if he does but keep in mind the *occasion* on which He was speaking, and the sense in which He must have known that his language would be understood. The *Importance of considering the occasion on which Jesus was speaking.*

---

[1] See *Essay* I. 2nd Series.

occasion on which He spoke was when on his trial before a Roman governor, for *treason*,—for a design to subvert, or in some way interfere with, the established government. To this charge, it is plain Pilate understood Him to plead *not guilty*; and gave credit to his plea. Pilate, therefore, must have taken the declaration that Christ's "kingdom is not of this world," as amounting to a renunciation of all secular coercion,—all forcible measures in behalf of his religion. And we cannot, without imputing to our blessed Lord a fraudulent evasion, suppose Him to have really meant anything different from the sense which He knew his words conveyed. Such is the conclusion which I cannot but think any man must come to who is not seeking, as in the interpretation of an Act of Parliament, for any sense most to his own purpose that the words can be made to bear, however remote that may be from the known design of the Legislator; but who with reverential love, is seeking with simplicity and in earnest to *learn* what is the description that Christ gave of his kingdom.

But the ingenuity which has been (as I said before) wasted in trying to explain our Lord's words in some other way, has been called forth by a desire to escape some of the *consequences* which follow from taking them in their simple and obvious sense. Those who are seeking not really to learn the true sense of our Lord's declarations, but to reconcile them with the conduct of some Christian States, and to justify the employment of secular force in behalf of religion, are driven to some ingenious special-pleading on the words employed, in order to draw from them such a sense as may suit their own purpose.

And all this ingenuity is (as I said before) wasted; because even supposing it proved that the words which Jesus uttered are, in themselves, capable of bearing some other meaning, still, nothing is gained (supposing our object is, not to *evade*, but to *understand*, Scripture) if that meaning be one which could not have been so understood at the time, or which would have been one utterly foreign to the occasion, and irrelevant to the question that was to be tried.

§ 10. For instance, I have heard it said that our Lord's description of his kingdom as "not of this world" meant *merely* that He claimed to possess a spiritual dominion (as undoubtedly He did) over the souls of men, and to be the distributor of the rewards and judgments of the other world. And such certainly *is* his claim: but the essential point, with a view to the trial then going on, was, that this was his *only* claim. He did not merely claim spiritual dominion, but He also *renounced* temporal. He declared not merely that his kingdom is of the *next* world; but that it is *not* of *this* world.

Other interpretations put forward.

In fact, the *mere* assertion of his spiritual dominion, and one extending beyond the grave, would have been, at that time, and in reference to the charge brought against Him, wholly irrelevant, and foreign to the question. He was charged with "speaking against Cæsar,"—with making Himself King in opposition to the Roman emperor. The Jews expected (as Pilate could hardly have been ignorant) a Christ who should be a heaven-sent "King of the Jews," possessing both temporal *and* spiritual authority; a kingdom, both of this world and of the next: for the great mass of the nation believed in a future state.

Mere assertion of spiritual dominion would have been irrelevant.

Whether this expected "King of the Jews" were about to establish the dominion of the *Jewish nation over the Gentiles*, (which was the expectation first formed) or whether

—as was soon afterwards apparent to all men—*Jews and Gentiles without distinction* of Race, were to be admitted as his subjects, was a question comparatively unimportant, as long as there was an apprehension that his subjects were to force on all men, as soon as they should be strong enough, submission to their Law, or to monopolize secular power; —in short, if they were to be, in either way, a political faction. Such they were represented to be, by the accusers of Paul before the Romans, long after he had been inviting the Gentiles to join the Church on equal terms:[1] "These all do contrary to the *decrees of Cæsar*, saying that there is *another king*, one Jesus."

Indeed it is plain that if in the rebellion of 1745 any adherent of the reigning King had suspected a design in the Pretender's partisans to establish a political ascendency of the *Scotch Highlanders* over all Britain, and had afterwards been convinced that there was no such design, but that Scotch and English, Highlanders and Lowlanders, alike, were to be on an equal footing, *provided* they would *embrace Jacobite-principles*, and submit to the Stuarts, this would not have diminished his opposition, or made him deem their procedure the less treasonable.

Any man therefore claiming to be, in either way, such a king of the Jews, would evidently be an opponent of the Roman government. His *spiritual* pretensions, the Romans did not concern themselves about. It was the assumption of *temporal* power that threatened danger to the Empire; and it was of this assumption that Jesus was accused. *Did He not distinctly deny it?* There was no question about the rewards and punishments of another world. The question was, whether He did or did not design to claim, for Himself, or his followers *as such*, any kind of secular empire:[2] could any words have disclaimed it more strongly

---

[1] Acts, xvii. 7.   [2] See Appendix.

than those He used? And can any one in his senses seriously believe that when Jesus said, "My kingdom is not of this world," He meant to be understood as saying that his kingdom was not only of this world, but of the next world too?

No,—I have heard it said by some other expounders,—He did mean to disclaim all personal dominion for *Himself personally*, and *at that time;* but that, hereafter, when " the kingdoms of this world should become kingdoms of the Lord," and when " kings should become nursing-fathers" of his Church, when " the Church should be in its complete development, by being perfectly identified with the State," then, all those Christians who should have attained power, should exercise that power in enforcing the profession of his Gospel, and in putting down idolatry, infidelity, heresy, dissent, and all false religion. In short, at the time when Christ stood before Pilate, his kingdom was not of this world, " because " (I am citing the words of one of the most celebrated ancient divines[1]) " that prophecy was not yet fulfilled, ' Be wise now, therefore, O ye kings, be learned, ye that are judges of the earth; serve the Lord with fear;'" the rulers of the earth, he adds, were at that time opposed to the Gospel; the Apostles and other early disciples were *unable* to compel men to conform to the true faith; and *therefore* it was that the secular arm was not yet called to aid against the Church's enemies.

Mere disclaimer of present personal claims would have been frivolous.

---

[1] Augustine. Some persons actually seem to understand the "*now*" in our Lord's answer as if it signified "at this time:" the sense being evidently, in this and in several other places, "as it is," or "as the case stands." Thus we have, in John, xv. 24, " If I had not done among them the works that none other man did, they had not had sin; but *now*, they have both seen," &c. So also, here, "If my kingdom were of this world, *then* would my servants fight; * * * but now is my Kingdom not from hence."

To claim temporal power for his followers would have been to plead guilty.

Now, without entering into the question whether our Lord's words could, in themselves, bear such a meaning; let us confine ourselves to the principle we set out with, and merely consider whether He could possibly have meant to be so *understood*. For this, we should observe, would clearly have been to *plead guilty to the charge*. It mattered nothing to the Roman Government whether it were Jesus *Himself*, or his *followers*,— whether it were Jews alone, or Jews and Gentiles conjointly, —that should revolt against Cæsar's power, and set up a rival kingdom. And therefore, when our Lord Himself, and afterwards Paul and the other Apostles, *defended* themselves against the imputation of seditious designs, it is impossible they could have meant to be understood as merely disclaiming such designs *for the present*, and renouncing temporal dominion only for *themselves, personally*, but reserving for their followers, when these should have become strong enough, the right to establish by force a christian political ascendency, and to put down all other religions. To have defended themselves against their accusers by acknowledging the very designs which those accusers imputed to them, would have been downright insanity.

Grounds on which Roman magistrates persecuted Christians.

The grounds on which the several Roman magistrates, at various times, acted, or were called on to act, against Jesus and his followers, were probably very various. Some probably suspected, or professed to suspect them, of designs to subvert the existing Government, "saying that there is another King, one Jesus." Some perhaps were moved by mere *anger* at their daring obstinately to refuse conformity to the established religion; while others may have thought this obstinacy — however unimportant the subject of it—a proof of a disposition to insubordination, which, if unchecked, would be likely to break out in other ways: some may have given credit to the tales which imputed to them various abominable crimes, such as the burning of Rome in Nero's time:[1] and others again may have thought merely of gaining popularity with the rabble, or preventing "a tumult from being made."[2]

But we are not left to historical researches into profane authors, and conjectures as to the motives of Roman magistrates, for the determination of a question so practically important to every Christian as this is, of our great Master's meaning when He disclaimed a Kingdom of this World. The most unlearned Christian may be taught this in the Scriptures, if he approach them with an unbiassed and teachable mind. For this surely is clear to any man of ordinary understanding; that whatever any Roman governor did or did not suspect in any particular case that came before him, he could not fail to regard (and not without some reason) as *seditious*—as a treasonable design against the existing Government—*any* design to claim for the followers of Jesus (when they should become strong enough to assert the claim,) a political ascendency, and to punish, or hold in vassalage, all who would not embrace their religion.[3] And if he had understood them to disclaim *one* particular kind of treasonable design, in such terms as *not* to disclaim *another*, similar one, this would have been as unimportant a distinction as if those who had been forbidden to draw the *sword* in their Master's cause, had held themselves at liberty to fight for Him with spears.

---

[1] See Tacitus.
[2] See note to § 2.
[3] The monopoly of civil rights by those of a certain religion, if designed not to *force* the rest into *conformity*, but simply, to exclude them from those rights, is a violation indeed of the principle of Christ's Kingdom, but not, in the strict sense, a *punishment*, though likely to *operate* as such. See Note A.

If therefore they had entertained such a design as has been imputed to them, and had answered the accusations brought against them in terms which they themselves *meant to be understood as not disavowing* any such design, they would have been acting the part of madmen.

Parallel case of political revolutionists. But such absurdities as would, *in any other subject*, revolt every man of common sense, are sometimes tolerated in the interpretations of Scripture, that are framed in order to serve a purpose. For instance, suppose some emissaries of the Pretender in the last century, or, in later times, of the French revolutionists, or of the Chartists, or any set of revolutionists of the present day, to go about the Country proclaiming and disseminating their principles, and then to be arrested and brought to trial for sedition: can any one conceive them defending themselves against the charge, by pleading that they did not intend that *they themselves* but that their *disciples*, should obtain the government of the Country, and enforce their principles; that they aimed at the possession and the monopoly of civil rights[1] and privileges, not for themselves, but for their *successors;* that they did not mean to take up arms till they should have collected a sufficient number of followers; and that they taught all men to yield obedience to the existing government, *till* they should be strong enough to overthrow it? Who does not see at once that to urge such a plea would convince every one of their being madmen? And yet this is what must be imputed to Jesus and his disciples, by any one who can suppose that they *meant to be understood* by the Roman magistrates as merely disclaiming all interference with civil government, till they should become numerous enough to enforce the claim;—all resort to

---

[1] See Appendix.

secular coercion in religious matters, till they should have strength to employ it effectually;—all political monopoly, till they should be in a condition to maintain it by a strong hand.

Jesus then, it is plain, when He said "My kingdom *is* not of this world," could not have meant to be *understood* as implying that it *should* be so hereafter.

One of the modes in which it has been attempted to explain away the teaching of Christ and his Apostles, is by representing them as inculcating only the duty of *Subjects* towards Governors, and not meaning that the same principles should be applied in reference to the duty of *Governors* towards Subjects: so that though Christians were to "be subject, for conscience' sake," even to idolatrous rulers (as long as nothing at variance with christian duty was enjoined) the right was reserved, it seems, to Christians, whenever they might obtain political power, to employ this in forcibly maintaining and propagating their own religion,[1] and securing to its professors a monopoly of civil rights. As if a citizen, of whatever persuasion, had not the same claim to the rights of a *citizen*, that a ruler, of whatever persuasion, has to the rights of a *ruler!* As if the christian principles implied in "render unto Cæsar the things that are Cæsar's" ... "render unto *all* their *due*," were not equally applicable to the duties either of Subject or of Prince!

Corresponding rights and duties of Subjects and Rulers.

And supposing (what is inconceivable) that any such groundless and fanciful distinction had been in the mind of our Lord and his Apostles, and moreover that they had

---

[1] I know not how the oppression under which the Vaudois are now suffering (see the Pamphlet referred to in the Preface) can be objected to by Protestants who hold these principles, unless they renounce altogether the rule of doing as we would be done by.

meant the Roman magistrates so to understand them, and also that those magistrates had given them credit for sincerity, still, after all, nothing is gained by these suppositions: since there could be no security against a Christian's obtaining political power, or against a man's embracing Christianity who was already in power. And if this power was to be exerted in propagating or supporting the Religion by those coercive means which a civil magistrate is enabled to employ, no one in his senses can doubt, that had Christ and his Apostles been understood as acknowledging this, they would have been *pleading guilty* to the charges brought against them.[1]

Supposed hidden meaning of our Lord's declaration.

§ 11. But had He then some *hidden* meaning, which He did *not* intend to be understood at the time? Did He design to convey one sense to the Roman governor, and another to his own disciples?—to reserve for his followers in future times, that power to enforce the acknowledgment of his gospel, which He *pretended* to disclaim.[2]

It seems almost too shocking even to ask such a question: and yet it is but too true, that such, in substance, (however glossed over in words) must be the meaning attributed to our blessed Lord by those who would reconcile his declarations before Pilate with that which they represent as the right and the duty of every christian Governor. "The magistrate" they say (I am giving the very words that have been employed) "who restrains, coerces, and punishes any one who opposes the true faith, obeys the command of God:" and they contend that a christian Governor is not only authorized, but bound, to secure to the

---

[1] See *Essays on the Dangers*, &c., pp. 210—213.
[2] See note to § 4.

professors of the true faith a monopoly of political power and civil rights. Now, to reconcile such doctrines with the declarations of Christ and his Apostles, a meaning must be attributed to those declarations which it would have been madness for them to have *avowed* at the time;—in short, a *hidden* meaning.

It is recorded of an ancient king of Egypt,—one of the Ptolemies—that he employed a celebrated architect to build a magnificent Light-House, for the benefit of shipping, and ordered an inscription in honour of himself to be engraved on it: the architect, it is said, though inwardly coveting the honour of such a record for *himself,* was obliged to comply ; but made the inscription on a plaster resembling stone, but of perishable substance: in the course of years this crumbled away; and the next generation saw *another* inscription, recording the name, not of the King, but of the architect, which had been secretly engraved on the durable stone below.

Now, just such a device as this is attributed to our Lord and his Apostles by those who believe them to have designed that secular power should hereafter be called in to enforce the christian Faith, though all such designs were *apparently* disavowed, in order to serve a present purpose. According to such interpreters, " My kingdom is not of this world," was only an inscription on the perishable plaster ; the design of " coercing and punishing " by secular power all opponents of the true faith, was, it seems, the engraving on the stone beneath. " Render unto Cæsar the things that be Cæsar's," was but the outward part of the inscription ; the addition was an inner hidden engraving, directing that Christians, when become strong enough, should compel both Cæsar and his subjects,—all Rulers and all citizens— either to acknowledge the true faith, or to forfeit their civil

Dishonesty of a double meaning.

rights. It was the *outside* inscription only that ran thus, "Submit yourselves to every ordinance of man; * * * the powers that be, are ordained of God:" the secret characters on the *stone* said, "Take care as soon as possible to make every ordinance of man submit to *you*," and to provide that none but those of your own Body shall *be* in authority; and that they shall use that authority in enforcing the profession of your religion.[1]

It might seem incredible, did we not know it to be the fact, that persons professing a deep reverence for Christ and his Apostles as heaven-sent messengers, should attribute to them this double-dealing;—should believe them to have secretly entertained and taught the very views of which their adversaries accused them, and which they uniformly disclaimed: that the blessed Jesus Himself, who rebukes *hypocrisy* more strongly than perhaps any other sin, should be regarded by his professed followers as having pretended to disavow that which was his real design, and which He imparted to his Apostles; teaching *them* in like manner to keep the secret till they should be strong enough to assert the political supremacy of the Gospel, and to extirpate, or hold in subjection as vassals, all professors of false religions.

Impiety of attributing double-dealing to our Lord.

All this, I say, might seem hardly credible, did not daily experience show us how easily (not only in this but in other cases also) even intelligent men are satisfied with the slightest pretences of argument—with the most extravagant conclusions —when they are seeking not really for *instruction* as to what they *ought* to do, but for

---

[1] Of this subject I have treated more fully in the *Essay on Persecution*, 3rd Series; and in Appendix E. and F. to *Essays on the Dangers*, &c. 4th Series.

a *justification* of what they are *inclined* to do. Such a bias of inclination, is like the magnet which is said to have been once secretly placed near a ship's compass, by a traitor who purposed to deliver the crew into the enemy's hands. All their diligence and skill in working the ship and steering by this perverted compass, served only to further them on the wrong course.

Without presuming to pronounce judgment on the general moral character of others, I cannot forbear saying, for myself, that if I could believe Jesus to have been guilty of such subterfuges as I have been speaking of, I not only could not acknowledge Him as sent from God, but should reject Him with *the deepest moral indignation.*

How far this indignant disgust may have been excited in the breasts of some who have taken for granted, on the authority of learned and zealous divines, that the interpretation I have been reprobating is to be received, and who may in consequence have *rejected Christianity* with abhorrence, it is for those who maintain such an interpretation carefully to consider.

Infidelity promoted by such an interpretation.

It is to be expected that in proportion as civilization, in the highest sense of the word, gains ground, the number will ever increase of persons so disposed as to feel both an abhorrence of all oppression,—every thing approaching to religious persecution,—and also a disdain of every kind of disingenuousness and double-dealing. And some persons of this character, unfortunately, may have been content to take their notions of the Gospel from the accounts of those whom they suppose likely to be the best judges, instead of carefully comparing those accounts with the Scriptures themselves. Such persons will have, not their evil passions, but, their moral sentiments, in proportion as these are just, and elevated, and pure, enlisted against the Gospel.[1] Their procedure is indeed justly censurable, in not examining for themselves what the religion is, before they reject it: but this does not lessen the responsibility of those who place such a stumbling-block in another's path. " Woe unto that man by whom the offence cometh!"

Fallacious arguments adduced by generally intelligent men.

§ 12. It is in many respects important to observe and to keep in mind, to how great an extent both an obliquity of moral judgment, and a deficiency in the reasoning-powers, will often beset, on some *one or two particular points*, a man who may be, on the whole, and in other points, where his particular prejudices have not gained dominion, a person both morally and intellectually above the average. In the present case, for instance, one may find men of much intelligence, misled by a fallacy which in the ordinary concerns of life every person of common sense would see through at once.

Objections brought against the obvious interpretation.

Was it designed, they say, that Christians should never take any part in civil affairs;— should never be magistrates or legislators, and thus partake of political power? And if this is permitted, must they not, as civil magistrates, act on christian principles? No doubt; but they would *cease* to act on christian principles if they should employ the *coercive power* of civil magistrates *in the cause of Christianity;*—if they should not only take a part in civil affairs, but claim *as* Christians, or as members of a particular Church, a *monopoly* of civil rights. It is this, and this only, that tends to make Christ's kingdom "a kingdom of this world."

---

[1] I am speaking not from mere conjecture, but from personal knowledge of such cases.

The mistake that prevails in many minds as to this point, may conveniently be stated in the form of a "Fallacy of interrogations"[1] as thus: "Is it not the duty of every *man*, and consequently of a Magistrate or Legislator, to aim at promoting human good, generally?"

The answer is in the affirmative, supposing the meaning to be "to promote human good, *as every human Being* ought, by such means as are legitimate, and appropriate to each particular kind of good, respectively:" but if the meaning be, "to aim at promoting every kind of human good in *his capacity of Magistrate*, by means of the *coercive power* with which, *as* a Magistrate, he is entrusted," then, the answer should be in the negative.

The same persons may be members of distinct Societies.

Now this is a distinction which in all other cases is readily perceived by every man of common sense. For instance, there are many well-known Societies in this and in most other Countries, which no one would call in any degree political Societies; such as Academies for the cultivation of mathematical and other sciences,—Agricultural Societies,—Antiquarian Societies, and the like; now it would be reckoned silly, even to ask respecting any one of these Societies, whether the members of it were excluded from taking any part in civil affairs, and whether a magistrate or a legislator could be admitted as a member of it. Every one would see the absurdity of even entertaining any doubt on this point: and it would be reckoned no less silly to inquire whether the admission of such persons as members, constituted that Academy a political Society. It would at once be answered that the Society itself, (whether possessing endowments or not) and the members of it, *as such*, had nothing to do with political, but only

---

[1] See *Logic*, B. iii. § 9.

with scientific matters; and that though individual members of it might be also members of the legislature, the provinces of the two Societies, *as* Societies,—of a scientific association, and a political community,—are altogether distinct.

What was taught by the Apostles to their converts.
Now this is just the non-interference in political affairs which Christ and his Apostles professed, and taught, and carried into practice, in respect of the religion of the Gospel.

As the Apostle Peter converted to the Faith Cornelius the *Centurion,* so likewise Paul,—who avowed his practice of "witnessing both to small and *great,*"—converted Sergius Paulus the Roman Governor at Paphos, and Dionysius the Areopagite, a Judge of the highest court at Athens; and expressed his ardent wish to convert King Agrippa, and also all "who heard him that day." Yet neither Peter nor Paul ever thought of desiring the Centurion—the Governor—the Judge and the King, to lay down their offices, and renounce all concern with secular business; nor did they ever dream that their holding such offices when Christians, would make Christ's a "kingdom of this world." They wished, and they openly endeavoured, to make "the kingdoms of this world the kingdoms of the Lord,"[1] and "kings the nursing-fathers of the Church," in the sense of making the *individuals* of every nation members of Christ;—of inducing kings and magistrates, and subjects too, to abstain from persecuting Christians, and voluntarily to *become* Christians, and to act so as to induce others *voluntarily* to follow their example.

---

[1] Some Millennarians understand this prophecy, as referring to a temporal reign of Christ on earth. See *Scripture Revelations of a Future State.* Lect. on Millennium.

It has been said that this passage respecting the "kingdoms of this world becoming the kingdoms of the Lord," describes the christian Church in its perfection, and "My kingdom is not of this world," describes it in its infancy. But what Jesus and his Apostles taught on this point, belongs, and ever did, and ever will belong, to the christian Church in *every* stage alike; namely, that the Christian is to act, in *all* the relations of life, in whatever circumstances he is placed, on christian principles. And what were the principles they inculcated? "Render unto Cæsar the things that are Cæsar's, and unto God the things that are God's:" "Render unto *all* their due; tribute to whom tribute is due; custom, to whom custom; fear, to whom fear; honour, to whom honour:" "Submit yourselves to every ordinance of man, for the Lord's sake:" "Ye must needs be subject, not only for wrath, but also for conscience' sake," &c. Never was the Christian required to do less than conform to such principles; never will he be called on to do more.[1]

All Christians required to act on christian principles, in all the relations of life.

The Apostles, we should observe, inculcated without any express limitations or exceptions, submission to Civil Rulers; who were, then, and for several Ages after, Pagans, and often persecutors of Christianity; and whom yet they described as "Powers *ordained by God*, for the *punishment of evil-doers*, and for the praise of them that do well." But in what regards *Religion*, these very Apostles taught men, both by precept and example, to hold fast their Faith in *disobedience* to the commands of the Rulers, and to brave persecution. It is quite evident therefore that their hearers must have understood them to mean that the *province of the*

Proper province of the Civil Magistrate.

---

[1] See Appendix.

Civil-Ruler is limited to secular concerns;—to the guardianship of men's persons and property from fraud and violence. The "evil-doers" whom these Rulers were divinely ordained to punish, could not have been understood to include such as transgressed the laws pertaining to *religion*.

This view, therefore, of the proper department of the Civil-Magistrate, and of the character and objects of a Political-Community, (which some are accustomed to allude to as "Warburton's theory," as if to insinuate that it originated with *him*,) must have been fully impressed on the minds of the early Christians, and perfectly familiar to them, as the interpretation and development of their Master's precept, "Render to Cæsar the things that are Cæsar's, and to God, the things that are God's."

Christian Rulers have not, as such, any rights beyond Pagan.
And when christian Emperors arose, the principle was not thereby altered, though it was too often lost sight of. The christian Rulers often became as fierce persecutors as the Pagans had been, not only of their Pagan, but of a portion of their *christian* subjects;—the Arians, for instance, or Athanasians, as the case might be—who differed in creed from themselves.

Now, it would be absurd to suppose the Apostles to have meant that a man ought indeed to disobey a Magistrate's command to renounce *Christianity* for *Paganism*, but should obey, if commanded to renounce what he believed to be *pure and genuine* Christianity, for what he considered as an heretical *corruption* of it.

Evidently, therefore, the Apostles must always have been understood by such as would interpret them in candid simplicity, as teaching that universally, the Christian is to "hold fast his Faith without wavering," in opposition to any commands to the contrary, of *any* Rulers, Pagan or

Christian;—that the dutiful submission to the " ordinances of men " which they inculcated, related to secular matters only;—and, that to these, accordingly, must we limit the rightful power of the Magistrate, and the proper province of Civil Government.

Different kinds of societies to be kept distinct as to their end and means.

If Sergius Paulus and other converted Roman governors had consulted Paul, whether they should use their *power as Roman Governors* to put down Paganism by force, or if Dionysius, after having induced (suppose) the other Judges of the Areopagus to embrace the Gospel, had proposed to the Apostle that that Court should sit in judgment on religious offences, and inflict punishments[1] on all persons opposing or rejecting the true Faith, or deprive them of civil rights,—if the Apostle Paul, I say, had been *thus* consulted, what answer, think you, he would have given? What answer *must* he have given, if we believe him sincere in his professions, and if we believe his great Master to have really meant exactly what He declared? The Apostle would surely have explained to such inquirers that Christ meant the reception of his Gospel to rest on sincere inward conviction, not on constrained outward profession, which is all that legal penalties *can* produce:—that their office as governors and judges, was to take cognizance of men's *overt acts*, and to punish and restrain crimes against the civil community; but that their duty as Christians was to regulate, and try to persuade others to regulate, the inward motives and dispositions of the heart, according to Gospel-principles; and to keep themselves not from *crimes* merely, but from *sins* against God; and to " exercise themselves in having them-

---

[1] The error of speaking of *excommunication* as a "punishment" is noticed in *Note A* to *Essay II.*

selves a conscience void of offence, before God and man," (Acts, xxiv. 16) not in seeking to force another to speak or act against his conscience. He would not have forbidden them to take a part (as it is most fit that the laity should) in the government of the Church, or to hold any ecclesiastical or spiritual office in it; or again, to retain their civil offices: but he would have deprecated with abhorrence their blending the two classes of offices together, and attempting to employ the power of *coercion* which essentially belongs to the civil magistrate, in the cause of Christ's religion. He would have told them to strive to convert and reclaim their neighbours from superstitious error (even as *he* had converted *them*) by instruction and *persuasion;* never losing sight of their great Master's rule, of doing as they would be done by; not inflicting therefore on the unbeliever the persecution which they had disapproved when directed against Christians; but leaving to every man that liberty of conscience which they desired to enjoy themselves.[1]

Such would have been the answer, I think we cannot doubt, which the Apostles would have given to such inquirers; and which, if Peter and Paul were now on earth, they *would* give to any like questions at this day. For such surely must be the decision of any one who is convinced that Jesus Himself was perfectly sincere in the declaration He made at his trial, and that He "left us an example, that we should follow his steps, who did no sin, neither was *guile* found in his mouth."

---

[1] Warburton in his *Alliance of Church and State* has most clearly laid down the characters and proper provinces respectively of these two kinds of Societies. His error is, that he has supposed the one Society to confer on the other a right which neither of them *had* to confer, and which neither of them (as he has himself proved) can, consistently with its own proper character, legitimately exercise.

§ 13. Yet if the Apostle Paul, with these sentiments, were now on earth, would there not be some danger of his being accounted a *latitudinarian* — a person nearly indifferent about religious distinctions, — regarding one Religion nearly as good as another ;—ready to profess any,—and believing little or nothing of any? For such is the character often attributed to any one who disapproves of the employment of secular force in behalf of the true Faith, or the monopoly, by its professors, of civil rights.

Alleged latitudinarian tendency of the above principles.

That there are persons indifferent about all religions, is true; and it is true that *some* of them are, from humanity of disposition, averse to persecution and coercion. For, many persons,—perhaps most,—are tolerant or intolerant according to their respective *tempers*, and not according to their *principles*. But as far as principles are concerned, certainly the latitudinarian is the more likely to be intolerant, and the sincerely conscientious, tolerant. A man who is careless about religious *sincerity*, may clearly see and appreciate the political convenience of religious *uniformity ;* and if he has no religious scruples of his own, he will not be the more likely to be tender of the religious scruples of others: if he is ready himself to profess what he does not believe, he will see no reason why others should not do the same.

Latitudinarian principles, intolerant.

Mr. Brydone mentions in his travels the case of an Englishman who attended Mass at a church in Naples, through curiosity, (which I am far from justifying,) and on the elevation of the Host, remained standing, while those around knelt: for this he was reproved by a gentleman near him, as a violation of the rules of delicacy and good breeding, in thus shocking the feelings of the congregation:

he answered that he did not believe in the real presence; "*No more do I, Sir,*" was the reply; "and yet you see I kneel."

Now without attempting to vindicate the conduct of the Englishman (who was under no compulsion to be present at a Service in which he scrupled to join) it may be remarked that the Neapolitan, or Mr. Brydone, would probably have been disposed, if entrusted with the government of any Country, to *compel* every one's compliance, in all points, with whatever the feelings of the people required; not only to kneel before the Host, but to attend in processions the image of St. Januarius, &c. if their omitting it would be likely to give offence. The plea of conscientious scruple, they would not have understood. "I do not *believe* so and so," would have been met by the ready answer, ". No more do I; and yet I *kneel.*"

Conscientious sincerity, friendly to tolerance.

That man on the contrary whose own conscience is tender, and his sense of religion deepfelt and sincere, will be (so far) the more disposed to respect the conscience of another, and to avoid giving occasion to hypocritical professions. His own faith being founded on genuine conviction, he will seek for the genuine conviction of others, and not their forced conformity. He will remember that "*the highest truth, if professed by one who believes it not in his heart, is to him, a lie,* and that he sins greatly by professing it. Let us try as much as we will, to convince our neighbours; but let us *beware of influencing their conduct, when we fail in influencing their convictions.* He who bribes or frightens his neighbour into doing an act which no good man would do for reward, or from fear, is tempting his neighbour to sin; he is assisting to lower and to harden his conscience;—to make him act for the favour or from the fear of man, instead of for the favour and from the fear of God: and if this be a sin in him, it is a double sin in us to tempt him to it."[1]

And above all, in proportion as any man has a right understanding of the Gospel, and a deep veneration for his great Master, and an earnest desire to tread in his steps, and a full confidence in his promises, in the same degree will he perceive that the employment of secular coercion in the cause of the Gospel is at variance with the true spirit of the Gospel; and will be convinced that Christ's declarations are to be interpreted as He Himself knew them to be understood, then, and are to be the guide of his followers, now.

Real knowledge of the Gospel conducive to toleration.

And finally, such a man will feel that it implies a sinful distrust,—a want of faith in Christ's wisdom, and goodness, and power,— to call in the aid of the arm of flesh,—of military or civil force,—in the cause of Him who declared that He *could* have called in the aid of "more than twelve legions of angels;" and who, when " all power was given unto Him

Tolerance one fruit of faith.

---

[1] Arnold's *Christian Life*, p. 435. No words could express more distinctly, more completely, or more forcibly than these, my own sentiments; and I have the more pleasure in citing them, because other passages in the Works of the same justly-esteemed author have been understood as inculcating an opposite principle; as making it the duty of a Government to enforce conformity to the established religion, by punishing, or by excluding from civil rights, all who refuse so to conform. It is plain from the above-cited passage, either that the meaning of those other passages which have been understood as at variance with it, has been mistaken, or else that the principles advocated in them, if really tending to such a conclusion, would have been at once rejected by the author, as soon as he perceived that tendency. For it is incredible that any one should *designedly and avowedly* recommend such a system of government as would, *in his own opinion*, tend to lead subjects into " a great sin," (involving the rulers in a "double sin,") by " bribing or frightening them into doing what no good man would do for reward or fear," and thus "hardening and lowering their conscience." This, I say, is what no man in his senses, much less, an able and a virtuous man, would knowingly and avowedly recommend.

in Heaven and in Earth," sent forth his disciples—not to *subjugate*, or to coerce, but to "*teach* all nations;" and "sent them forth as sheep among wolves," forewarned of persecutions, and instructed to "bless them that cursed them," to return "good for evil;" and to "endure all things,—hope all things,—believe all things," for which He, their Master, had prepared them;—to believe *all* that He had taught,—to hope *all* that He had promised,—and to endure and do *all* that He had commanded.

# APPENDIX TO ESSAY I.

IN maintaining that Christ and his Apostles aimed at no secular empire, or monopoly of civil rights, I have said, "*secular* empire" and a "monopoly of *civil* privileges and powers," because the rule does not apply to such as are purely *ecclesiastical*. The government of a *Church* (except so far as relates to temporalities, which are clearly the property of the Nation) *ought* to be monopolized by members of that Church. It is an unseemly, and in many respects, mischievous, anomaly, that, in purely religious matters, any authority should be possessed (as is the case in this country) by those who are not members of the Religious Community. [See *Appeal on behalf of Church-government*, a valuable and well-written pamphlet. Houlston and Co.][1]

It is true that the *greatest* of the evils that *might* arise from such an anomaly,—vexatious and oppressive interference in matters that affect the conscience—do *not* arise in this country. No greater evil does result in practice than that (no small one, however) of leaving the Church virtually *without any* legislative government. But even if this were a less evil than it is, it would not be the less true as a principle, that none ought to have any share in the government of a Church (except—as I have said—in respect of secular matters) who are not members of that Church.

There are some however who, from want of the habit of attentive reflection, are with difficulty brought to perceive

---

[1] Since re-published in Bishop Dickinson's *Remains*. [Fellowes.] See also *Thoughts on Church-government:* Charge of 1844.

the unsoundness of any false principle, except when it is fully developed in practice, and produces, *actually*, *all* the ill effects that it can consistently lead to. They cannot perceive which way a wind is blowing unless it blows a perfect gale. They not merely know a tree only by its fruits, but, except when it is actually bearing its fruits, and when it has brought them to the full perfection of poisonous maturity, they do not recognize the tree.

This defect may often be observed in men's judgments on another point also,—the employment of secular coercion in religious matters, with a view either to compel men to conform to the faith and mode of worship prescribed by the Civil-government, or to give more or less of political ascendancy, and monopoly of civil rights and power, to those of a particular persuasion. To burn Dissenters under the title of heretics,—or to put them to a less cruel death,— or to banish, or fine and imprison them,—or to exclude from all, or from some, of the rights of citizens, and reduce, more or less, to the condition of vassals or Helots, those who do not profess the religion which the State, as such, enjoins, —these are widely different indeed, in respect of the *actual amount* of evil inflicted, or of good denied, to individuals; but the *principle* is in all these cases, the same; viz.: the assumed right of the Secular Government, as such, to interfere with men's conscience, and consequently (when the Government calls itself christian) to make Christ's kingdom, so far, "a kingdom of this world."[1]

One of the causes that have contributed to the prevalence of this error, is, a mistaken view of the nature of that *supremacy* which is possessed by a *political* Community.

The office of a Political Society or State—which is, to

---

[1] See *Essays*, 3rd and 4th Series. See also Note O to *Essay II*.

afford *protection* (as all admit it is bound to do) to the citizens, necessarily implies a *coercive* power over *all* of them; and thence, over other Societies of which any of them may be members. Hence, the Political Society must be (in respect of *power*) the "highest;" and the Secular Government—the person or persons in whom that power is vested, being as it were the *centre of gravity* in which the whole physical force of the Community is collected, and acts,—must be, in this sense, "Supreme" or "Sovereign;"[1] as not being *responsible* or *subject* to any other.

Much confusion of thought, and practical error has thence arisen in some minds; especially, since, in any question that may arise whether the State (the Political Society) have gone beyond its own proper province, it must *itself* be, in practice, the judge; there being no higher authority, on earth, to appeal to. It *can* do nothing (humanly speaking) *unlawful;* since it has the power to make, and absolutely enforce, laws; and again, to alter, or repeal them.

Indistinct and confused views on these points have led to various wrong conclusions. It has been supposed, for instance, that since the Political Society is the *highest* (which in a certain sense it is) it must have for its ends the *highest objects;*—that it ought to propose to itself, not, like any other kind of Society, some *particular* good, but, *human good, generally;*—the welfare, in all respects, of the citizens;—and that since every human good is therefore equally within the province of the Secular Government, the *greatest* good,—the moral welfare of the citizens, and the salvation of their souls,—must be especially its care: and hence follows the right, and the duty, of putting down heresy by the civil sword; since if it would be unjustifiable

---

[1] Κύριον, according to the ancient Greek Philosophers.

for the Magistrate to tolerate the circulation of counterfeit money, much more, that of false doctrine. And the *moral* as well as *religious* welfare of the citizens being entrusted to his care, he must take upon himself to determine both what is *true Religion*, and what is *morally right;* according to the doctrine of Hobbes, in his *Leviathan.*

I have no doubt that many advocates of the principle in question do not *mean* to advocate either religious persecution, or Hobbism: but I am speaking of the logical connexion of these consequences with that principle.

All this perplexity and error might be escaped by merely recollecting that the Political Society has,[1] like any other, its own appropriate objects; and that any other desirable objects which it may be enabled, incidentally, to promote, more effectually than could otherwise be done, and without interfering with its main objects, are yet (however intrinsically important) only secondary and subordinate;[2] and that it is "*Sovereign*" only in this sense, that its proper and main object is one which necessarily implies the exercise of *coercive power.*

In fact, the very circumstance which gives to the Political Community that kind of sovereignty which it does possess, is exactly what places beyond its own proper province the very noblest and highest objects of all. For, pure *Morality* as existing in the motives and not in mere outward acts, and sincere belief in a true *Religion*, are precisely what cannot be produced, directly and immediately, by the coercive power of the Civil Magistrate. "The quality of mercy is not strained:" and the same may be

---

[1] See § 12.

[2] The reader is referred, for an able development of just views on this point, to the *Edinburgh Review,* No. 139; especially a passage in p. 273, cited in the Appendix to the *Elements of Rhetoric,* Note (F). See also note to § 2 of the *Second Essay.*

said, with equal truth, of every other moral virtue also, and of genuine Christian "Hope, Faith, and Charity."

Moreover, the very circumstance that there exists *no higher Power on earth* to appeal to, from the decisions of a political "Government," ought, instead of leading us at once to acquiesce in the justice of whatever may be claimed for it, to render us on the contrary the more cautiously distrustful in our examination of its claims; and ought to make those holding the reins of that Government doubly careful in pronouncing decisions; because from these decisions there is *no appeal*. The "*supremacy*" of the Political-Community is not such as places *all* matters *without exception* under the proper province of the Civil-Legislator; but it is such as leaves the State to *decide what does* and what does not, come under that province; constituting, in short, the State the judge in its own cause.

Now it is universally believed that every class of men,—the Agricultural,—the Mercantile,—the Legal,—the Clerical,—the Military, &c., are liable to a bias, each in favour of itself:—that all men are disposed to lean towards an over-estimate of the importance, and an undue extension of the department, each, of his own Class. Every one accordingly would demur to the decision of any one of these Classes as to its own claims; and there seems no reason why those engaged in Legislation and Government should be exempt from such a bias. Now all *other* Classes are checked *by each other*, in any attempt to put forth unreasonable claims: Legislators and Governors alone, as representing the whole Nation,—the Political Community,—and as entrusted consequently with the physical force of it,—have to decide in each case what the just claims are,—what the proper department—of that Community.

From this cause, combined with a laudable desire to employ the greatest power for the promotion of the greatest and noblest ends, too often unaccompanied by calm reflection on the wisest and best and most legitimate mode of accomplishing those ends;—and again, the feeling of hostility natural to Man[1] against those opposed to us on points of faith;—these, and other circumstances, conspire to produce a tendency towards those notions of the functions and duties of a Civil Government, which have been above alluded to:—towards the System (so opposite to that taught by the Apostles) which places under the Control of the Secular Power the Religion of the Subjects.[2]

There has always been accordingly a majority, actually great, and *apparently* still greater, on that side.[3] It is but too true, that if we are to be guided by *authorities*, we must be prepared to admit, not only the right of secular coercion in religious matters, but also, an Order of Sacrificing (Sacerdotal) Priests under the Gospel-dispensation; deriving a sacramental virtue through imposition of hands, in regular succession from the Apostles, and, more or less, acting as substitutes for the People in the Service of God. For, *both* these views have been maintained by a great majority, in most Ages and Regions of Christendom; and so far from being, as some have imagined, incompatible, are for the most part, as all History testifies, found together.[4]

The prevalence of these views, in consequence of the natural tendencies of the human heart, I have, in several places,[5] dwelt on, illustrated, and endeavoured to explain. When a prevailing current in a particular spot sets strongly towards certain shoals, we must expect that many vessels will strike on them. When the passions and prejudices of

---

[1] See *Essay on Persecution*, 3rd Series, § 7.

[2] See § 12.

[3] And (formerly) against the Gospel. For "as for this way, we know that it is everywhere spoken against."—Acts, xxviii. 22.

[4] See *Essay II.*, § 14, note.

[5] Especially in *Essays II.* and *V.*, 3rd Series.

Man tend towards some particular errors, it must be expected that such errors will prevail among those not especially on their guard against them. In such cases therefore the presumption is rather if anything *against* the prevailing opinions. They may fairly be in some degree suspected of being what Bacon calls " Idola Tribus,"—errors of the Human Race.

I have said however that the weight of authorities on the side of that theory of Government I have been alluding to, is *apparently* even greater than in reality. For I am convinced that it has been advocated by many from their not perceiving what it really amounts to;—that it is in fact the theory of *intolerance :*—from their not recollecting, that, if men's spiritual concerns do properly come under the legitimate province of the Civil Magistrate, he can have no more right to *tolerate Heresy or Dissent*, than Theft or Murder. The man who vends poisoned food, or who fires his neighbour's houses, all would allow, ought to be arrested and punished : and he who, by his preaching or his example, disseminates doctrines and precepts which, in the Ruler's opinion, tend to poison not the bodies, but the souls of men, and which instead of destroying only their material earthly houses, tend to exclude them from " everlasting habitations," is even still more a fitting subject of secular coercion and punishment, if the concerns of Religion be the appropriate and primary care of the Secular Ruler.

And yet there are, I have no doubt, many who would not in practice follow up this most indisputable conclusion, by drawing the Civil Sword against heretics ; and who yet maintain, from not perceiving its tendency, the principle which leads to that conclusion. And it is certainly better that men should be inconsistently right, than consistently wrong.

The true character and legitimate consequences of the

theory, they often conceal from themselves by the employment of a vague and inaccurate kind of language. The moral and spiritual well-being of men, being confessedly of incomparably *higher importance* than the protection of their persons and property, many do not like to hear the terms "subordinate" and "secondary" applied to the former object, in reference to the Political Community, which is "sovereign" and exercises "*supremacy*" over all the individuals in the Country. They like to speak therefore of the Government of the Country as being entrusted with the care of the *welfare*, generally of the Subjects; and accordingly, of the right and duty of a christian Nation to make the Gospel the foundation of its laws,—to identify the State with the Church, &c.

But if, quitting vague generalities, we come to particulars, and inquire whether all this means, that "*conformity to the established Religion is to be enforced on all citizens*, or on all who are to partake of civil rights," or what else it does mean, this, which is the practically important question, we find kept very much out of sight.

It has been alleged that the question "whether the State has a right to dictate to every citizen what religion he shall profess," is much the same as the question "whether it has a right to impose *laws*." And this is no unfair statement of the case; supposing, of course, that by "laws" is meant "*any* laws whatever, that the Legislature may see fit to enact." *Some* laws, no one could deny a State's right to impose; since without laws of some kind, no State could subsist: and the concession of *this* right would not affect the present question. But if a State has the right to enact *all* laws whatever that the Legislative Body,—or, these, backed by the great mass of the population—may deem advisable, it is plain that a Government *may* enact laws prescribing to the citizens what their religion shall be. One Government may enjoin men to adore a Crucifix, and another, (as the Japanese) to trample on it: the laws may compel every one to attend Mass, or a Protestant-Service, or to worship in the Mosque, or in the Pagoda; or, like Nebuchadnezzar, (who seems to have found only three recusants,) to " fall down and worship the golden image."

The laws indeed cannot operate directly on the *belief* of the People, but can only control *outward acts:* but these outward acts may be such as greatly to interfere (as for example, in such points as those just alluded to) with men's conscientious sense of duty. The early Christians were not required to believe Jesus a false prophet, but only " not to *teach* in that name:" the laws did not require them to believe in Jupiter, but merely to burn incense before the Idol.[1]

And there is this peculiarity in the case of the outward acts of *Religion,* as distinguished from all others; that in this case, outward compliance, unaccompanied by inward conviction, is a pure, *unmixed* evil. One who abstains from crime, or who relieves the indigent, not from pure motives, but from fear of punishment, or for the sake of worldly credit or other advantages, benefits Society at least, though not himself. *Religious* hypocrisy, on the contrary, has no counterbalancing advantages;[2] so that outward religious observances, when practised under compulsion, whether we think them, in themselves, bad or good ones, must, in either case, be an evil.

Few therefore I suppose would admit the unlimited right of enacting laws on these points.

And if any should say that the professors of the *true* religion, have a right to compel all men to profess the same, though Heretics or Idolaters have not, this is plainly to admit the principle of persecution. For, each Government will of course pronounce to be true, the religion it enforces,

---

[1] Gibbon alludes to this circumstance, with a sneer at their unreasonable scrupulosity.

[2] See *Essays on the Dangers, &c.,* 4th Series, p. 206.

and will refuse to admit of any appeal from its decision. And if the Heretic, Mahometan, or Pagan ruler, in compelling all to profess his religion, is doing only that which *would* be right, supposing his religion were the true one, those who censure him must evidently be censuring, not, his employment of *coercion*, but his *theological error*. It is not a correct and allowable use of language to profess to condemn a sovereign for banishing, or putting to death, or disfranchising, one half of his subjects, if in reality we blame him only for not deciding as we think he ought, *which* half it shall be.[1]

If again any one *denies* to a Government the right to proceed thus, he has evidently answered in the negative the question whether a Government has the (unlimited) right of enforcing laws on the People.[2] And most persons, in these days, probably *would*, in practice, give such an answer; though, by vague generalities of language, and by the employment of words in an unusual sense, many leave it doubtful what their real meaning is.

For instance, it has been said that a man should be allowed the right of private judgment, *provided he decides in a certain way*, but *not otherwise;* and that religious liberty does not imply *irreligious liberty*. As if there could be *liberty* where no *alternative* is allowed;—where a man has only what, according to the homely proverb, is called in derision, "Hobson's choice!" A man OUGHT of course, in every case where there is a right and a wrong, to chuse what is right: but he cannot be said to be at *liberty*, or to exercise

---

[1] See *Essays on the Dangers, &c.*, Appendix.

[2] The case of a People who should unanimously agree in professing a certain religion, need not be considered; because it would be manifestly *superfluous* for *them* to pass a law that, as long as this agreement should continue, all civil rights should be exclusively enjoyed by the professors of that religion. If they did pass any law on the subject, it must be in reference to the future contingency of such spontaneous unanimity *not* continuing.

his own judgment, if *another*—however rightly—decide *for* him;—if he is not left to decide for himself which is the right and which the wrong, and to take which side he thinks fit. And though there may be various *degrees* of liberty and of constraint, so that the same person may to a certain degree be both free and constrained, it is evident he cannot at once be *both*, as to the *same* point.

In many other matters also, men's incautiously eager desire that others should do what is in itself right, often leads them to proceed in such a way as completely to defeat their own object. For instance, it is, of course, desirable that all who have the ability should contribute towards the relief of the poor; and that the amount each bestows, and the mode of bestowing it, should be such as a wise and good man, not biassed by any selfish, or any weak feelings, would prescribe. If reasoning, and exhortation, and entreaty, can induce them to do this, a great point is gained. But supposing these fail: then comes the temptation to *compel* men by Law to give as they ought. Immediately, there is an end of *giving*,—an end of all *charity*,—not only in the illiberal, but in the bountiful also; since what the Law enjoins, becomes not a *gift*, but a *payment* of a tax.

So also in the present case: it seems so desirable to transfer the decision as to the most important points of religion, from those who may be unlearned, weak, rash, prejudiced,—to those who are learned, able, careful, candid, wise, and good, that we are of course naturally led to exhort all men to pay due deference to the judgment of such persons; and we urge them to adopt such conclusions as seem to us agreeable to that wisdom and goodness. And then, if any one cannot satisfy himself of the truth of these conclusions, many are thereupon tempted to urge him to stifle his own convictions, and to resolve to believe on man's authority that that is divine truth which to himself appears the reverse. And henceforward, the decision, though it may be a *right* one, is none of *his*.

As some have an excessive, or a misdirected, deference for the decisions of some person, party, or Church, so, others are defective in that point. But whatever course we may think the right one in this respect, it is at least plain that when any one does resolve to stifle his own convictions as far as they may be at variance with those of another, and to assent to another's interpretation of Scripture whether it appear to his own mind a true or a false one, this man, however right he may be, cannot be said, without an abuse of language, to be exercising "private judgment:" not even though he should bring himself (as most likely he will) to a full conviction of the truth of what he had resolved to maintain.[1] For if a man does not earnestly seek truth, as such, and strenuously and steadily strive to follow it, he will seldom fail to satisfy himself of the truth of what he is already predisposed or predetermined, to believe.

Lastly, when any one cannot or will not bring himself to do this, many are tempted to *force* him by Law to profess a truth (as they think it) which he does not believe; or at least, to abstain from openly professing what he does believe. And as soon as this is done, there is an end at once of that which the Apostles were all along labouring to effect,—the *voluntary* reception of the truth. Not only no one can be sure that his neighbours sincerely believe what they profess, but he cannot call his own profession, however sincere, a *voluntary* profession,—a free testimony borne to the truth. However *well-contented* he may be to do that which he is compelled to do, it is an abuse of language to call that contentment, "liberty."

Restrictions on liberty are, it is true, sometimes necessary

---

[1] See *Essay on Truth*, No. I., 2nd Series.

and justifiable; but it is always best to call "liberty," and "restriction," each by its own name. It will often happen that the public good requires even the confinement of an individual in prison; but then it is best to say plainly that he *is* confined, instead of saying that "he is at liberty to remain within the walls of the prison, though not at liberty to leave it." The employment of words in new and unauthorized senses only tends to produce confusion of thought, and to screen fallacies from the observation both of the writer and the reader. If intelligent and well-intentioned men had not bewildered themselves in the inaccuracies of their own language, I should have been spared the necessity of dwelling on what, to most readers, will appear self-evident truisms, such as would not need even to be stated, were not doctrines that are in reality at variance with them, circulated and maintained at the present day.

Again, some persons seem to have been so confused by the employment of the term "voluntary," as to confound together in their minds the *voluntary reception* of a religion, and, what is termed in modern times, the "voluntary system;" i. e., the *support of the Clergy* by the *voluntary contributions* of their congregations:[1] as if it were necessary to reject, or to explain away, the prohibition to make Christ's a kingdom of this world, or else to renounce all right in a Church to hold such possessions, or to receive such grants of public money, as are enjoyed by many Hospitals, Almshouses, Schools, &c."[2]—as if there were some connexion between the absence of *endowments*, and the absence of *coer-*

---

[1] See Sermon delivered before the Curates-Fund-Society and published at their request. See also correspondence between the late Bishop Dickinson and the Rev. M. James, since reprinted in Bp. Dickinson's *Remains*.

[2] As for instance, by National Schools in England and Ireland; to which no one is constrained to send his children. See above, Note, p. 52.

cion. Yet the two things are not only quite distinct, but unconnected. On the one hand, it is well known that there are endowments (in the hands of trustees) for Chapels not only Episcopalian but Presbyterian, &c., though no one is now constrained to profess any religion contrary to his conscience. And on the other hand, it is perfectly conceivable (historical instances of it might be adduced) that a State might require all the subjects, or all who would enjoy their full share of civil privileges, to profess a certain religion, and yet might leave whole districts unprovided with the instructions and ordinances of that very religion, except so far as the inhabitants might chuse to provide ministers by their own voluntary contributions.

Some again there are,—I believe not a few—who conceive that to renounce all right of resorting to secular force in behalf of religion, would imply a renunciation of the right of self-defence against such as might assail or threaten our own religious liberty; and a tame submission to an invasion such as that of the Spanish Armada,—or to a tyrant such as James the Second, endeavouring to extirpate by force the religion of his subjects, or to a Body of insurgents like the German Anabaptists. To resist such attempts, is not unfrequently called " fighting for one's religion : " and those who insist on the right of taking measures to resist, or to prevent, such persecution or oppression as proceeds on religious grounds, are apt to fancy themselves bound to oppose the principles I have been inculcating, and to explain away the declaration of Christ as to the character of his kingdom.

But there is no ground for such inferences. These persons should be warned against confusing together in their minds, questions concerning the right of *resistance to unjust aggression*, and questions as to the *motives which influence the aggressors;* which latter we have nothing to do with. To defend our liberty, our persons, and property, by forcible means, when no others can avail, is a natural right of Man, which the Gospel, I conceive, never meant to take away.[1] If oppression, spoliation, or wrongful violence of any kind, be exercised or manifestly designed against us, we are justified in resistance; and we have nothing to do with the motives which have influenced the wrong-doer. Whether we are attacked by men who are acting only from avarice or ambition, or by bigoted Mahometans seeking to suppress Christianity, or by professed Christians designing to put down heresy, or by insurgent Negroes seeking to extirpate, or to subjugate, all White-men, all this makes no difference to us. We are authorized to defend our lives, our liberties, and our rights, against unjust aggression, whatever may be the ground, or the pretext, of that aggression. But we cannot with propriety be said to be "fighting for our *religion*" against a Mahometan oppressor in the one case, or "fighting for the *White race*" in the other, when we are resisting Negro oppressors. In all the cases alike, we are fighting *for our lives*, property, and other rights; however different may be the motives which may actuate the *assailants*. A person is then, and then only, properly said to be fighting (or in whatever other way, employing secular force) in *behalf* of his religion,

---

[1] This seems to be implied, according to the simplest and plainest sense of the words, in the passage (among others) which records our Saviour's directions to his disciples preparatory to his separation from them [Luke, xxii. 38]. That He did *not* mean them to use their swords in *fighting for Him*, is perfectly plain. And if we set aside all mystical and fanciful interpretations, his obvious meaning seems to have been, simply to warn them that they must no longer expect the protection of that special providence which, in their first mission, had superseded all ordinary care and provision; but were to use the customary means and precautions of ordinary travellers; providing themselves accordingly with "Scrips" for carrying provisions, and with weapons for defence against robbers. In a country so imperfectly governed and regulated as theirs appears to have been at that time, it is probable that a party of travellers would ordinarily consider it no less natural and necessary that one or two of their number should be armed, than we do, to bolt our house-doors at night.

when he is striving, by coercive means, to propagate it,—to compel the profession of it, or to establish its political ascendancy. And it is this, that, as I have endeavoured to show, is clearly contrary both to the letter and the spirit of our Lord's doctrine.[1]

How far, in each case that arises, the use of coercive means is necessary, and *therefore* justifiable, against those who invade, or who, we are convinced, are preparing to invade, our rights, is a question which must, of course, be settled according to the particular circumstances of the particular case. Whatever may be the motives that actuate the aggressor, it is evident that no greater violence or severity should be resorted to,—no greater restraints imposed,—than are clearly indispensable to our own defence. But the main point to be kept in mind (in reference to the immediate question now before us) is, that we are not to be influenced by

---

[1] Besides the other passages in Scripture in which this is so plainly declared or implied, there is one (of more doubtful interpretation) which does seem to me to signify that our Lord's especial divine protection would be withdrawn from such of his followers as should resort to force in the cause of their Religion : "Put up thy sword into its sheath; for all *they that take the sword shall perish with the sword.*" That is, (I conceive,) "those who wage *war*, shall be left to the *ordinary risks* of war, and be *liable* to defeat, and even to the total overthrow of their cause, if overmatched, in numbers, or other military advantages, by their adversaries."

A *liability* to such defeat, seems plainly to be all that we are to understand : for we know that *every* one does not *actually suffer* a violent death who "takes the sword" even in the cause of religion. Nor again were *individual* Christians, however peaceable and patient, exempted from violent death. But the *cause of Christianity* has been most wonderfully supported against persecuting violence. And on the other hand, the Crusaders, and others who have *waged wars* under the banner of the Cross, have never been (like the Israelites of old) supported by any extraordinary Providence against superiority of numbers or of military skill. When they *appealed to the sword, to the sword the decision was left*, according to that ordinary course of Providence which we call "the fortune of war."

But whatever may be the sense of the particular passage above-mentioned, the prohibition of force in the cause of Christianity is quite clear from numerous others, and from the whole tenour of the New Testament.

any considerations as to what is the magnitude of an assailant's religious errors; or whether religion has, or has not, anything to do with his invasion of our rights. We are only to consider, and to consider dispassionately, and with a deep sense of the responsibility of those who resort to forcible means,—the magnitude and the character of the danger apprehended. The insurgent Anabaptists at Munster, *e.g.* it was clearly necessary to put down by force; and it would have been equally necessary had their avowed object been that of the Jacquerie in France, and Jack Cade's followers in England,— to extirpate all who possessed property. And the same may be said of the no-popery rioters in London, stirred up by Lord George Gordon. The question was not whether Romanism or Protestantism were the better religion, but whether the lives and property of peaceable citizens should be protected.

If in any case we are fully convinced that the religious opinions of certain persons,—whether Jews, or professed Christians, or of any other persuasion,—are incompatible, —not only in *our* opinion but in *theirs*,—with the duties of " loyal and peaceable subjects," and that they meditate, and are, from their numbers, likely to accomplish, designs subversive of the ends of the Political community, it would be a folly to allow them free access to high offices; and, I should add, a still greater folly (for the reasons which I have stated at large elsewhere[1]) to allow them to live in the Country, and to acquire property, and exercise, in person, or through others, the elective franchise, or other political influence.

We must be very careful, however, how we judge men by the conclusions—(disavowed by themselves)—which *we* deduce from their tenets; and impose penalties or restrictions on them for acts which they neither commit nor justify,

---

[1] See *Essays on the Dangers, &c.*, Appendix.

because we think that *we*, if we held their tenets, should commit such. Ingenious and plausible arguments have been adduced to show that no Roman Catholic can consistently be a loyal subject : (though they came forward zealously against the Spanish Armada)—that every consistent Roman Catholic must approve of persecution ;— that no Calvinist can consistently exert himself in the practice of duty ;—that no Calvinist,—and, again, that no one who is *not* a Calvinist,—can be a consistent member of the Church of England, &c. In short, there is hardly any shade of opinion that may not be, and that has not been, thus denounced. Let any one who has convinced himself, by any of these trains of reasoning, recollect, that, after all, Man is not a uniformly *consistent* Being ; —that as most men are often in practice worse, so, they are not unfrequently better, than their principles : and that it is clearly more desirable that a man should be inconsistently right than consistently wrong.

In many cases, however, it is impossible for a man to be even *consistently wrong*. For instance, the christian Scriptures are clearly inconsistent with persecution : if, therefore, a man be an adherent of any church which inculcates persecuting dogmas, and which also acknowledges the christian Scriptures, it is evident he has only his choice between two inconsistencies ; since, whether he approve or disapprove persecution, he must at any rate be inconsistent. And it is to be hoped, in charity, that he may chuse the better of the two.[1]

Lastly, there are some, I believe, who, in speaking of a christian State, as *upholding Christianity*, mean no more than to vindicate the prohibition by law of sundry crimes

---

[1] See *Thoughts on the Grant to a Roman-catholic Seminary.*

which were permitted among the ancient Heathens, such as Gladiatorial-shows, Infanticide, and other enormities. But as no plea of *conscience* is urged in behalf of such practices, the consideration of any laws prohibiting them is wholly irrelevant to any question concerning *religious liberty*. Cases indeed may conceivably arise, (such as I have adverted to in *Essay V.* § 10, 3rd Series) in which even the plea of conscience ought not to be admitted by the Legislator: as, for instance, if a man should conceive himself religiously bound to offer human sacrifices, or to do any other such acts detrimental to the temporal well-being of his fellow-citizens. But cases in which *no* such plea can be urged, are evidently foreign from all questions as to the interference, in religious matters, of the Secular Government. There may even be much of unwise and troublesome legislation, (such as many of the sumptuary-laws and police regulations of our ancestors,) which may be objected to as absurd, or oppressive, but not on the ground of the spiritual character of Christ's Kingdom. The laws which forbade men to have more than so many dishes of meat on their tables, or to have a light in their houses after the curfew-bell, were doubtless very objectionable; but no one could plead that he was bound in conscience to disobey them.

But in proportion as men advance in civilization, and become more enlightened, humane, and moral, (an advance which any tolerably-pure form of Christianity evidently tends to promote) their Laws and Institutions will not fail to exhibit a corresponding improvement. Some things will be prohibited, which, in a ruder and more vicious state of Society[1] were permitted, or even enjoined: and again, many prohibitions will be removed, which were either founded

---

[1] See Taylor's *Natural History of Society*.

in error, or cannot be effectually enforced, and which, in the attempt to enforce them, will do more harm than good.[1]

And, among others, we may expect to find a continual diminution of the laws dictating to men in religious matters. For it is a fact, that, generally speaking, in proportion as any nation is found to have been making such advancement as I have been alluding to, it will be found to have been advancing also in *religious toleration*. Instead of becoming more and more disposed towards the system of placing the religion of the citizens under the control of the Secular Government, the direct reverse is found to take place. The history of mankind, imperfect as men are, evinces the truth of this, as a general proposition. And difficult as it must be for the advocates of an opposite theory to account for the fact, that such *is* the fact, they can hardly deny.

Although, therefore, the prevailing opinion should, even still, be in favour of that system, this is a case in which the Authority of Mankind (which, though not entitled to implicit acquiescence, must be admitted to have great weight) may be appealed to even *against* the opinion of the majority. I mean, the Authority of men, *as* rational Beings, and considered in reference to the exercise of judgment, uninfluenced by passion and prejudice. Indeed it is in this way only, that rectitude, generally, can be said to have the suffrages of Mankind in its favour. It is not that the majority of mankind adhere to it in cases where their feel-

---

[1] Hardly any one can have had intercourse with intelligent *children*, (and many persons,—in a semibarbarian Country, nearly all—never advance beyond this condition) without observing that their first thought usually is to suggest that there "should be a law" to oblige men to do so and so, or to prohibit such and such conduct. It is characteristic of the puerile and the semibarbarian condition of mind, to be disposed to violate the wise maxim of "pas trop gouverner."

ings or interests are concerned; but they approve of it, for the most part, in cases where they have to judge without any selfish bias ;—*so far forth as* they are *rational* agents.

Now, in the present question, if we inquire what is the lesson that Scripture is calculated to convey to mankind, we should look not to the conclusions adopted by the majority of mankind, but, to the conclusions towards which there has been more or less *tendency*, in proportion as men have been more or less attentive, intelligent, and candid searchers into Scripture.

Before the Gospel appeared, we find all Legislators and Philosophers agreed in regarding " *human good* universally," as coming under the cognizance of the Civil Magistrate; who accordingly was to have a complete control over the moral and religious conduct of the citizens.

We find again that, when the Scriptures were wholly unread by all but one in ten thousand of professed Christians, the duty of Rulers to wage war against Infidels and to extirpate Heretics, was undisputed.

When the Scriptures began to be a popular study, but were studied crudely and rashly, and when men were dazzled by being brought suddenly from darkness into light, intolerant principles did indeed still prevail, but some notions of religious liberty began to appear. As, towards the close of a rigorous winter, the earliest trees begin to open their buds, so, a few distinguished characters begun to break the icy fetters of bigotry; and principles of tolerance were gradually developed.

As the study—and the intelligent study—of Scripture, extended, in the same degree, the opening buds, as it were, made continually further advances. In every Age and Country, as a general rule, tolerant principles have (however imperfectly) gained ground wherever scriptural knowledge has gained ground. And a presumption is thus afforded that a still further advance of the one would lead to a corresponding advance in the other.[1]

The story is well known, of the woman who appealed from the decision of king Philip when half-intoxicated, to that of "Philip when sober." In like manner we may here appeal from the judgment of men ignorant of Scripture, to that of men acquainted with it;—from the judgment of men ill-read in Scripture, to that of more diligent and attentive students; —from the decision of Man's passions, and prejudices, and apparent interests, to that of his sober and unbiassed reason; —to that of Man, in short, so far forth as he is a rational Being, and an intelligent student and humble follower of God's Word.

And even should any one be convinced that not only the apparent but the actual majority, even of good and enlightened Christians, retain more or less of intolerant principles, still, if he is also convinced that *in proportion as* they are more enlightened and better, they recede more and more from such principles, his inference as to the *tendency* of Christianity will be the same.

Although however the above reasons appear to me to be amply sufficient, alone, to warrant the conclusion drawn, they are adduced chiefly as suggesting a satisfactory *confirmation* to one who has already ascertained, by examination of the christian Scriptures, his christian duty on this point. All others will generally be driven out of the true course by that current above alluded to, of human prejudices and passions. For, arguments, even the strongest and clearest, will usually prove too weak to overthrow the "Idols of the

---

[1] This is an instance of the kind of argument which is described in the *Elements of Rhetoric*, (Part I. ch. ii. § 6,) as the argument from "progressive approach;" by which we are often enabled to form reasonable conjectures as to cases of which we have no complete experience.

Race" (Idola Tribus) as Bacon calls them:—the errors springing out of Man's nature—in those who either neglect altogether the teaching of Scripture, or approach the study with a ready-framed theory in their minds, and a secret wish to be able to make out that this theory is reconcileable with Scripture. If, like Balaam, they do not acquiesce at once in the divine prohibition, but try once more " what the Lord will say," they will, like him, be indulged in finding something more conformable to their sinful wish; even as Balaam, on his second application, received permission to "go with the men," and yet " the Lord's anger was kindled against him because he went."

But those who consult the Sacred Writings with a truly inquiring, humble and teachable mind, and a resolution to comply, readily and implicitly, with their directions, will be rewarded by perceiving afterwards that what they have decided on as the most christian course, is also the most expedient; the most conformable to the general maxims of political Wisdom and natural Justice.

ESSAY II.

ON THE

CONSTITUTION OF A CHRISTIAN CHURCH,
ITS POWERS AND MINISTRY.

Οὐ γὰρ ἑαυτοὺς κηρύσσομεν, ἀλλὰ Χριστὸν Ἰησοῦν Κύριον· ἑαυτοὺς δὲ, δούλους ὑμῶν διὰ Ἰησοῦν. 2 Cor. iv. 5.

ESSAY II.

§ 1. OF all who acknowledge Jesus of Nazareth as their Master, "the Author and Finisher of their faith," there are scarcely any who do not agree in regarding Him as the Founder and perpetual Head of a religious *Society* also;—as having instituted and designed for permanent continuance, a Community or system of Communities, to which his Disciples here on earth were to belong. The religion He introduced was manifestly designed by Him,—and so understood by his immediate followers,—to be a *social* Religion.[1] It was not merely a revelation of certain truths to be received, and of practical rules to be observed,—it was not a mere system of doctrines and precepts to be embraced by each individual independently of others; and in which his agreement or co-operation with any others would be accidental; as when several men have come to the same conclusions in some Science, or have adopted the same system of Agriculture or of Medicine; but it was to be a *combination* of men who should be "members of the body of Christ,"—living stones of one Spiritual Temple;[2] "edifying" (*i. e.* building up) "one another in their Faith;"—and brethren of one holy Family.

Christianity designed to be a social Religion.

This "Kingdom of Heaven," as it is called, which the

---

[1] See "Use and Abuse of Party-feeling:" *Bampton Lectures*, Lect. I.

[2] See Sermon IV., *On a Christian Place of Worship*, and also Dr. Hinds's *Three Temples*.

Lord Jesus established, was proclaimed (*i. e.* preached)[1] by his forerunner John the Baptist as "*at hand.*" And the same, in this respect, was the preaching of our Lord Himself, and of his Disciples,—first the Twelve, and afterwards the Seventy,—whom He sent out during his ministry on earth. The good tidings they were to proclaim, were only of the *approaching* Kingdom of Heaven ; it was a joyful *expectation* only that they were commissioned to spread : it was a preparation of men's hearts for the coming of that Kingdom, that they were to teach.

But when the personal ministry of Christ came to a close, the Gospel they were thenceforward to preach was the good tidings of that Kingdom not *approaching* merely, but actually *begun,*—of the first christian Community set on foot,—of a kingdom which their Master had "*appointed unto them.*" Thenceforward, they were not merely to *announce* that kingdom, but to *establish* it, and invite all men to enrol themselves in it : they were not merely to make known, but to execute, their Master's design, of commencing that Society of which He is the Head, and which He has promised to be with "always, even unto the end of the world."[2]

---

[1] This word has come to be ordinarily applied to religious *instruction ;* from which, however, it is always clearly distinguished in Scripture. It signifies, properly, to *announce* as a *herald.* Our Lord's "*preaching* that the Kingdom of Heaven was at hand," and his *teaching* the People, are always expressed by different words.

[2] It is likely that the Doxology at the end of the Lord's Prayer, "Thine *is* the kingdom, and the power, and the glory," (which all the soundest critics, I believe, are now agreed, does not exist in the best MSS. of the Gospels,) was adopted by the Disciples very soon after our Lord's departure from earth. At the time when He first taught the prayer to his Disciples, it would have been premature to speak of the heavenly kingdom in the present tense, as actually established. They were taught to pray for its coming as a thing future. At a later period, it was no less proper to allude to it as already existing ; and the prayer for its "coming" would be, from the circumstances of the case, a prayer for its continued extension and firmer hold on men's hearts.

We find Him, accordingly, directing them not only to " go into all the world, and preach to every creature,"¹ but further, to " teach" (" make disciples of," as in the margin of the Bible) " all nations ;" admitting them as members of the Body of Disciples, by " baptizing them into² the name of the Father, and the Son, and the Holy Ghost."

Institution of a Christian Society.

Of his design to establish what should be emphatically a Social Religion,—a " Fellowship" or " Communion (*i. e.* Community) of Saints," there can be, I think, no doubt in the mind of any reflecting reader of our sacred books. Besides our Lord's general promise of " coming unto, and dwelling in, *any man* who should love Him and keep his saying," there is a distinct promise also of an especial presence in any *Assembly*—even of " two or three—gathered together in his name." Besides the general promises made to prayer,—to the prayer of an individual " in the closet," —there is a distinct promise also to those who shall " *agree together* touching something they shall ask." And it is in conformity with his own institution that Christians have, ever since, celebrated what they designate as, emphatically, *the Communion*, by " meeting together to break bread," in commemoration of his redemption of his People.

His design, in short, manifestly was, to adapt his Reli-

---

¹ See a Sermon by Dr. Dickinson, (afterwards Bishop of Meath,) on *Our Lord's Two Charges to his Disciples*. It has since been republished in his *Remains*.

² " In the name," is a manifest mis-translation, originating, apparently, with the Vulgate Latin, which has " in nomine." The preposition, in the original, is not ἐν but εἰς, " into" or " to."

The command to " baptize into the Name," &c., is derived (in point of expression) from the language of the Old Testament in several passages; one of which is referred to by the Apostle James, (Acts, xv. 17,) where he speaks of " all the Gentiles upon whom my Name is called," &c.

See Discourse on *The Name Emmanuel*.

gion to the *social* principles of man's nature;[1] and to bind his disciples, throughout all Ages, to each other, by those ties of mutual attachment, sympathy, and co-operation, which, in every human Community and Association, of whatever kind, are found so powerful.

Properties of a Community.

§ 2. Obvious, and indeed trite, as these remarks may appear, most persons are apt, I think, not sufficiently to consider what important conclusions result from them;—how much is implied in the constituting of a *Community*. It is worth while, therefore, to pause at this point, and inquire what are the inherent properties and universal character naturally and necessarily belonging to any regularly-constituted Society, as such, for whatever purpose formed. For I think it will appear, on a very simple examination, that several points which have been denied or disregarded by some, and elaborately, but not alawys satisfactorily maintained by others, arise, as obvious consequences, out of the very intrinsic character,—the universal and necessary description of a regular *community*.[2]

A Community requires OFFICERS, RULES, *and power to admit* MEMBERS.

It seems to belong to the very essence of a Community that it should have — 1st, *Officers* of some kind; 2ndly, *Rules* enforced by some kind of penalties; and, 3rdly, Some power of admitting and excluding persons as *Members*.

---

[1] See *Bampton Lectures* for the year 1822, Lect. I.

[2] I wish it to be understood, once for all, that I all along speak of a "Society" or "Community" in the received and customary sense. To apply the term to a Police-force, or to an Army, &c., which are manifestly only *instruments employed by* a Community, would be as great and as uncalled-for an innovation in language as it would be to call the limbs or other *organs* of the animal frame, "animals."

For, 1st, whatever may be the character, and whatever the proposed objects of a regularly-constituted Community, Officers of some kind are essential to it. *Officers necessary to a Community.* In whatever manner they may be appointed,—whether by hereditary succession, or by rotation, or by election of any kind,—whatever be the number or titles of them, and whatever the distribution of their functions,—(all which are matters of detail,) Officers of some kind every Community *must* have. And these, or some of these, while acting in their proper capacity, *represent* the Community; and are, so far, invested with whatever powers and rights belong to *it;* so that their acts, their rights, their claims, are considered as those of the whole Body. We speak, *e. g.* indifferently of this or that having been done by the Athenians, the Romans, the Carthaginians; or by the Athenian, the Roman, or Carthaginian *Government*, or *Rulers*.[1] And so also when we speak of the acts of some University, or of the *Governors* of that University, we are using two equivalent expressions.

2ndly. It seems equally essential to every Community that it should have certain Regulations or Bye-laws, binding on its own members. *Bye-laws of a Community binding on its members.* And if it be not wholly subjected to the control, and regulated by the directions of some extraneous Power, but is in any degree an *independent* Community, it must so far have power to enact, and abrogate,—to suspend, alter, and restore bye-laws for itself; namely, such regulations, extending to matters intrinsically indifferent, as are not at variance with the

---

[1] And it is to be observed that it makes no difference, as to this point, whether the Governors are *elected by* the governed, and in any degree restrained by them, or are hereditary and unlimited. In all cases, the *established and recognised* Rulers of any Community are considered as *representing* it.

enactments of any superior authority. The enforcement also of the regulations of a Community by some kind of Penalties, is evidently implied by the very existence of Regulations. To say of any Community that its Laws are valid, and binding on its members, is to say that the violators of them may justly be visited with Penalties:[1] and to recognise Officers in any Community, is to recognise, as among its Laws, submission to those Officers while in the exercise of their legitimate functions.

Coercive power belongs to Political Communities.

In the case of *Political* Communities, which is a peculiar one, inasmuch as they necessarily exercise an *absolutely-coercive* power,—the Penalties must be determined according to the wisdom and justice of each Government, and can have no other limit. But in a purely *voluntary* Community, the *ultimate* Penalty must be expulsion; all others, short of this, being submitted to as the *alternative*.[2] But in every Community, of whatever description (or in those under whose control it is placed) there must reside a power of enacting, enforcing, and remitting, the Penalties by which due submission to its laws and to its officers is to be secured.

Admission to membership of a Community.

3rdly. Lastly, no less essential to a Community seems to be a power, lodged somewhere, of determining questions of Membership. Whatever may be the claims or qualifications on which that may depend,—nay, even whether the community be a voluntary Association, or (as is the case with political Communities) one claiming compulsory

---

[1] That is, be it observed, penalties *voluntarily* submitted to by its members, as the condition of their *continuing such*: the ultimate penalty being *expulsion*; except in the case of a Political Community, (a State) which alone has the right of *absolute* compulsion. See *Appendix* to *Essay I.*

[2] See *Note A* to *Essay II.*

power,—and whatever may be its purpose—in all cases, the admission to it, or exclusion from it, of each individual, must be determined by some recognised authority.

Since therefore this point, and also those others above-mentioned, seem, naturally and necessarily, to belong to every regular Community,—since it must, in short, consist of regularly-constituted *Members*, subject to certain *Rules*, and having certain *Officers*, it follows, that whoever directs or sanctions the establishment of a Community, (as our Lord certainly did in respect of christian Churches) must be understood as thereby sanctioning those institutions which belong to the essence of a Community. To recognise a Community as actually having a legitimate existence, or as allowably to be formed, is to recognise it as having *Officers*,—as having *Regulations* enforced by certain Penalties, and as admitting or refusing to admit *Members*.

§ 3. All this, I say, seems to be implied by the very nature of the case. But, on purpose, as it should seem, to provide against any misapprehension or uncertainty, our Lord did not stop at the mere general sanction given by Him to the formation of a christian Community, but He also particularized all the points I have been speaking of. He appointed or ordained the first *Officers;* He recognised the power of enacting and abrogating *Rules;* and He gave authority for the admitting of *Members*.

Rights divinely conferred on a christian Community.

Such is the obvious sense of his directions to his Apostles: obvious, I mean, *to them*, with such habits of thought and of expression as they had, and as He must have known them to have. He must have known well what meaning his words would convey to his own countrymen, at that time. But some things which would appear plain and obvious to a Jew,—even an unlearned Jew,—in

G

those days, may be such as to require some examination and careful reflection to enable *us*, of a distinct Age and Country, to apprehend them in the same sense. When however we do examine and reflect, we can hardly doubt, I think—considering to whom, and at what time, He was speaking—that our Lord did sanction and enjoin the formation of a permanent religious Community or Communities, possessing all those powers which have been above alluded to.

Power to bind and loose, power of the keys, and power of remission of sins.
 The power of "binding and loosing;"— *i. e.* enacting and enforcing, and of abrogating or suspending regulations, for a christian Society,—was recognised by his promise[1] of the *divine ratification* of those acts,—the "binding and loosing in heaven." The "Keys of the Kingdom of Heaven," denote the power of admitting persons Members of the Church, and excluding them from it. And the expression respecting the "remitting and retaining of sins," if it is to be understood (as I think it is) as extending to anything beyond the power of admitting members into Christ's Church by "Baptism for the remission of sins," must relate to the enforcement or remission of *ecclesiastical* censures for offences against a christian Community.

By attentive reflection on the two topics I have here suggested — namely, on the rights and powers essentially inherent in a Community, and consequently implied in the very institution of a Community, so far as they are not expressly excluded; and again, on the declarations of our Lord, as they must have been understood by his Disciples, —by reflection, I say, on these two topics, we shall be

---

[1] See *Note B* to *Essay II*.

enabled, I think, to simplify and clear up several questions which have been sometimes involved in much artificial obscurity and difficulty.

§ 4. And our view of the sense in which our Lord's directions are to be understood will be the more clear and decided, if we reflect that all the circumstances which have been noticed as naturally pertaining to every Community, are to be found *in that religious Community, in which the Disciples had been brought up;*—the Jewish Church, or (as it is called in the Old Testament) the "Congregation," or Ecclesia,[1] of which each Synagogue was a branch.[2] It had regular *Officers;*—the Elders or Presbyters, the Rulers of Synagogues, Ministers or Deacons, &c.—it had Bye-laws; being not only under the Levitical Law, but also having authority, within certain limits, of *making* regulations, and enforcing them by penalties (among others, that which we find alluded to in the New Testament, of excommunicating or "casting out of the Synagogue"): and it had power to admit Proselytes.

Constitution of the Jewish Church.

With all these points, then, the Disciples of Jesus had long been familiar. And He spoke of them in terms with which they must have been well acquainted. For instance, the expression "binding and loosing"[3] was, and still is, perfectly familiar to the Jews, in the sense of enforcing and abrogating rules; or,—which

Rights exercised by the Jewish Church, familiar to the Disciples.

---

[1] Septuagint.
[2] See Vitringa *on the Synagogue,* of which an excellent abridged translation by the Rev. J. Bernard has appeared : [published by Fellowes, Ludgate-street.]
[3] See Lightfoot on this subject, and also Dr. Wotton's valuable work on *the Mishna.*

amounts precisely to the same thing,—deciding as to the manner, and the extent, in which a previously existing law is to be considered as binding: as is done by our Judges in their recorded Decisions.

The Jewish Church was indeed subject, by divine authority, to the Levitical Law. But minute as were the directions of that Law, there were still many points of detail, connected with the observance of it, which required to be settled by some competent authority: such as, for instance, what was, or was not, to be regarded as "work," forbidden on the Sabbath:—what was to be considered as "servile work," forbidden on certain other days;—and in what way the injunctions respecting their food, their garments, the sowing of their fields, and several other matters, were to be observed.[1]

Authority of Jewish Rulers recognised by Christ.

In regard to regulations of this kind, our Lord recognises the authority of the Jewish Rulers, as being so far successors of Moses; for He tells his hearers, "The Scribes and Pharisees sit in Moses's seat; all, therefore, whatsoever they bid you observe, that observe, and do." And though He adds a caution not to "do after their works, for they say, and do not," He does not teach that their personal demerits, or even the gross abuse of their power, which He so strongly reprobates, could invalidate the legitimate exercise of that power. Indeed, since there is hardly any human Government that has not, at some time or other, abused, more or less, the power entrusted to it, to deny on that ground all claims whatever to submission, would be the very principle of anarchy.

---

[1] Those who can procure, or gain access to Dr. W. Wotton's *Selections from the Mishna*, will find in it much curious and interesting information relative to these and several other particulars, which throws great light on many passages of the New Testament.

The Jewish Rulers went beyond their proper province, when, instead of merely making such regulations as were necessary with a view to the due observance of the Mosaic Law, they superadded, on the authority of their supposed Tradition, commandments foreign to that Law; and, still more, evasions of the spirit of it.[1]

Abuse of power by Jewish Rulers.

Jesus accordingly censures them severely, as "teaching for doctrines the commandments of men;" and again, as "making the Word of God of none effect, by their Tradition." But still He distinctly recognises their legitimate authority in making such regulations as were necessarily left to their determination.

§ 5. And his disciples, therefore, who heard *both* of these his declarations, could not have been at any loss to understand what He meant by giving to themselves and the succeeding Officers of a christian Church, the power to "bind and loose." He charged them to "teach every one to observe all things whatsoever He had commanded them;" promising to be "with them always, even to the end of the world;" and He also gave them the power of "binding and loosing;" saying, "Whatsoever ye shall bind on earth shall be bound in heaven;" (*i. e.* ratified by the divine sanction;) "and whatsoever ye shall loose on earth, shall be loosed in heaven."

How the disciples would understand the Commission given them.

They would of course understand by this, not that they, or any of their successors, could have authority to dispense with their Master's commandments,—to add to or alter the terms of Gospel-salvation,—to teach them, in short, *not* to "observe

Power to make regulations.

---

[1] See Wotton *on the Mishna.*

what He had commanded them,"—but, to enact, from time to time, to alter, to abrogate, or to restore, regulations respecting matters of detail, not expressly determined in Scripture, but which yet *must* be determined in some way or other, with a view to the good order of the Community, and the furtherance of its great objects.

Power of remitting sins. So, also, we cannot suppose they would even suspect that they, or any mortal *man*, can have " power to forgive sins," *as against God ;*—that a *man* could be authorized either to absolve the *im*penitent, or to shut out from divine mercy the penitent; or again, to read the heart, so as to distinguish between the two, without an express inspiration in each particular case.

Power of reading all men's hearts, not given. And this express inspiration in particular cases, whatever may have been their original expectations, they must soon have learnt they were *not* always to look for. They were to use their best discretion,— to exercise due caution, in guarding against the admission of " false brethren,"— " deceitful workers,"—hypocritical pretenders to christian faith and purity;—but they had not, universally at least, any supernatural safeguard against such hypocrisy.

The example of Simon Magus would alone show this, even if there were no others to be found. He was, we find, baptized along with the other Samaritans (Acts, viii. 18), professing, as of course he must have done, sincere repentance, and devotion to Christ: and yet the Apostles find him, after this, to be still " in the gall of bitterness and in the bond of iniquity."[1]

But still the Gospel or good-tidings which they were authorized and enjoined to proclaim, being most especially tidings of " remission of sins " to all who should accept the

---

[1] Acts, viii. 21.

invitation made to them by the preachers of that Gospel, they might properly be said to "remit" or "retain" according as they admitted to Baptism the attentive and professedly-penitent and believing hearers, and left out of the number of the subjects of Christ's kingdom those who neglected or opposed Him.[1] "Repent and be baptized every one of you *for the remission of sins*," is accordingly the kind of language in which they invite their hearers every where to join the Body of their Master's People; and yet it is certain the remission of sins was *conditional only*, and dependent on a condition of which they—the Apostles themselves—had no infallible knowledge; the condition being, the real sincerity of that penitence and faith which the converts *appeared* and *professed* to have.[2]

§ 6. But although this is the only sense in which the Apostles, or of course, any of their successors in the christian ministry, can be empowered to "forgive sins" *as against God;* *i. e.* though they can only pronounce *A Community may pardon offences against itself.* and proclaim *his* forgiveness of all those who come to Him through Christ, and assure each individual of his acceptance with God, *supposing* him to be one of "those who truly repent and unfeignedly believe," yet offences *as against a Community* may, it is plain, be pardoned, or pardon for

---

[1] Of course, if there had been a distinct divine appointment of such a sacrament as that of Penance, as it is called (including private Confession and priestly Absolution) we should have been found to regard *that* in the same light as we do the sacraments of Baptism and of the Eucharist. Without presuming to set limits to the divine favour, we feel bound to resort to, and to administer, these, as appointed means of grace. And if again there had *not* been that divine appointment of those sacraments, a Church would have no more authority to confer on *them* a sacramental character, than on the pretended sacrament of Penance.

[2] See Speech of Bishop Stanley in the House of Lords, May 26, 1840.

them withheld, *by* that Community, or by those its officers who duly represent it.[1]

Penalties for Ecclesiastical offences. Whether our Lord intended, in what He said of " remitting and retaining sins," to include (as seems to me the probable supposition) this power of inflicting or removing *ecclesiastical censures* for transgressions of the regulations of a Society, we may be perhaps not authorized positively to conclude; but at any rate, such a power is *inherent* necessarily in every Community, so far as not expressly reserved for some superior jurisdiction: *regulations* of some sort or other, and consequently *enforcement* of those regulations by some kind of penalties, being essential to a Community, and implied in the very nature of it.

Different views of the same act, as a SIN *and as a* CRIME. But what leads to confusion of thought in some minds, is, that the same action may often have two distinct characters, according to the light in which it is viewed: whether as a *sin*[2] against God, or as a *crime* in reference to the Community; and hence they are sometimes led to confound together the pardoning of the *crime*—the *offence* against the Community—with the pardoning of the *sin*. Now the regularly-appointed Ministers—the Officers of a Community—may be authorized to enforce or remit penalties against the ecclesiastical offence,—the crime,—in reference to the Community; and may pronounce an *absolute* and complete pardon of a particular offender, for a particular act, on his making the requisite submission and reparation, and appearing outwardly, as far as Man can judge, a proper subject for such pardon. And we are commanded to "forgive one another;" namely, offences against *ourselves*. But the pardon of sin as against God, must *be*

---

[1] See *Lessons on the History of Religious Worship*, l. v., § 6.
[2] See Warburton's *Div. Leg.*

conditional on that hearty inward repentance, of which, in each case, God only, or those to whom He may impart the knowledge, can adequately judge.

When Paul says to the Corinthians in reference[1] to that member of their Church who had caused a scandal by his offence, "To whomsoever ye forgive anything, I forgive it also," though I am far from saying that the offender's sin against God was *not* pardoned, it is quite plain *this* is not what the Apostle is here speaking of. He is speaking of a case in which they and he were not merely to *announce*, but to *bestow* forgiveness. They were to receive back the offender, who had scandalized the Society, into the bosom of that Society, on his professing with sincerity, or rather *apparent* sincerity (for of that alone they could be judges) his contrition. They would, of course—as believing those his professions—cherish a confident hope that his sin against God was pardoned. But doubtless they did not pretend either to an omniscient discernment of his sincerity, or to the power either of granting divine pardon to the impenitent, or of excluding from God's mercy the repentant sinner.

§ 7. Then again, with respect to the "Keys of the Kingdom of Heaven" which our Lord promised (Matt. xvi. 19) to give to Peter,[2] the

Power of the Keys.

---

[1] 2 Cor. ii. 10.

[2] There seems good reason to believe,—though it would be most unwarrantable to make it an article of faith,—that Peter really was the chief of the Apostles; not, certainly, in the sense of exercising any supremacy and absolute control over them,—as dictating to their consciences,—as finally deciding all cases of doubt—or as claiming any right to interfere in the Churches other Apostles had founded, (See Gal. ii. 7—9 and 11—14,) but as the chief in dignity; taking precedence of the rest, and acting as President, Chairman, or Speaker in their meetings. Peter, and James, and John, and sometimes Peter, and James, —always with Peter placed foremost, —were certainly distinguished (as appears from numerous passages in the Gospels) from the rest of the Apostles. He was apparently the chief Spokesman on the day of Pentecost, when the *Jewish* Believers were first called on to unite themselves into a Church;

Apostles could not, I conceive, doubt that He was fulfilling that promise to Peter and to the rest of them conjointly, when He " appointed unto them a Kingdom," and when, on the day of Pentecost He began the building of his Church, and enabled them, with Peter as their leader and chief spokesman, to open a door for the entrance of about three thousand converts at once; who received daily accessions to their number. The Apostles, and those commissioned by them, had the office of granting admission into the Society from time to time, to such as they judged qualified.[1]

Christian Church the Kingdom of Heaven. And that this Society or Church—was that "Kingdom of Heaven" of which the keys were committed to Peter, and which the Apostles had before proclaimed as "at hand," they could not doubt. They could not have been in any danger of cherishing any such presumptuous dream, as that they or any one else, except their divine Master, could have power to give or refuse admittance to the mansions of immortal bliss.[2]

---

and he was the chosen instrument in founding the first Church of the (" devout") *Gentiles ;* opening the door of the Kingdom of Heaven to Cornelius and his friends.

I need hardly add, that to claim on that account for Peter's supposed *successors* such supreme jurisdiction over the whole Church-universal, as he himself neither exercised nor claimed, would be most extravagant. Moreover, since whatever pre-eminence he did possess, was, confessedly, not conferred on him *as* Bishop of Rome, his supposed successors in that See cannot, manifestly have any claim to *that* pre-eminence; any more than the successors of King William the Third, in the office of Stadtholder, could claim the English throne. And to speak of a *succession* of men, as being, each, a *foundation* on which the Church is built, is not only extravagant but unmeaning. [See *Lectures on the Apostles.*]

[1] σωζομένους, rendered in our version " such as should be saved;" by which our Translators probably meant, according to the idiom of their day, (which is the true sense of the original,) " persons entering on the road of salvation."

[2] " He that openeth, and no man shutteth ; and shutteth, and no man openeth," (Rev. iii. 7,) is the Lord.

On the whole then, one who reads the Scriptures with attention and with candour, will be at no loss, I conceive, to ascertain what was the sense, generally, in which our Lord's Disciples would understand his directions and injunctions. Besides what is implied, naturally and necessarily, in the very institution of a Community, we know also, what the instructions were which the Disciples had already been accustomed to receive from their Master, and what was the sense they had been used from childhood to attach to the expressions He employed. And as we may be sure, I think, how *they* would understand his words, so, we may be equally sure that He would not have *failed to undeceive* them, had they mistaken his real meaning; which therefore, we cannot doubt, must have been that which these Disciples apprehended.

§ 8. As for the mode in which the Apostles and other early Christian Ministers carried into effect the directions they had received, we have indeed but a few, and those generally scanty and incidental, notices in the sacred writers; but all the notices we do find, go to confirm—if confirmation could be wanted—what has been just said, as to the sense in which our Lord must have been understood—and, consequently, in which He must have *meant* to be understood—by his Disciples.

Procedure of the Disciples in conformity to their Master's directions.

And among the important facts which we can collect and fully ascertain from the sacred historians, scanty and irregular and imperfect as are their records of particulars, one of the most important is, *that very scantiness* and incompleteness in the detail;—that absence of any full and systematic description of the formation and regulation of christian Communities, that has been just noticed. For we may plainly infer, from this very circumstance, the design of the Holy Spirit, that those details, concerning which no precise directions, accompanied with strict injunctions, are to be found in Scripture, were meant to be left to the regulation of each Church, in each Age and Country. On any point in which it was designed that all Christians should be, everywhere, and at all times, bound as strictly as the Jews were by the Levitical Law, we may fairly conclude they would have received directions no less precise, and descriptions no less minute, than had been afforded to the Jews.

Importance of noticing the omissions in any work.

It has often occurred to my mind that the generality of even studious readers are apt, for want of sufficient reflection, to fail of drawing such important inferences as they often might, from the *omissions* occurring in any work they are perusing;—from its *not* containing such and such things relative to the subject treated of. There are many cases in which the non-insertion of some particulars which, under other circumstances, we might have calculated on meeting with, in a certain book, will be hardly less instructive than the things we do meet with.

And this is much more especially the case when we are studying works which we believe to have been composed under divine guidance. For, in the case of mere human compositions, one may conceive an author to have left out some important circumstances, either through error of judgment, or inadvertency, or from having written merely for the use of a particular class of readers in his own time and country, without any thought of what might be necessary information for persons at a distance and in after ages; but we cannot, of course, attribute to any *such* causes omissions in the *inspired* Writers.

On no supposition whatever can we account for the omission, by all of them, of many points which they do omit, and of their scanty and slight mention of others, except by considering them as withheld by the express design and will (*whether communicated* to each of them or not) of their Heavenly Master, restraining them from committing to writing many things which, naturally, some or other of them, at least, would not have failed so to record.

The Sacred Writers supernaturally withheld from recording some things.

I have set forth accordingly, in a distinct Treatise,[1] these views respecting the *Omissions* in the Sacred Books of the New Testament, and the important inferences thence to be deduced. We seek in vain there for many things which, humanly speaking, we should have most surely calculated on finding. "No such thing is to be found in our Scriptures as a Catechism, or regular *Elementary Introduction* to the Christian Religion; nor do they furnish us with anything of the nature of a systematic Creed, set of Articles, Confession of Faith, or by whatever other name one may designate a regular, complete Compendium of christian doctrines: nor, again, do they supply us with a Liturgy for ordinary Public Worship, or with Forms for administering the Sacraments, or for conferring Holy Orders; nor do they even give any precise *directions* as to these and other ecclesiastical matters;—anything that at all corresponds to a Rubric, or set of Canons."

Now these omissions present,—as I have, in that Treatise, endeavoured to show,—a complete moral demonstration that the Apostles and their followers must have been *supernaturally withheld* from recording great part of

---

[1] *Essay VI.* First Series. See also *Note C* to *Essay II.*

the institutions, instructions, and regulations, which must, in point of fact, have proceeded from them;—withheld, *on purpose* that other Churches, in other Ages and Regions, might not be led to consider themselves bound to adhere to several formularies, customs, and rules, that were of local and temporary appointment; but might be left to their own discretion in matters in which it seemed best to divine wisdom that they should be so left.[1]

Christian Churches derived from Synagogues.

§ 9. With respect to one class of those points that have been alluded to, it is probable that one cause—humanly speaking— why we find in the Sacred Books less information concerning the Christian Ministry and the Constitution of Church-Governments than we otherwise might have found, is that these institutions had less of *novelty* than some would at first sight suppose, and that many portions of them did not wholly originate with the Apostles. It appears highly probable—I might say morally certain[2]— that wherever a Jewish synagogue existed that was brought, —the whole or the chief part of it,—to embrace the Gospel, the Apostles did not, there, so much *form* a christian Church, (or Congregation;[3] Ecclesia,) as *make an existing Congregation christian*; by introducing the christian Sacraments and Worship, and establishing whatever regulations were requisite for the newly-adopted Faith; leaving

---

[1] See *Note C* to *Essay II.*

[2] See Lightfoot, as cited in *Note B* to *Essay II.*

[3] The word "*Congregation*," as it stands in our Version of the Old Testament, (and it is one of very frequent occurrence in the Books of Moses,) is found to correspond, in the Septuagint, which was familiar to the New-Testament Writers, to Ecclesia; the word which, in our Version of these last, is always rendered — not "Congregation," but "*Church*." This, or its equivalent "Kirk," is probably no other than "circle;" *i. e.* Assembly, Ecclesia. In James, (ch. ii. ver. 2,) "synagogue" is the word he uses for a christian assembly.

the machinery (if I may so speak) of government, unchanged; the Rulers of Synagogues, Elders, and other Officers (whether spiritual or ecclesiastical, or both) being already provided in the existing institutions. And it is likely that several of the earliest christian Churches did originate in this way; that is, that they were *converted synagogues;* which became christian Churches as soon as the members, or the main part of the members, acknowledged Jesus as the Messiah.

The Apostles, we know, acted on the rule of "becoming all things to all men;" that is, of complying with men's habits, and avoiding all shock to their feelings, as far as this could be done without any sacrifice of principle, or detriment to the great objects proposed. It is incredible therefore, especially considering that for several years the only converts were persons frequenting the Synagogues,—Jews or "devout Gentiles"—that they should have utterly disregarded all the existing and long-reverenced Institutions and Offices, which could so easily be accommodated to the new dispensation. To have established everything on a perfectly new system, through mere love of novelty,—to have erected, as it were, a fresh building from the very ground, when there was one standing which with small and easy alterations would answer all the same purposes, would have been to raise up, wantonly, difficulties, and obstacles to their own success. They did not indeed, no doubt, think themselves bound, or authorized, to adhere blindly to existing institutions in any points in which these were at variance with the spirit of the Gospel, or were capable of being changed for the better: and doubtless they introduced from time to time (and designed that their successors should do the same) such alterations in the functions of the several officers, and in all regulations respecting other, non-essential points, as

Compliance with existing usages.

circumstances of time and place might require. But we cannot suppose that they aimed at originality for its own sake, or altered for the sake of altering. And the correspondence accordingly which has been traced by learned men between the Synagogue and the Church,[1] is no more than what we might antecedently have expected.

Precedence allowed to the Jews. The attempt to effect this conversion of a Jewish Synagogue into a christian Church, seems always to have been made, in the first instance, in every place where there was an opening for *it.* Even after the call of the idolatrous Gentiles, it appears plainly to have been the practice of the Apostles Paul and Barnabas,[2] when they came to any city in which there was a Synagogue, to go thither first and deliver their sacred message to the Jews and "devout (or proselyte) Gentiles;" —according to their own expression, (Acts, xiii. 16,) to the "men of Israel and those *that feared* God;" adding, that "it was necessary that the Word of God should first be preached to them."

And when they founded a Church in any of those cities in which (and such were, probably, a very large majority) there was no Jewish Synagogue that received the Gospel, it is

---

[1] See extract from Lightfoot in *Note B* to *Essay II.*, and also Bernard's *Vitringa.*

[2] These were the first who were employed in converting the *idolatrous* Gentiles to Christianity (see Barrington's *Miscellanea Sacra*); and that their first considerable harvest among these was at Antioch in Pisidia, may be seen by any one who attentively reads the 13th Chapter of Acts. Peter was sent to Cornelius, a *"devout"* Gentile;—one of those who had renounced idolatry and frequented the Synagogues. And these seem to have been regarded by him as in an especial manner his particular charge. His Epistles appear to have been addressed to them; as may be seen both by the general tenor of his expressions, (as remarked in Dr. Hinds's *History*, vol. ii.) and especially in the opening address; which is not (as would appear from our Version) to the dispersed *Jews*, but to the "Sojourners of the dispersion," παρεπιδήμους διασπορᾶς, *i. e.* the *devout Gentiles living among the* "Dispersion."

likely they would still conform, in a great measure, to the same model.

But though, as has been said, the circumstance just mentioned was probably the cause—humanly speaking—why some particulars are not recorded in our existing Sacred Books, which otherwise we might have found there, still, it does seem to me perfectly incredible on any supposition but that of supernatural interference, that neither the Apostles nor any of their many followers should have committed to writing any of the multitude of particulars which we do *not* find in Scripture, and concerning which we are perfectly certain the Apostles did give instructions, relative to Church-Government, the christian Ministry, and Public-Worship. When we consider how large a proportion of the Churches and of the ministers, were Gentiles, and strangers to the constitution of Jewish Synagogues, and also how much was introduced that was new and strange, even to Jewish Christians (as well as highly important)— the christian Sacraments being wholly new, and the Prayers in a great measure so—we may judge how great a number of particular directions must have been indispensably necessary for all;—directions which it would have been natural, humanly speaking, for the Apostles or their attendants to have recorded in writing; and which, if this had not been done, would naturally have been so recorded by the persons to whom they were delivered. "Suppose we could make out the possibility or probability, of Paul's having left no Creed, Catechism, or Canons, why have we none from the pen of Luke, or of Mark? Suppose this also explained, why did not John or Peter supply the deficiency? And why again did none of the numerous Bishops and Presbyters whom they ordained, undertake the work under their

New directions needed even for converted Synagogues.

direction?"[1] "And that there is nothing in the christian Religion considered in itself, that stands in the way of such a procedure, is plain from the number of works of this description which have appeared from the earliest times, (*after the age of inspiration*) down to the present;—from the writings entitled the 'Apostles' Creed,' and the 'Apostolical Constitutions,' &c., (compositions of uncertain authors, and, amidst the variety of opinions respecting them, never regarded as Scripture) down to the modern Formularies and Confessions of Faith. Nor again can it be said that there was anything in the *founders* of the religion, any more than in the religion itself, which, humanly speaking, should seem likely to preclude them from transmitting to us such compositions. On the contrary, the Apostles, and the rest of the earlier preachers of Christianity, were brought up Jews; accustomed in their earliest notions of religion, to refer to the Books of the Law, as containing precise statements of their Belief, and most minute directions as to religious Worship and Ceremonies. So that to give complete and regular instructions as to the character and the requisitions of the new Religion, as it would have been natural, for any one, was more especially to be expected of these men."[2]

We are left then, and indeed unavoidably led, to the conclusion, that, in respect of these points, the Apostles and their followers were, during the age of inspiration, *supernaturally withheld* from recording those circumstantial details which were not intended by divine Providence to be absolutely binding on all Churches, in every Age and Country, but were meant to be left to the discretion of each particular Church.[3]

---

[1] *Essay on Omissions*, p. 19. [2] Ibid. pp. 7, 8.
[3] See some valuable remarks on this subject, in a pamphlet by Dean Hoare, entitled *Letters on the Tendency and Principles advocated in the 'Tracts for the Times.'*

§ 10. The absence of such detailed descriptions and instructions as I have been adverting to, is the more striking when contrasted with the earnest and frequent inculcations we do meet with, of the great fundamental Gospel-doctrines and moral duties, which are dwelt upon in so many passages, both generally, and in reference to various classes of persons, and various occasions. *Scanty records of what relates to Church government, and copious, of moral and doctrinal instructions.* Our sacred writers have not recorded their Creeds,—their Catechisms for the elementary instruction of converts,—their forms of Public Prayer and Psalmody,—or their modes of administering the Sacraments; or whether either, or both of them should be, or usually were, administered by Presbyters exclusively:—they have not even described the posture in which the Eucharist was received, or the use of leavened or unleavened Bread; (two points on which, in after-ages, bitter controversies were raised,) nor many other things which we are certain Paul (as well as the other Apostles) " set in order, when he came" to each Church.

But, on the other hand, it is plainly recorded that they did establish Churches wherever they introduced the Gospel; that they " ordained Elders in every city," and that the Apostles again delegated to others that office of ordaining; that they did administer the rite of Baptism to their converts; and that they celebrated the Communion of the Lord's Supper.[1] *Clear records of the fact that christian Churches were founded.* 'And besides the general

---

[1] One very remarkable circumstance is, that they have nowhere laid down any injunction as to the *exclusive administration of these Sacraments* by the *Ministers.* It is indeed quite natural,—and accordingly appears to have been the original and universal custom—that the most prominent part in the celebration of christian Rites should be assigned to a christian Elder. And a Church would deserve blame which should lightly depart from an an-

principles of christian Faith and Morality which they sedulously set forth, they have recorded the most earnest exhortations to avoid "confusion"[1] in their public worship; to do "all things decently and in order;" to "let all things be done to edifying," and not for vain-glorious display; they inculcate the duty of Christians "assembling themselves together" for joint worship;[2] they record distinctly the solemn sanction given to a christian Community; they inculcate[3] due reverence and obedience to those that "bear rule" in such a Community, with censure of such as "walk disorderly" and "cause divisions;" and they dwell earnestly on the care with which christian Ministers, both male and female, should be selected, and on the zeal, and discretion, and blameless life required in them, and on their solemn obligation to "exhort, rebuke, and admonish:" yet with all this, they do not record even the number of distinct Orders of them, or the functions appropriated to each, or the degree, and kind, and mode, of control they exercised in the Churches.

Principles which are to guide Christian Societies clearly recorded.

While the *principles*, in short, are clearly recognised, and strongly inculcated, which christian Communities and individual members of them are to keep in mind and act upon, with a view to the great objects for which these Communities were established, the *precise modes* in which these objects are, in each case, to be promoted, are left,—one can hardly doubt, studiously left—undefined.

---

cient and wholesome precedent. But still, the practice is one of those left to rest on Church-authority, not, on any express injunction in Scripture.

[1] 1 Cor. and 1 Tim.
[2] Heb. x. 25.
[3] See Ep. to Hebrews, and to Timothy.

§ 11. Many of the omissions I have alluded to, will appear even the more striking in proportion as we contemplate with the more minute attention each part of the sacred narrative. For instance, it is worth remarking that the matters concerning which the Apostle Paul's Epistles do contain the most detailed directions, are most of them precisely those which every one perceives to have relation only to the times in which he wrote; such as the eating or abstaining from "meats offered to idols," and the use and abuse of supernatural gifts. He was left, it should seem, *unrestrained* in recording—and hence he does record,—particular directions in *those cases where there was no danger* of those his directions being applied in *all* Ages and Countries, as binding on *every* Church *for ever*.

Remarkable circumstance in the matters of detail which the Scriptures do record.

Again, almost every attentive reader must have been struck with the circumstance, that there is no such description on record of the first appointment of the higher Orders of christian Ministers as there is (in Acts, vi.) of the ordination of an *inferior* Class.[1] And this consideration alone would lead a reflecting mind to conclude, or at least strongly suspect, that the particular notice of this appointment of those seven officers is *incidental* only, and that probably there would have been as little said of these, as of the Presbyters, but for the circumstance of the extraordinary effect produced by two of them, Stephen and Philip, as preachers: the narrative of their appointment being a natural, and almost necessary introduction to that of two

---

[1] Commonly called Deacons; though it may reasonably be doubted whether they were Deacons in the sense in which Paul speaks of Deacons in the Epistle to Timothy. See the Article "Deacon" in Eden's *Theological Dictionary;* and also Bernard's *Vitringa.*

most important events, the great outbreak of persecution consequent on Stephen's martyrdom (which seems to have led, through the dispersion of the Disciples, to the founding of the first Gentile Church, at Antioch[1]), and the conversion of Samaria.

The Seven Deacons not the first appointed. But this conclusion is greatly strengthened, when, on a closer examination, we find reason to be convinced that these, so-called, first seven Deacons, (or rather Treasurers,) who are usually assumed (for I never met with even any attempt at proof,) to have been the first that ever held such an office, were, in reality, only the first Grecian[2] Treasurers, and that there were *Hebrew* Treasurers before; or at least Hebrew officers having duties answering to those of these Seven.

The following extract from an able Article in the *Encyclopædia Metropolitana* on Ecclesiastical History, will make this point, I think, perfectly clear.

" Meanwhile within the Church itself were displayed some slight symptoms of discontent, which deserve to be noticed particularly, on account of the measure to which they gave rise. The complaint is called ' a murmuring of the Grecians (or foreign Jews) against the Hebrews, (or native Jews,) because their widows were neglected in the daily ministration.' Who these widows probably were has already been suggested; and if the suggestion, that they were deaconesses, be admitted, the grounds of the complaint may be readily surmised. As the greater share of duty would at this time devolve on the Hebrew widows or

---

[1] See *Encyclop. Metrop.* (*Ecclesiastical History*) on the designation of Christians first given to the Disciples at that place.

[2] Hellenist, or "Grecian," is the term constantly used for the *Jews* who used the Greek *language;* as distinguished from Hellen, a *Greek* or Gentile by *nation.*

deaconesses, they might have been paid more liberally, as their services seemed to require; and hence the discontent.

"This, it is true, supposes that the order of deacons and deaconesses already existed, and may seem at first to contradict the statement of St. Luke, that in consequence of this murmuring, deacons were appointed. It does not however really contradict it; for evidently some *dispensers* there must have been, and if so, either the Apostles must have officiated as deacons, or special deacons there must have been, by whatever name they went. That the Apostles did not officiate, is plain from the tenor of the narrative, which indicates that the appeal was made to them, and that they excused themselves from presiding personally at the 'ministration,' (as was probably desired by the discontented party,) alleging that it was incompatible with their proper duties. 'It is not reason that we should *leave the word of God*, and serve tables.' This very assertion, then, is proof certain that they did not officiate. Again, on reading over the names of the seven deacons, we find them all of the Grecian or Hellenistic party; Stephen, Philip, Prochorus, Nicanor, Timon, Parmenas, and Nicolas, the last of whom is expressly described as 'a proselyte of Antioch.' Now this surely would have produced, in turn, a murmuring of the Hebrews against the Grecians, unless they had *already* had some in office interested in looking after their rights. With these presumptions in favour of a previous appointment of deacons, it would seem then, that these seven were *added* to the former number, because of the complaint.

"All that is thus far intimated of their office is, that they were employed in the daily distribution of the alms and the stipends due from the public fund. Whether, even at the first, their duties were limited to this department of *service*, may be reasonably doubted. Of this portion of their duties we are now informed; obviously, because to the unsatisfactory mode in which this had been hitherto performed it was owing, that the new appointment took place, and that the subject was noticed at all. It is, however, by no means improbable, that the young men who carried out the dead bodies of Ananias and Sapphira, and who are described as 'ready' in attendance, were of the same order; in other words, deacons by office, if not by name. What may serve to confirm this view of it is, the opposition between what would seem to have been their original title, and another order in the Church. They are called 'juniors' and 'young men,' (νεώτεροι and νεανίσκοι,) terms so strongly opposed to presbyters or elders as to incline one at the first glance to consider them as expressive of the two orders of the ministry, the seniors and the juniors, (the πρεσβύτεροι διάκονοι and the νεώτεροι διάκονοι;) the two orders, in short, which at length received the fixed and perpetual titles of presbyters and deacons.

"Accordingly, there is no just ground for supposing, that when the same term deacon occurs in the Epistles of St. Paul, a different order of men is intended: first, because an office may preserve its original name long after the duties originally attached to it have been changed; and, secondly, because, whatever duties may have been added to the office of deacons, it is certain that the duty of attending to the poor was for several centuries attached to it. Even after the deacons ceased to hold the office of treasurers, and the Bishops began to receive the revenues of their respective sees, the distribution of that portion which was allotted to charity still passed through the hands of the deacons. Hence in a still later period, the title of cardinal deacon; and hence, too, the appropriation of the term *diaconiæ* to those Churches wherein alms used to be collected and distributed to the poor.

"Not that it is possible to point out, with anything like precision, the course of duty which belonged to the primitive deacons. That it corresponded entirely with that of our present order of deacons is very unlikely, whatever analogy be allowed from their relative situation in the Church. As the Church during the greater part of the first century was a shifting, and progressive institution, their duties probably underwent continual change and modification. If we were to be guided, for instance, by the office in which we find the 'young men,' ($\nu\epsilon\alpha\nu\iota\sigma\kappa\text{o}\iota$,) engaged, when the dead bodies of Ananias and Sapphira were removed, we should say that they performed the business, which in the present day would devolve on the inferior attendants of our churches. If, again, we were to judge of their character from the occasion on which we find them acting as stewards of the Church fund, a higher station would be doubtless assigned to them, but still, one not more nearly connected with the ministry of the word nor approaching more to the sphere of duty which belongs to our deacons. On the other hand, the instances of Stephen and Philip prove, that the title was applied to those who were engaged in the higher departments of the ministry, although not in the highest.

"After all, it is most likely that the word deacon was originally applied, as its etymology suggests, to all the *ministers* of the Gospel establishment. But the Apostles having from the first a specific title, it more properly denoted any minister inferior to them,—any, however employed in the *service* of the Church. Between these, also, there soon obtained a distinction. If we suppose, then, that the *seniors*, or superior class, were distinguished by the obvious title of Elder deacons, ($\pi\rho\epsilon\sigma\beta\acute{\upsilon}\tau\epsilon\rho\text{o}\iota\ \delta\iota\acute{\alpha}\kappa\text{o}\nu\text{o}\iota$) the generic and unappropriated term 'deacon' would devolve on the remaining class. And thus the present Order in the Church, to which that name is applied, may be truly asserted to be deacons in the apostolical and primitive sense of the word; and yet, nevertheless, much may be said about deacons, both in the New Testament and in the writings of the early fathers, which will not apply to them."¹

Importance of the question. If any one should be disposed to think it a question of small moment whether Stephen and his companions were or were not the first Deacons ever appointed, or were, properly speaking, Deacons at all, let him consider that, however unimportant in itself, it is one which throws much additional light on the subject now before us. We not only find few and scanty records of those details of the Church-government established by the Apostles, which, if they had designed to leave a model absolutely binding on all Christians for ever, we might have expected to find fully and clearly particularized, but also we find that a part even of what the

---

¹ The writer has proceeded on the supposition of the correctness of the general belief that the SEVEN men spoken of did belong to that Order called *Deacons*, alluded to by Paul in writing to Timothy. But this is far from certain. The office indeed of "ministering" or "serving" at tables, (διακονεῖν) is alluded to in reference to them: and in a certain sense, all *ministers*, of whatever kind, may be called "Deacons:" (διάκονοι) but "the SEVEN" are *nowhere in Scripture* designated by this title. They are referred to in Acts* not as the "seven Deacons" but simply as *The Seven*. And the primary and especial Office for which they were appointed, —that of Stewards and Almoners,— is not referred to at all, in what Paul says of the Office of a Deacon.†

Hence some have inferred that "*the seven*" persons mentioned in Acts ‡ were appointed to a *temporary* Office, for a temporary and local emergency, and did not belong to the Order of Deacons strictly so called.

Be this as it may; at all events, it is plain, 1st, that we have, on either supposition, no distinct record of the *first* appointment of Deacons, any more than of Presbyters and Bishops; and 2dly, that the Churches appear always to have had, and to have exercised, full liberty to appoint various Orders of Ministers, under several titles, and for various Offices, and to determine from time to time, what should be the functions and titles of the several orders. — See Bernard's Abridgment of *Vitringa on the Church and Synagogue*.

---

* Ch. xxi. 8. † 1 Tim. iii. ‡ Ch. vi.

inspired writers do record, is recorded incidentally only, for the elucidation of the rest of the narrative; and not in pursuance of any design to give a detailed statement of such particulars. Thus a further confirmation is furnished of the view that has been taken; viz. that it was the plan of the Sacred Writers to lay down clearly the *principles* on which christian Churches were to be formed and governed, leaving the mode of application of those principles undetermined and discretionary.

§ 12. Now what did the Holy Spirit design that we should learn from all this? In the first place, "he that hath ears to hear," may draw from it, as has been already observed, a strong internal evidence of the genuineness and of the inspired character of our Sacred Books; inasmuch as they do not contain what would surely have been found in the works of men (whether impostors or sincere) left to themselves to record whatever seemed interesting and important. *Internal evidence of the Gospel resulting from the above views.*

And this point of evidence presents itself to the mind at once, before we have even begun to inquire into the particular object proposed in the omission; because we may be sure, in this case, that what did *not* come from Man must have come from God.[1]

But besides this, we may fairly infer, I think, the different characters of the several points connected with our religion. Since what is *essential* may be expected to be found clearly laid down in Scripture (for we could not properly be said to have any *revelation*, if we were left to seek among varying and doubtful traditions what *Of Essentials a distinct revelation in Scripture to be expected.*

---

[1] See *Note D*.

are the fundamentals of our religion) we may conclude that whatever is *not* thus laid down, must be of a different character. We may infer that those points which are either wholly passed over in silence (when they are such that we are certain from the nature of the case, the Apostles must have given *some* directions relative to them) or are slightly mentioned, imperfectly described, and incidentally alluded to, must belong to the class of things either altogether indifferent, or so far non-essential in their character that "it is not necessary" (as our 34th article expresses it,) "they should be in all places one and utterly alike;"—such in short that divine wisdom judged it best they should be left to the discretion of each Church in each Age and Country,[1] and should be determined according to the *principles* which had been distinctly laid down by divine authority; while the *application* of those principles in particular cases, was left (as is the case with our moral conduct also)[2] to the responsible judgment of Man.

Extent and limits of the power of a Church.
It was designed in short that a Church should have (as our 34th Article expresses it) " authority to ordain, change, and abolish ceremonies and rites resting on Man's authority only:" (this, be it observed, including things which may have been enjoined by the Apostles *to those among whom they were living,* and which, *to those persons,* had a divine authority; but which are not recorded by the sacred writers as enjoined *universally*) " so that all things be done to edifying:" but that " as no Church ought to decree anything *against* Holy Writ, so, *besides* the same ought it not to enforce the belief of anything as necessary to salvation."

---

[1] See *Note E.*
[2] *Essay on Abolition of the Law.* Second Series.

§ 13. And we may also infer very clearly from an attentive and candid survey of the Sacred Writings, not only that some things were intended to be absolutely enjoined as essential, and others left to the discretion of the rulers of each Church, but also that some things, again, were absolutely *excluded*, as inconsistent with the character of a christian Community.

Things enjoined, things excluded, and things left at large.

It is very important therefore, and to a diligent, and reflective, and unprejudiced reader, not difficult,—by observing what the Sacred Writers have omitted, and what they have mentioned, and in what manner they have mentioned each, to form in his mind distinctly the three classes just alluded to: viz. 1st, of things essential to Christianity, and *enjoined* as universally requisite; 2ndly, those left to the *discretion* of the governors of each Church; and 3rdly, those *excluded* as *inconsistent* with the character of the Gospel-religion.

Points essential, incompatible, and indifferent.

These last points are not least deserving of a careful examination; especially on account of the misconceptions relative to them that have prevailed and still prevail, in a large portion of the christian world. It would lead me too far from the subject now immediately under consideration, to enter into a full examination of all the features that are to be found in most religions except the christian, and which might have been expected to appear in that, supposing it of human origin; but which are expressly excluded from it. It may be worth while however to advert to a few of the most remarkable.

The christian Religion, then, arose, be it remembered, among a People who not only looked for a temporal Deliverer and Prince in their Messiah, but who had been accus-

Temporal sanctions succeeded by those of a future state.

tomed to the sanction of temporal rewards and judgments to the divine Law;[1] whose Laws, in religious and in secular matters alike, claimed to be an immediate revelation from Heaven—whose civil Rulers were regarded as delegates from "the Lord their God, who was their king," and were enjoined to punish with death, as a revolt from the supreme Civil Authority,—as a crime of the character of high treason,—any departure from the prescribed religion. It arose in a Nation regarding themselves as subjects of a "Kingdom of God" that *was*, emphatically, a kingdom of this world: and its most prominent character was its being "a Kingdom *not* of this world." It was in all respects the very reverse in respect of the points just mentioned, of what *might* have been expected, humanly speaking, from Jewish individuals, and of what *was* expected by the Jewish *Nation;* and it may be added, of what many Christians have in every Age laboured to represent, and to make it. While the mass of his own People were seeking to "take Jesus by force to make Him a King" (a procedure which has been, virtually, imitated by a large proportion of his professed followers ever since) He Himself and his Apostles, uniformly and sedulously, both in their precepts, and in their conduct, rejected as alien from the character of the Gospel, all employment of secular coercion in behalf of their religion,—all encroachment on "the things that be Cæsar's;" and maintained the purely spiritual character of that "Kingdom of Heaven" which they proclaimed.

On this, every way most important, point, I have treated at large in the first Essay in this volume, and also, in the *Essay on Persecution* (3rd Series), and the *Essays on the Dangers to Christianity,* (4th Series.)

---

[1] See *Essay I.*, 1st Series: *On the Peculiarities,* &c. And also Discourse *On National Blessings.*

§ 14. Moreover the Gospel religion was introduced by men, and among men—whether Jews or Gentiles,—who had never heard of or conceived such a thing as a religion without a Sacrificing *Priest*,—without Altars for *Sacrifice*,—without *Sacrifices* themselves,—without either a *Temple*, or at least some High Place, Grove, or other sacred spot answering to a Temple;—some place, that is, in which the Deity worshipped was supposed more especially to dwell.[1]

Christianity a religion without Sacrifice, Altar or Temple.

The Apostles preached, for the first time—the first both to Jew and Gentile—a religion quite opposite in all these respects to all that had ever been heard of before:—a religion without any Sacrifice but that offered up by its Founder in his own person;—without any Sacrificing-Priest (Hiereus or Sacerdos)[2] except Him, the great and

---

[1] Hence the name of Ναὸς from ναίειν, "to dwell." See Hinds's *Three Temples*.

[2] See Discourse *On the christian Priesthood*, appended to Bampton Lectures. See also Eden's *Theological Dictionary*, Articles, "Temple," "Altar," &c.

It is worthy of remark that the notion of a *Sacerdotal-Priesthood* in the christian Church, and that of *Apostolical Succession*, (in the sense of the Romanists, and of a certain party among Protestants) are generally maintained *together*. And yet they are not naturally and intrinsically connected; and there are some few persons,—though but very few, —who hold the latter doctrine, and not the former.

The conjunction of these two notions (which, as I have said, one generally meets with) may, I think, be thus accounted for.

A conceivable supposition, it certainly is, though at variance with the fact, that the Apostles might have left us directions as precise, and injunctions as strict, respecting the mode of ordaining christian-Ministers,—the rules for their succession —and the functions they were to exercise—as were given in the Mosaic Law relative to the Levitical Priesthood; and might yet have left the two Offices as distinct and unlike as in fact they are. This, I say, is what the Apostles *might* conceivably have done. But it is manifest they have not. And in the *absence* of any such precise directions in the *New*-Testament,—which is what the advocates of Apostolic succession (in the above sense) cannot quite conceal from themselves, they are naturally driven to resort to the *analogy of the Mosaic Law;* which does give (in respect of a *Sacerdotal* priesthood)

true High Priest,[1] and consequently with no Priest (in that sense) on Earth: except so far as every one of the worshippers was required to present himself as a "living Sacrifice, holy, acceptable to God;"[2] and a religion without any Temple, except the collected Congregation of the Worshippers themselves.[3]

Let any one but contemplate the striking contrast, between the confined—the local character,—of the Mosaic system, and the character of boundless extension stamped on the Gospel of Christ. "In the place which the Lord shall chuse" (says Moses[4]) "to set his Name therein, there shalt thou offer thy Sacrifices." "The hour cometh" (says Jesus[5]) "when men shall neither on this mountain, nor yet at Jerusalem, worship the Father:" ..... "wheresoever two or three are gathered together in my name, there am I in the midst of them."[6] "In his *Temple*" (says the Psalmist;[7] *i. e.* in his temple at Jerusalem) "doth every one speak of his glory:" ..... "there will I" (Jehovah) "*dwell*, for I have a delight therein:" "*Ye* are the *Temple*" (says the Apostle Paul) "of the Holy Ghost, which *dwelleth* in you."[8]

---

just such precise directions, and strict injunctions as are wanted for the purpose of the argument. And thence it is, I conceive, that men have been so often led to represent the christian-ministers as the regular successors of the Levitical, and christian Places of Worship, of the Temple; and in short to *judaize* Christianity all through.

This will account for the fact (which I never heard accounted for in any other way) that almost every Church, Sect, or Party, that have adopted the above view of Apostolical-succession, has also adopted,—either at once, or gradually—that of a Sacerdotal-priesthood also.

[1] Hebrews, ch. iv.
[2] Rom. xii. This offering the Apostle calls θυσίαν ζῶσαν, "a living Sacrifice," as distinguished from the *slain* animals offered up in other religions; and also λογικὴ λατρεία, "a *reasonable* (*i. e.* rational) service," as opposed to the *irrational* animals slain on the altars.
[3] I have treated of this point in one of a volume of Discourses delivered in Dublin.
[4] Deut. xii.
[5] John, iv.
[6] Matt. xviii.
[7] Ps. xxix.
[8] 1 Cor. iii.

Now all this is deserving of attentive reflection, both as important in reference to a right knowledge of the true character of the religion of the Gospel, and also as furnishing a strong internal evidence as to its origin. For not only is it inconceivable that any impostor or enthusiast would have ever *devised* or dreamed of anything both so strange, and so unacceptable, as must have seemed, in those days, a religion without Priest, Altar, Sacrifice, or Temple, (in the sense in which men had always been accustomed to them;) but also it is no less incredible that any persons unaided by miraculous powers, should have *succeeded*—as the Apostles did—in propagating such a religion.

Christianity such a system as Man would not have devised, nor could have succeeded in propagating.

But what is most to our present purpose to remark, is, that the Sacred Writers did not *omit* the mention of these things, and leave it to the discretion of each Church to introduce them or not; but they plainly appear to have distinctly *excluded* them. It is not that they made little or no mention of Temples, Sacrifices, and sacrificing Priests; they mention them, and allude to them, perpetually; as existing, in the ordinary sense of the terms, among the Jews, and also among the Pagans; and again, they also perpetually mention and allude to them in reference to the religion of the Gospel, invariably, and manifestly, *in a different sense*. Jesus Christ as the christian Priest, and christian Sacrifice,—Christians themselves as "living Sacrifices,"—the sacrifice of beneficence to the Poor,[1]—the Temple composed of the christian worshippers themselves; who are exhorted to "build up" (or edify,

Sacrifices, and sacrificing Priests, excluded from Christianity.

---

[1] "To do good and to distribute, forget not, for with such sacrifices, (θυσίαις,) God is well pleased."

οἰκοδομεῖν) one another, as "living stones"[1] of the Temple of the Holy Ghost;—all these are spoken of and alluded to continually; while, in the primary and customary sense, the same terms are perpetually used by the same writers, in reference to the Jewish and to the Pagan religions, and never to the Christian.[2]

I cannot well conceive any proof more complete than is here afforded that Christ and his Apostles intended distinctly to exclude and forbid, as inconsistent with his religion, those things which I have been speaking of. It being the natural and inherent office of any Community to make bye-laws for its own regulation, *where not restricted by some higher Authority*, these points are precisely those which come under that restriction; being distinctly excluded by the Founder and Supreme Governor of the Universal Church, as inconsistent with the character of his Religion.

It seems something strange, therefore,—though in

---

[1] 1 Peter, ii. 5, &c.

[2] It is worth observing how distinctly our Church repudiates the notions of "Sacrifice," "Temple," &c., not merely by *omitting* the application of those terms in the Rubrics and Communion-Service, and not merely by dwelling on the "sufficiency" of the "*one* oblation of Christ *once* offered," but also by studiously introducing in that service the word "Sacrifice" in the *other* senses in which it *is* applicable; viz.; first, in the offertory, to "*alms*" ("with such *sacrifices* God is well pleased") and afterwards, to the "sacrifice of praise and thanksgiving," and again to the "sacrifice of ourselves, our souls and bodies." And in addition to this, a distinct Rubric is subjoined to explain that "no adoration is intended or allowed" of the bread and wine of the Eucharist.

Will it be credited that in the nineteenth century the principles here inculcated have been gravely stated, in print, to be "subversive of our Church" with "its *Altars*, *Temples*, *Sacrificing*-Priests, and *adoration* of the Eucharistical bread and wine?"—all of which the writer would have seen, in simply looking over the Prayer-Book, to be utterly alien from our Church! The mistake of Tacitus, who represents the Jews as adoring the effigy of an Ass, was nothing to this; because Gentiles not being admitted into the Temple at Jerusalem, had nothing but hearsay to trust to.

other matters also experience shows the liability of men to maintain at once opposite errors,—that the very persons who are for restricting the most narrowly,—or rather, annulling,—the natural right of a Community to make and alter bye-laws in matters not determined by a superior authority, and who deny that any Church is at liberty to depart, *Unreasonable restriction, and unreasonable extension of Church-powers, advocated by the same persons.* even in matters left undecided in Scripture, from the supposed, or even conjectured practice of the Apostles,— these very persons are found advocating the introduction into Christianity of practices and institutions and doctrines not only unauthorized, but plainly excluded, by its inspired promulgators;—such as Sacrifices and Sacrificing Priests; thus, at once, denying the rights which do belong to a christian community, and asserting those which do not: at once fettering the Church by a pretended obligation to conform strictly to some supposed precedents of antiquity, and boldly casting off the obligation to adhere to the plainest injunctions of God's written Word. "Full well do ye reject the commandment of God, that ye may keep your own tradition."[1]

§ 15. Among the things excluded from the christian system, we are fully authorized to include all subjection of the christian World, permanently, and from generation to generation, to some one Spiritual-Ruler (whether an individual man or a Church) the *The christian Church universal has no Spiritual Head on Earth.* delegate, representative and vicegerent of Christ; whose authority should be binding on the conscience of all, and decisive on every point of faith. Jesus Himself, who told

---

[1] Mark, vii. 9.

his Disciples that it was "expedient for them that He should go away, that He might send them another Comforter, who should abide with them for ever," could not possibly have failed, had such been his design, to refer them to the man, or Body of Men, who should, in perpetual succession, be the depositary of this divine consolation and supremacy. And it is wholly incredible that He Himself should be perpetually spoken of and alluded to as the Head of His Church, without any reference to any Supreme Head on Earth, as fully representing Him, and bearing universal rule in his name,—whether Peter or any other Apostle, or any successor of one of these,—this, I say, is utterly incredible, supposing the Apostles or their Master had really designed that there should be for the universal Church any institution answering to the oracle of God under the Old Dispensation, at the Tabernacle or the Temple.

The miraculous Signs of an Apostle requisite for any claimant of apostolical power.

The Apostle Paul, in speaking of miracles as "the signs of an Apostle," evidently implies that no one NOT possessing such miraculous gifts as his,[1] much less, without possessing any at all,—could be entitled to be regarded as even on a level with the Apostles; yet he does not, by virtue of that his high office, claim for himself, or allow to Peter or any other, supreme rule over all the Churches.[2] And while he claims and exercises the right to decide authoritatively on points of faith and of practice on which he had received express revelations, he does not leave his converts any injunction to apply, hereafter, when he shall be removed from them, to the Bishop or Rulers of any other Church, for such decisions; or to any kind of permanent living Oracle to dictate to all Christians in all Ages. Nor does he even ever hint at any subjection of one

---

[1] 1 Cor. xiv. 18.   Gal. ii. 7—9.

Church to another, singly, or to any number of others collectively;—to that of Jerusalem, for instance, or of Rome; or to any kind of General Council.[1]

It appears plainly from the sacred narrative, that though the many Churches which the Apostles founded were branches of one *Spiritual* Brotherhood, of which the Lord Jesus Christ is the Heavenly Head,—though there was " one Lord, one Faith, one Baptism," for all of them, yet they were each a distinct, independent community *on Earth,* united by the common principles on which they were founded, and by their mutual agreement, affection, and respect; but not having any one recognised Head on Earth, or acknowledging any sovereignty of one of these Societies over others.[2]

No one Community on Earth possessing power over all Christians.

And as for—so-called—General Councils, we find not even any mention of them, or allusion to any such expedient. The pretended first Council, at Jerusalem, does seem to me[3] a most extraordinary chimera, without any warrant whatever from Sacred History. We find in the narrative, that certain persons, coming from Jerusalem to Antioch, endeavoured to impose on the Gentile converts the yoke of the Mosaic Law; pretending—as appears plainly from the context[4]—to have the sanction of the Apostles for this. Nothing could be more natural than the step which was thereupon taken,—to send a deputation to Jerusalem, to inquire whether these pretensions were well founded. The

General Councils not authorized by Scripture.

---

[1] See the *Search after Infallibility.*
[2] Generally speaking, the Apostles appear to have established a distinct Church in each considerable city; so that there were several even in a single Province; as for instance, in Macedonia, those of Philippi, Thessalonica, Beræa, Amphipolis, &c.: and the like in the Province of Achaia, and elsewhere.
[3] See Burnet on Art. 21.
[4] Acts, xv. 24.

Apostles, in the midst of an Assembly of the Elders (or Clergy, as they would now be called) of Jerusalem, decided that no such burden ought to be imposed, and that their pretended sanction had not been given. The Church at Jerusalem, even independently of the Apostles, had of course, power to decide this last point; *i. e.* to declare the fact, whether they had or had not given the pretended sanction: and the Apostles, confessedly, had plenary power to declare the will of the Lord Jesus. And the deputation, accordingly, retired satisfied. There is no hint, throughout,

Pretended first general Council, not of that character. of any summons to the several Churches in Judea and Galilee, in Samaria, Cyprus, Cyrene, &c. to send deputations, as to a general Council; nor any assumption of a right in the *Church* of Jerusalem, as such, to govern the rest, or to decide on points of faith.

Ordination of Saul and Barnabas. It is worth remarking also, that, as if on purpose to guard against the assumption, which might, not unnaturally, have taken place, of some supremacy—such as no Church was designed to enjoy,—on the part of Jerusalem, the fountain-head of the religion, it was by the *special appointment* of the Holy Spirit that Saul[1] and Barnabas were *ordained* to the very highest office, the Apostleship, *not by the hands of the other Apostles*, or of any persons at *Jerusalem*, but by the *Elders of Antioch*. This would have been the less remarkable had *no human* ordination at all taken place, but merely a special immediate appointment of them by divine revela-

---

[1] For whether Saul's previous call to the Apostleship by Jesus Christ Himself, were, or were not, already *publicly known to the Church*, it is plain that both he and Barnabas were, at this time, by divine command, "separated," and solemnly ordained to the "work to which the Lord had appointed them," and were thereupon and thenceforward recognised as Apostles.

tion. But the command given was, "separate me .... let them go."[1] *Some* reason for such a procedure there must have been; and it does seem probable that it was designed for the very purpose (among others) of impressing on men's minds the independence and equality of the several Churches on Earth.

We should consider too, in addition to all these circumstances, the number and the variety of the Epistles of Paul, (to say nothing of those of the other Apostles) and the deep anxiety he manifests for the continuance of his converts in the right faith, and his earnest warnings of them[2] against the dangers to their faith, which he foresaw. And we should con- *Impossibility of Paul's having omitted to notice a supreme universal tribunal, had there been any.*
sider also the incalculable importance of such an institution (supposing it to exist) as a permanent living Oracle and supreme Ruler of the Church, on Earth; and the necessity of pointing it out so clearly that no one could possibly, except through wilful blindness and obstinacy, be in any doubt as to the place and persons whom the Lord should have thus "chosen to cause his name to dwell" therein—especially, as a plain reference to this infallible judge, guide, and governor, would have been so obvious, easy, short, and decisive a mode of guarding against the doubts, errors, and dissensions which he so anxiously apprehended. And when we consider all this, it does seem a perfect moral impossibility, that Paul and the other sacred writers should have written as they have done, without any mention or allusion to any thing of the kind, if it had been a part (and it must have been a most *essential* part, if it were any) of the christian System. They do not merely omit all reference to any supreme and infallible Head and Oracle of the

---

[1] Acts, xiii. 2, 3.   [2] Acts, xx.

Universal Church,—to any Man or Body, as the representative and Vicegerent of Christ, but they omit it in such a manner, and under such circumstances, as plainly to amount to an exclusion.[1]

Commencement of christian Church; deferred till Christ's departure.

It may be added, that the circumstance of our Lord's having *deferred* the Commencement of his Church till after his own *departure* in bodily person, from the Earth, seems to have been designed as a further safeguard against the notion I have been alluding to. Had He publicly presided in bodily person subsequently to the completion of the Redemption by his death, over a Church in Jerusalem or elsewhere, there would have been more plausibility in the claim to *supremacy* which might have been set up and admitted, on behalf of that Church, and of his own successors in the Government of it. His previously withdrawing, made it the more easily to be understood that He was to remain the spiritual Head in Heaven, of the spiritual Church-universal; and consequently of all particular Churches, equally, in all parts of the world.

---

[1] It is worthy of remark that the pretensions of the Church of Rome to be at once "the Catholic [or Universal] Church," and also to be divinely *exempted from errors and dissensions*, are overthrown by the very *existence* of Protestants, and of the Greek and some other Churches. If these do *not* properly belong to the Church of Rome, as subjects, though revolted and disobedient subjects, then, it is not *Universal;* if,—which is what is actually alleged—they do thus belong to it, then, it is manifestly not exempt from *error and dissension.* It is true the Authorities of that Church condemn all who disown her supremacy: but this does not affect the argument. For, an *exemption* from any evil does not consist in its being censured, but in its *not arising* at all. It would be absurd to call a certain town incombustible, on the ground that a cry of "fire" is raised in it whenever a conflagration breaks out. It would be easy,—and nugatory—for any Body of men, however few, to boast that all *ought* to submit to them; that all do submit, *except* those who disobey; and that all agree with their doctrines except those who dissent.

§ 16. This therefore, and the other points just mentioned, must be regarded as *negatively* characteristic of the christian religion, no less than it is positively characterised by those truths and those enactments which the inspired Writers lay down as essential. Their prohibitions in the one case, are as plain as their injunctions in the other.

Importance of points excluded.

There is not indeed any systematic enumeration of the several points that are excluded as inconsistent with the character of the religion; answering to the prohibition of Idolatry in the Decalogue, the enumeration of forbidden meats, and other such enactments of the Levitical Law. But the same may be said no less of the affirmative directions also that are to be found in the New Testament. The fundamental doctrines and the great moral principles of the Gospel, are there taught,—for wise reasons no doubt, and which I think we may in part perceive,[1] not in Creeds or other regular formularies, but incidentally, irregularly, and often by oblique allusions; less striking indeed at first sight than distinct enunciations and enactments, but often even the more decisive and satisfactory from that very circumstance; because the Apostles frequently allude to some truth as not only essential, but indisputably admitted, and familiarly *known to be* essential by those they were addressing.[2]

On the whole then, I cannot but think an attentive and candid inquirer, who brings to the study of Scripture no extraordinary learning or acuteness, but an unprejudiced and docile mind, may ascertain with reasonable certainty, that there are points—and what

Certainty with which things enjoined, forbidden and discretionary, may be distinguished.

---

[1] See *Note F*.
[2] See *Rhetoric*, 6th Edition, Part I. ch. 2. § 4.

those points are—which are insisted on by our sacred writers as *essential;* and again, which are excluded as *inconsistent* with the religion they taught; and again, that there are many other points,—some of them such that the Apostles cannot but have practically decided them in one way or another *on particular occasions,* (such as the mode of administering the Eucharist, and many others) respecting which they have not *recorded* their decisions, or made any *general* enactment to be observed in all Ages and Countries.

And the inference seems to be inevitable, that they *purposely* left these points to be decided in each Age and Country according to the discretion of the several Churches, by a careful *application* of the *principles* laid down by Christ and his Apostles.

Opposite errors at variance with the above principles.

§ 17. At variance with what has been now said, and also at variance with each other, are some opinions which are to be found among different classes of Christians, in these, as well as in former times. The opposite errors (as they appear to me to be) of those opinions, may in many instances be traced, I conceive, in great measure, to the same cause; to the neglect, namely, of the distinction—obvious as it is to any tolerably attentive reader—which has been just noticed, between those things on the one hand, which are either plainly declared and strictly *enjoined,* or distinctly *excluded,* by the Sacred Writers, and on the other hand, those on which they give no distinct decision, injunction, or prohibition; and which I have thence concluded they meant to place under the jurisdiction of each Church. To the neglect of this distinction, and again, to a want of due consideration of the character, offices, and rights of a christian Community, may be attributed, in a great degree, the prevalence of errors the most opposite to each other.

There are persons, it is well known, who from not finding in Scripture precise directions, and strict commands, as to the constitution and regulation of a christian Church, —the several Orders of christian Ministers, —the distinct functions of each,—and other such details, have adopted the conclusion,—or at least seem to lean, more or less, towards the conclusion—that it is a matter entirely left to each individual's fancy or convenience to join one christian Society, or another, or none at all ;— to take upon himself, or confer on another, the ministerial office, or to repudiate altogether any christian Ministry whatever :—to join, or withdraw from, any, or every religious Assembly for joint christian worship, according to the suggestion of his individual taste :—in short, (for this is what it really amounts to when plainly stated) to proceed as if the sanction manifestly given by our Lord and his Apostles to the establishment of christian Communities, and consequently, to all the privileges and powers implied in the very nature of a Community, and also the inculcation in Scripture of the *principles* on which christian Churches are to be conducted, were all *to go for nothing*, unless the application of these principles to each particular point of the details of Church-government, can also be found no less plainly laid down in Scripture.

Error of those who regard no Church-ordinances, &c., as binding.

Now though I would not be understood as insinuating anything against the *actual* morality of life of those who take such views, I cannot but remark, that their *mode of reasoning* does seem to me perfectly analogous to that of men who should set at nought all the moral principles of the Gospel, and account nothing a sin that is

Mistake of expecting precise directions on each point of detail.

not expressly particularized as forbidden,—nothing a duty, that is not, in so many words, enjoined. Persons who entertain such lax notions as I have been alluding to, respecting Church-enactments, should be exhorted to reflect carefully on the obvious and self-evident, but often-forgotten truth—the oftener forgotten, perhaps, in practice, from its *being* self-evident—that *right* and *duty* are reciprocal; and, consequently, that since a Church has a *right* (derived, as has been shown, both from the very nature of a Community, and from Christ's sanction) to *make* regulations, &c. not at variance with Scripture-principles, it follows that *compliance* with such regulations must be a *duty* to the individual members of that Church.

Error of those who seek in Scripture or Tradition for a sanction to each Church-enactment.

On the other hand, there are some who, in their abhorrence and dread of principles and practices subversive of all good order, and tending to anarchy and to every kind of extravagance, have thought,—or at least professed to think,—that we are bound to seek for a distinct authoritative sanction, in the Scriptures, or *in some other ancient*[1] *writings*—some *Tradition* in short—for each separate point which we would maintain. They assume that whatever doctrines or practices, whatever institutions, whatever regulations respecting Church-govern-

---

[1] By "ancient" some persons understand what belongs to the first *three* centuries of the Christian era; some, the first four; some, seven; so arbitrary and uncertain is the standard by which some would persuade us to try questions, on which they, at the same time, teach us to believe our Christian Faith and Christian Hope are staked!

" Scire velim, pretium chartis quotus arroget annus:
* * * * * *
Est vetus atque probus, centum qui perficit annos.
Quid ? qui deperiit minor uno mense vel anno,
Inter quos referendus erit? veteresne?" * * *

Horace, Epist. I. b. 2.

ment, we can conclude, either with certainty, or with any degree of probability, to have been either introduced by the Apostles, or to have prevailed in their time, or in the time of their immediate successors, are to be considered as absolutely binding on all Christians for ever;—as a model from which no Church is at liberty to depart. And they make our membership of the Church of Christ, and our hopes of the Gospel-salvation, depend on an exact adherence to everything that is proved, or believed, or even suspected, to be an apostolical usage; and on our possessing what they call Apostolical Succession; that is, on our having a Ministry whose descent can be traced up in an unbroken and undoubted chain, to the Apostles themselves, through men regularly ordained by them or their successors, according to the exact forms originally appointed. And all Christians (so called) who do not come under this description, are to be regarded either as outcasts from "the Household of Faith," or at best as in a condition "analogous to that of the Samaritans of old" who worshipped on Mount Gerizim,[1] or as in "an intermediate state between Christianity and Heathenism," and as "left to the uncovenanted mercies of God."

Ambiguity of "divine origin," &c. These notions are fostered by the ambiguous employment of the phrases "*divine appointment*," "*divine institution*," "*divine origin*," &c.: that which is proved in one sense, being often assumed in another. Whatever is, strictly speaking, a *divine* appointment,—*i. e.* enjoined by a plain revelation, as binding on all Christians—from this, evidently, nothing short of a fresh revelation can authorize a departure. On the other hand, many things, we are sure, must have been enacted, from time to time, by the Apostles, doubtless under

---

[1] John, iv.

divine guidance, but which have not been laid down by them as of perpetual and universal obligation. Of many of these, such as, for instance, the particular mode in which they celebrated the Eucharist—we are left ignorant: of some institutions again of this character,—as for instance the observance of the Love-feasts [Agapæ]—we have some knowledge from incidental allusions in the Sacred writings, and from uninspired authors.

Now to prove, as certain or as probable, the "divine origin" of any institution, in this latter sense,—*i.e.* simply that it had the sanction of the Apostles,—is often put forward as if it were a proof of its "divine origin" in the *other* sense;—as a proof that they must have designed it to be of *universal and perpetual obligation;* even where they have omitted to indicate any such design, and where such omission, had that design existed, would have been unaccountable. It is surely not showing reverence for the Apostles, either as inspired servants of God, or even as men of ordinary good sense, to suppose that they would leave the *essentials of Christianity* to be collected from *incidental allusions,* or from *doubtful traditions,* quite inaccessible to the generality of Christians, and about which the learned few are far from being agreed.

Church-ordinances removed from a firm foundation, and rested on a basis of sand.

§ 18. Those who on such grounds as I have been speaking of defend the Institutions and Ordinances, and vindicate the Apostolical Character, of our own (or indeed of any) Church,—whether on their own sincere conviction, or, as believing that such arguments are the best calculated to inspire the mass of mankind with becoming reverence, and to repress the evil of schism,—do seem to me, in proportion as they proceed on those principles, to be, in the same degree, removing our institutions from a foundation on a rock, to place them on sand. Instead of a clearly-intelligible, well-established, and *accessible* proof of divine sanction for the claims of our Church, they would substitute one that is not only obscure, disputable, and out of the reach of the mass of mankind, but even self-contradictory, subversive of our own and every Church's claims, and leading to the very evils of doubt, and schismatical division, which it is desired to guard against.

The Rock on which I am persuaded our Reformers intended, and rightly intended, to rest the Ordinances of our Church, is, the warrant to be found in the Holy Scriptures written by, or under the direction of, those to whom our Lord has entrusted the duty of "teaching men to observe all things whatsoever He had commanded them." For in those Scriptures we find a divine sanction clearly given to a regular christian Community,—a Church; which is, according to the definition in our 19th Article,[1] "a congregation (*i. e.* Society or Community; Ecclesia) of faithful men,[2] in the which the pure Word of God is preached, and the Sacraments duly administered according to Christ's

True foundation of Church-enactments.

---

[1] In our Article as it stands in the English, it is "*The* visible Church of Christ is," &c.; but there can be no doubt, I think, that the more correct version from the Latin (the *Latin* Articles appear to have been the original, and the English a translation—in some few places, a careless translation—from the Latin) would have been "*A* visible Church*," &c. The Latin " Ecclesia Christi visibilis" would indeed answer to either phrase; the want of an *article*, definite or indefinite, in that language rendering it liable to such ambiguity. But the context plainly shows that the writer is not speaking of the Universal Church, but of particular Churches, such as the "Churches of Jerusalem, Alexandria, and Rome." The English translator probably either erred from momentary inattention, or, (more likely) understood by "Ecclesia," and by "the Church," the particular Church whose Articles were before him, — the Church of England. If it had been designed, and deliberately designed, to describe "*The* Universal Church" it would most likely have been called "*The* Congregation," &c., instead of "*A* Congregation." See note to § 24.

[2] *i. e.* believers in Christ;—fideles; —πιστοί.

ordinance, in all those things which of necessity are requisite to the same." Now since, from the very nature of the case, every Society must have Officers, appointed in some way or other, and every Society that is to be *permanent*, a perpetual *succession* of Officers, in whatever manner kept up, and must have also a power of enacting, abrogating, and enforcing on its own members, such regulations or bye-laws as are not opposed to some higher authority, it follows inevitably (as I have above observed) that any one who sanctions a Society, gives, in so doing, his sanction to those essentials of a Society, its Governments,—its Officers,—its Regulations. Accordingly, even if our Lord had *not* expressly said anything about "binding and loosing," still the very circumstance of his sanctioning a christian Community would necessarily have implied his sanction of the Institutions, Ministers, and Government, of a christian Church, so long as nothing is introduced at variance with the positive enactments, and the fundamental principles, laid down by Himself and his Apostles.

The English reformers chose the true foundation.

§ 19. This, which I have called a foundation on a rock, is evidently that on which (as has been just observed) our Reformers designed to place our Church.

While they strongly deny to any Church the power to "ordain anything contrary to God's Word," or to require, as essential to salvation, belief in anything not resting on scriptural authority, they claim the power for each Church of ordaining and altering "rites and ceremonies," "so that all things be done to edifying," and nothing "contrary to God's Word." They claim on that ground for our own Church a recognition of that power in respect of the Forms of Public Service;—on the ground, that is (Art. 36) that these "contain nothing that is in itself superstitious and ungodly."

And they rest the claims of Ministers, not on some supposed sacramental virtue, transmitted from hand to hand in unbroken succession from the Apostles, in a chain, of which if any one link be even doubtful, a distressing uncertainty is thrown over all christian Ordinances, Sacraments, and Church-privileges for ever; but, on the fact of those Ministers being the *regularly-appointed officers of a regular christian Community.* "It is not lawful" (says the 23rd Article) "for any man to take upon him the office of public preaching, or ministering the sacraments in the congregation, before he be *lawfully called and sent* to execute the same. And those we ought to judge lawfully called and sent which be chosen and called to this work by men who have *public authority given unto them in the Congregation*, to call and send Ministers into the Lord's Vineyard."[1]

Claim of the Ministers of the Auglican Church.

Those who are not satisfied with the foundation thus laid,—and which, as I have endeavoured to show, is the very foundation which Christ and his Apostles have prepared for us,—who seek to take higher ground, as the phrase is, and maintain what are called according to the modern fashion "Church-principles," or "Church-of-England principles," are in fact subverting the principles both of our own Church in particular, and of every christian Church that claims the inherent rights belonging to a Community, and confirmed by the sanction of God's Word as contained in the Holy Scriptures. It is advancing, but not in the right road,—it is advancing not

Pretended Church-principles subversive of the functions and rights of a Church.

---

[1] See § 23.

in sound learning, but error,—not in faith, but in superstitious credulity, to seek for some higher and better ground on which to rest our doctrines and institutions than that on which they were placed by "the Author and Finisher of our Faith."[1]

On this point I will take the liberty of inserting an extract from a Charge delivered a few years ago; because I wish to point out, that the views I am taking, whether sound or unsound—and this I sincerely wish to be decided according to the reasons adduced—are at least not hastily but deliberately adopted, and have undergone no change in that interval.

Christian advancement.
"When I speak of unceasing progress,—of continual improvement in all that pertains to the christian life,—as what we ought to aim at, both in ourselves, and in those with whom we have influence, it may perhaps be proper to add, that this does not imply any attempt 'to be wise above that which is written,'—any expectation of a new and additional revelation, or of the discovery of new doctrines, any pretensions

---

[1] It is curious to observe how very common it is for any Sect or Party to assume a title indicative of the very excellence in which they are especially deficient, or strongly condemnatory of the very errors with which they are especially chargeable. Thus, those who from time to time have designated themselves "Gnostics," *i. e.* persons "*knowing*" the Gospel, in a far superior degree to other professed Christians,—have been generally remarkable for their *want* of knowledge of the very first rudiments of evangelical truth. The phrase "Catholic" religion"(*i.e.* "Universal") is the most commonly in the mouths of those who are the most limited and *exclusive* in their views, and who seek to shut out the largest number of christian Communities from the Gospel-covenant. "Schism," again, is by none more loudly reprobated than by those who are not only the immediate authors of schism, but the advocates of principles tending to generate and perpetuate schisms without end. And "Church-principles,"—"High-church principles," —" Church-of-England principles,"— are the favourite terms of those who go the furthest in subverting all these.

Obvious as this fallacy is, there is none more commonly successful in throwing men off their guard.

to inspiration,—or hopes of a fresh outpouring of that, or of any other miraculous gifts. It seemed needful to make this remark, because such hopes have been cherished,—such pretensions put forth,—from time to time, in various ages of the Church, and not least in the present.

"I have coupled together these two things, —miraculous gifts, and a new revelation, because I conceive them to be in reality inseparable. Miracles are the only sufficient credentials on which any one can reasonably demand assent to doctrines not clearly revealed *(to the understanding of his hearers)* in Scripture. The promulgation of new articles of faith, or of articles which, though not avowedly new, are yet not obviously contained in Scripture, is most presumptuous, unless so authenticated. And again, pretensions to miraculous powers such as those of Moses and the Prophets,—of Christ and the Apostles, seem to imply some such object to be furthered by them. At any rate, those who shall have thus established their claim to be considered as messengers from Heaven *may* evidently demand assent to whatever they may, in that character, promulgate. If any persons therefore pretend to such a mark of a divine commission as the gift of tongues, or any such power, no one who admits their pretensions can consistently withhold assent from any thing they may declare themselves commissioned to teach.

Miraculous gifts, and revelation inseparable.

"And, again, if any persons claim for any traditions of the Church, an authority, either paramount to Scripture, or equal to Scripture, or concurrent with it,—or, which comes to the very same thing, *decisive as to the interpretation of Scripture*,[1]—taking on themselves to decide what *is* 'the Church,' and *what* tradition is to be thus received,—these

---

[1] See *Note G.*

persons are plainly called on to establish by miraculous evidence the claims they advance. And if they make their appeal not to miracles wrought by themselves, but to those which originally formed the evidence of the Gospel, they are bound to show by some decisive proof, that that evidence can fairly be brought to bear upon and authenticate their pretension;—that they are, by Christ's decree, the rightful depositaries of the power they claim.

Improved understanding of what is written, to be distinguished from additions to the Gospel.

" But to such as reject and protest against all such groundless claims, an interminable field is still open for the application of all the faculties, intellectual and moral, with which God has endowed us, for the fuller understanding and development of the truths revealed in his written Word. To learn and to teach what is there to be found;—to develop more and more fully to your own minds and to those of your hearers, what the Evangelists and Apostles have conveyed to us, will be enough and more than enough to occupy even a longer life than any of us can expect.

" The Mosaic Dispensation was the dawn of ' the dayspring from on high,' not yet arrived,—of a Sun only about to rise. It was a Revelation in itself imperfect. The Sun of the Gospel arose; 'the true Light, which lighteth every one that cometh into the world,' appeared: but it was partially hidden, and is so, still, by a veil of clouds;—by prejudices of various kinds,—by the passions, and infirmities, and ignorance, of mankind. We may advance, and we may lead others to advance, indefinitely, in the full development of Gospel-truth,—of the real character and meaning and design of Christ's religion; not by seeking to *superadd* something to the Gospel-revelation; but by a more correct and fuller comprehension of it;—not by increasing, absolutely, the light of the noonday-sun, but by clearing away the mists which obscure our view of it. Christianity itself cannot be improved;· but men's views, and estimate, and comprehension of Christianity, may be indefinitely improved.

"Vigilant discretion however is no less needful than zeal and perseverance, if we would really advance in the Christian course. The most active and patient traveller, if he be not also watchfully careful to keep in the right road, may, after having once diverged from it into some other track, be expending his energies in going further and further astray, while he fancies himself making progress in his journey. *Caution necessary against erroneous pursuit of religious knowledge.*

"In various ways is the Christian, and not least, the christian Minister, liable to this kind of self-deception. I am not now, you will observe, adverting chiefly to the danger of mistaking what is absolutely false, for true, or wrong for right; but rather to that of mistaking the real character of some description of truth or of valuable knowledge. We have to guard against mistake, for instance, as to what is or is not a part of the Christian-*Revelation ;*—a truth *belonging* to the Gospel, and resting, properly, on divine authority. While advancing in the attainment of what may be in itself very valuable and important knowledge we may be in fact going further and further in error, if we confound together the inspired and the uninspired,— the sacred text, with the human comment.

"There are persons (such as I have above alluded to) who in their zeal—in itself laudable—to advance towards a full comprehension of the Gospel-revelation, have conceived that they are to seek for this by diligent research into the tenets and practices of what is called the Primitive Church; *i. e.* the christian world during the first three or first four Ages. *Pretended developments of the Gospel.*

And some have even gone so far as to represent the revelation of the christian-scheme contained in the New Testament as a mere imperfect and uncompleted outline, which was to be filled up by the Church in the succeeding three centuries;—as a mere beginning of that which the early Fathers were empowered and commissioned to finish: though on what grounds any kind of authority is claimed for the Church *then*, which does not equally belong to it at this day, or at any intermediate period, no one, as far as I know, has even attempted to make out.

" Now to learn what has been said and done by eminent men in every Age of the Church, is of course interesting and valuable to a theological student. And a man of modesty and candour will not fail to pay great attention to their opinions, in whatever period they may have lived. He will also inquire with peculiar interest into the belief and the practices of those who had been instructed by the immediate disciples and other contemporaries of the Apostles themselves. But the mistake is, to assume, on the ground of presumptuous conjecture (for of proof, there is not even a shadow) that these men were infallible interpreters of the Apostles, and had received from them by tradition something not contained, or not plainly set forth, in their writings, but which yet were designed by those very Apostles as a necessary portion of Christianity.

No essentials of Christianity omitted by the Sacred Writers.

" Not only are all these assumptions utterly groundless and unwarrantable, but, on the contrary, even if there is anything which we can be morally certain *was* practised in the time of the Apostles, and with their sanction (as is the case for instance with the Agapæ or Love-feasts) we must yet consider it as not designed by them to be of universal and perpetual obligation, where they have not distinctly laid it down as such in their writings. By omitting, in any case, thus to record certain of their practices or directions, they have given us as clear an indication as we could have looked for, of their design to leave these to the free choice and decision of each Church in each Age and Country. And there seems every reason to think that it was on purpose to avoid misapprehensions of this kind, that they did leave unrecorded so much of what we cannot but be sure they must have practised, and said, and established, in the Churches under their own immediate care.

"And it should be remembered that what some persons consider as the *safe* side in respect of such points,—as the extreme of scrupulous and cautious veneration—is in truth the reverse. A wise and right-minded reverence for divine authority will render us doubly scrupulous of reckoning any thing as a divine precept or institution, without sufficient warrant. Yet, at the first glance, a readiness to bestow religious veneration, with or without good grounds (which is the very characteristic of superstition) is apt to be mistaken for a sign of pre-eminent piety. Besides those who hold the 'double doctrine'—the 'disciplina arcani'[1]—and concerning whom therefore it would be rash to pronounce whether any particular tenet taught by them is one which they inwardly believe, or is one of the exoteric instructions deemed expedient for the multitude,—besides these persons, there are, no doubt, men of sincere though mistaken piety, who, as has been just intimated, consider it as the safe side in all doubtful cases, to adhere with unhesitating confidence to every thing that *may possibly* have been introduced or practised by the Apostles; —to make every thing an article of christian faith that could have been implied in any thing they may have taught.

The safe side.

---

[1] See Dr. West's *Discourse on Reserve*. And also Bishop Dickinson's *Remains*.

But such persons would perceive on more careful and sober reflection, that a rightly-scrupulous piety consists, as has been said, in drawing the line as distinctly as we are able, between what is, and what is not *designed* by our divine Instructors as a portion of their authoritative precepts and directions. It is by this careful anxiety to *comply with their intention with respect to us*, that we are to manifest a true veneration for them.

"Anything that does not fall within this rule, we may believe, but not as a part of the christian *revelation;*—we may practise, but not as a portion of the *divine institutions essential to a christian Church,* and binding on all men in all Ages: not, in short, as something placed beyond the bounds of that 'binding and loosing' power which belongs to *every* Church, in reference to things neither enjoined in Scripture nor at variance with it. Otherwise, even though what we believe should be, really, and in itself, true, and though what we practise, should chance to be in fact what the Apostles did practise, we should not be honouring, but dishonouring God, by taking upon ourselves to give the sanction of his authority to that from which He has thought fit to withhold that sanction. When the Apostle Paul gave his advice on matters respecting which he 'had no commandment from the Lord,' he of course thought that what he was recommending was good; but so far was he from presuming to put it forth as a divine command, that he expressly notified the contrary. Let us not think to manifest our pious humility by reversing the Apostle's procedure!

"I have thought it needful, in these times especially, to insert this caution against such mistaken efforts after advancement in christian knowledge and practice; against the delusions of those who, while they exult in their imagined progress in the christian cause, are, in reality, straying into other paths, and following a bewildering meteor."

§ 20. Those whose "Church-principles" lead them thus to remove from a firm foundation the institutions of a christian Church, and especially of our own, and to place them on the sand, are moreover compelled, as it were with their own hands, to dig away even that very foundation of sand. For, in respect of our own Church, since it inculcates repeatedly and earnestly as a fundamental principle,[1] that nothing is to be insisted on as an essential point of faith, that is not taught in Scripture, any member of our Church who should *make* essentials of points confessedly NOT found in Scripture, and who should consequently make it a point of necessary faith to *believe* that these *are* essentials, must unavoidably be pronouncing condemnation, either on himself, or on the very Church he belongs to, and whose claims he is professing to fortify.

Pretended Church-principles fatal to the christian hopes and privileges even of their advocates.

But moreover, not from our own Church only, but from the Universal Church,—from all the privileges and promises of the Gospel,—the principles I am condemning, go to exclude, if fairly followed out, the very persons who advocate them. For it is certain that our own institutions and practices (and the like may be said, I apprehend, of every other Church in the world) though not, we conceive, *at variance* with any Apostolical injunctions, or with any Gospel principle, are, in several points, not precisely *coincident* with those of the earliest Churches. The

Departures from Apostolical precedents, general.

---

[1] Besides the Articles, see, on this point, the Ordination Service.

Agapæ for instance, or "Love-feasts," alluded to just above, have, in most Churches, been long discontinued. The "Widows" again, whom we find mention of in Paul's Epistles, appear plainly to have been an Order of Deaconesses regularly appointed to particular functions in the earliest Churches: and their Deacons appear to have had an office considerably different from those of our Church.[1]

Each Bishop originally presided over one entire Church.

Again, it seems plainly to have been at least the general, if not the universal, practice of the Apostles, to appoint over each separate *Church* a *single* individual as a chief Governor, under the title of "*Angel*" (i. e. *Messenger* or *Legate* from the Apostles) or "BISHOP," i. e. *Superintendent* or Overseer. A CHURCH and a DIOCESE seem to have been for a considerable time *co-extensive* and *identical*. And each Church or Diocese (and consequently each Superintendent) though connected with the rest by ties of Faith and Hope and Charity, seems to have been (as has been already observed) perfectly independent as far as regards any power of control.

The plan pursued by the Apostles seems to have been, as has been above remarked, to establish a great number of small (in comparison with most modern Churches) distinct and independent Communities, each governed by its own single Bishop, consulting, no doubt, with his own Presbyters, and accustomed to act in concurrence with them, and occasionally conferring with the Brethren in other Churches, but owing no submission to the rulers of any other Church, or to any central common authority, except the Apostles themselves. And other points of difference might be added.

---

[1] See *The Church and the Synagogue*, an Abridgment from Vitringa, by Rev. J. Bernard.

Now to vindicate the institutions of our own or of some other Church, on the ground that they "are not in themselves superstitious or ungodly,"—that they are not at variance with Gospel-principles, or with any divine injunction that was designed to be of universal obligation, is intelligible and reasonable. But to vindicate them on the ground of the exact conformity, which it is notorious they do not possess, to the most ancient models, and even to go beyond this, and condemn all Christians whose institutions and ordinances are not "one and utterly like"[1] our own, on the ground of their departure from the apostolical precedents, which no Church has exactly adhered to,—does seem —to use no harsher expression,—not a little inconsistent and unreasonable.

And yet one may not unfrequently hear members of Episcopalian Churches pronouncing severe condemnation on those of other Communions, and even excluding them from the christian Body, on the ground, not of their not being under the *best* form of Ecclesiastical Government, but, of their wanting the very essentials of a christian Church; viz. the very same distinct Orders in the Hierarchy that the Apostles appointed: and this, while the Episcopalians themselves have, universally, so far varied from the Apostolical institution as to have in one Church several *Bishops;* each of whom consequently differs in the office he holds, as to a most important point, from one of the primitive Bishops, as much as the Governor of any one of our Colonies does from a Sovereign Prince.

Inconsistency of condemnations often pronounced by Christians on each other.

It is to be observed, too, that this is a point of difference, not only of some importance, generally, but, in

---

[1] See 34th Article.

reference to the *ordaining* power of a Bishop, apparently most essential. For this, it seems reasonable to suppose, must have been assigned to a Bishop *by virtue of* his being the single *supreme Head* (on earth) of a distinct Church; since it is to such a one—to the supreme Governor of a Community—that the office naturally appertains of appointing subordinate functionaries. If, therefore, the apostolical institutions were to be regarded as designed to be of universal and eternal obligation, on this hypothesis, there would be a great doubt whether Bishops of the present day have any right to *ordain*.

It is remarkable that there are *Presbyterians* also, who proceed on similar principles; who contend that originally the distinction between Bishops and Presbyters did not exist; and *consequently* (not that Episcopacy is not *essential* to a Church, but) that episcopal government is an *unwarrantable innovation*,—an usurpation—a profane departure from the divine ordinances![1]

Now whether the several alterations, and departures from the original institutions, were or were not, in each instance, made on good grounds, in accordance with an altered state of society, is a question which cannot even be entertained by those who hold that no Church is competent

---

[1] If we look to Scripture alone, we find, on the one hand, Titus and Timothy entrusted with what may fairly be reckoned episcopal control over the Churches, respectively, of Crete and of Ephesus; and, on the other hand, we find this appointment of Timothy to have been apparently only *temporary*. And, looking to other ancient writings, we find Clement's Epistle evidently written as from a *Bishop* of Rome, to the Church at Corinth, as apparently *not* under a Bishop. This Epistle (confessedly very *ancient*) is considered by several competent judges as genuine; but even supposing it spurious, the forger would have been very unlikely to depart from the existing traditions concerning notorious facts. Had the episcopalian, or again, the presbyterian form of government been known to have been always *universal*, a contrary representation would never have been made by a person writing what he meant to be received as genuine.

to vary at all from the ancient model. Their principle would go to exclude at once from the pale of Christ's Church almost every christian Body since the first two or three Centuries.

§ 21. Waiving however what may be called a personal argument, and supposing that some mode could be devised of explaining away all the inconsistencies I have been adverting to, still, if the essentials of Christianity,—at least a considerable portion of them—are not to be found in Scripture, but in a supplementary Tradition,[1] which is to be sought in the works of those early Fathers who were orthodox, the foundations of a christian's Faith and Hope become *inaccessible* to nearly the whole of the Laity, and to much the greater part of the Clergy.

Appeal to the practice of the early Churches, an argument inaccessible to the great mass of Christians.

This, it may be said, is just as it should be; and as it must be: the unlearned being necessarily dependent on the learned, in respect of several most important points; since the great mass of Christians cannot be supposed capable of even reading the Scriptures in the original tongues; much less of examining ancient manuscripts.

Now this necessity I see no reason for admitting, if it be understood in the sense that the unlearned must needs take the word of the learned, and place implicit reliance[2] on the good faith of certain individuals selected by them as their spiritual guides. It is in their power, and is surely their duty, to ascertain how far the assertions of certain learned men are to be safely relied on.

Supposed dependence on the word of learned men.

---

[1] See Prof. Powell's *Tradition unveiled.*
[2] See *Note H.*

A blind uninquiring assent, however, as to *all* points connected with religion, is the natural result—whether the designed result or not—(to those who do not reject the christian Faith altogether) of the inculcation of such principles as I have been speaking of. For if a man were directed to take *two* medicines, as being *both* essential for his health, he would most likely not take the pains to *analyse* the one, when it was out of his power to analyse the *other;* but would either take his physician's word for both, or at once reject both. So, also, if men be taught that it is essential to their salvation to belong to a Church, formed on the exact model of the Primitive Churches, and that this model can be, and has been, completely ascertained by the laborious researches of a few eminent theologians, who have devoted their lives to the study,—the mass of mankind being quite incompetent, either to make these researches for themselves, or even to judge of the competency and fidelity of their guides,—they will be induced— if they trust these guides *at all*—to take their word for *everything* alike, and to forego all inquiry as to anything pertaining to religion.

Doubtfulness of appeals to early Churches. But when, in the case now before us, men do come to consider and inquire what the foundation really is on which they are told (according to the above principles) to rest their own hopes of eternal life, and to pronounce condemnation on those who differ from them, it cannot be but that doubt and dissatisfaction, and perhaps disgust, and danger of ultimate infidelity, will beset them, in proportion as they are of a serious and reflective turn, and really anxious to attain religious truth. For when referred to the works of the orthodox ancient Fathers, they find that a very large portion of these works is lost; some fragments, or reports of them by other writers, alone remaining: they find again

§ 21.] *inaccessible to the People.* 143

that what *has* come down to us is so vast in amount that a life is not sufficient for the attentive study of even the chief part of it;[1] they find these Authors far from being agreed, on all points, with each other, or with themselves; and that learned men again are not agreed in the interpretation of *them;* and still less agreed as to the orthodoxy of each, and the degree of weight due to his judgment on several points; nor even agreed, by some centuries, as to the degree of *antiquity*[2] that is to make the authority of each, decisive, or more or less approaching to decisive.

Everything in short pertaining to this appeal is obscure,—uncertain,—disputable,— and actually disputed,—to such a degree, that even those who are not able to read the original authors, may yet be perfectly competent to perceive how unstable a foundation they furnish. They can perceive that the mass of Christians are called on to believe and to do what is essential to Christianity, in implicit reliance on the *reports* of their respective pastors, as to what certain deep theological antiquarians have *reported* to *them*, respecting the *reports* given by certain ancient Fathers, of the *reports* current in their times, concerning apostolical usages and institutions! And yet whoever departs in any degree from these, is to be regarded at best in an intermediate state between Christianity and Heathenism! Surely the tendency of this procedure must be to drive the

Uncertain foundation of faith based on reports.

---

[1] Would not the ingenuous course be, for those who refer to the authority of "The Fathers," to state distinctly, 1st, *which* of these ancient writers they mean; and, 2ndly, whether they have *read* these? For, a very large proportion, even of the higher classes, are far from being aware of the voluminous character of the works thus vaguely referred to: and being accustomed, when any one refers to "The *Scriptures,*" to understand him as speaking of a well-known book, which they presume he professes to have read, it is likely they should conclude, unless told to the contrary, that one who appeals to "The Fathers," has himself read them.

[2] See Note, p. 124.

doubting into confirmed (though perhaps secret) infidelity, and to fill with doubts the most sincerely pious, if they are anxiously desirous of attaining truth, and unhappily have sought it from such instructors.

Pretended decisions of the Catholic Church.

§ 22. But an attempt is usually made to silence all such doubts by a reference to the Catholic Church, or the "primitive" or the "ancient Catholic Church," as having authority to decide,—and as having in fact decided,— as to the degree of regard due to the opinions and testimony of individual writers among the Fathers. And a mere reference such as this, accompanied with unhesitating assertion, is not unfrequently found to satisfy or silence those who might be disposed to doubt. And while questions are eagerly discussed as to the degree of deference due to the "decisions of the universal Church," some preliminary questions are often overlooked: such as,—when, and where did any one visible Community, comprising all Christians as its members, exist? Does it exist still? Is its authority the same as formerly? or when, and how, was its authority suppressed, or curtailed? And again, who are its rulers and other officers, rightfully claiming to represent Him who is the acknowledged Head of the Universal (or Catholic) Church, Jesus Christ, and to act as his *Vicegerents* on Earth? For, it is plain that no society that has a *supreme Governor*, can perform any act, *as a Society*, and in its corporate capacity, *without* that supreme Governor, either in person, or represented by some one clearly deputed by him, and invested with his authority. And a Bishop, Presbyter, or other officer, of any particular Church, although he is a *member* of the Universal christian-Church, and also a *christian Ecclesiastical-Ruler*, is not a Ruler *of* the Universal Church; his jurisdiction not extending beyond his particular Diocese, Province, or Church: any more than a *European King* is King *of* Europe. Who then are to be recognised as Rulers *of* (not merely, *in*) the Universal Church? Where (on Earth) is its central supreme government, such as every single Community must have? Who is the accredited organ empowered to pronounce its decrees, in the name of the whole Community? And where are these decrees registered?

Yet many persons are accustomed to talk familiarly of the decisions of the Catholic Church, as if there were some accessible record of them, such as we have of the Acts of any Legislative Body; and " as if there existed some recognised functionaries, regularly authorized to govern and to represent that community, the Church of Christ; and answering to the king—senate—or other constituted authorities, in any secular community. And yet no shadow of proof can be offered, that the Church, in the above sense,— the Universal Church,—can possibly give any decision at all;—that it has any constituted Authorities as the organs by which such decision could be framed or promulgated;— or, in short, that there is, or ever was, any *one community on earth*, recognised, or having any claim to be recognised, as the Universal Church, bearing rule over and comprehending all particular Churches.

No accessible records of Catholic decisions.

" 'We are wont to speak of the foundation of the Church,—the authority of the Church,—the various characteristics of the Church,—and the like,—as if the Church were, originally at least, One Society in all respects. From the period in which the Gospel was planted beyond the precincts of Judæa, this manifestly ceased to be the case; and as christian Societies were formed among people more and more unconnected and

The Church-Universal, not a Single Society on Earth.

L

dissimilar in character and circumstances, the difficulty of considering the Church as One Society increases. Still from the habitual and unreflecting use of this phrase, " the Church," it is no uncommon case to confound the two notions; and occasionally to speak of the various societies of Christians as *one*, occasionally as *distinct* bodies. The mischief which has been grafted on this inadvertency in the use of the term, has already been noticed; and it is no singular instance of the enormous practical results which may be traced to mere ambiguity of expression. The Church is undoubtedly *one*, and so is the Human Race *one;* but not as a *Society*. It was from the first composed of distinct societies; which were called one, because formed on *common principles*. It is One Society only when considered as to its *future* existence. The circumstance of its having one common Head, (Christ,) one Spirit, one Father, are points of unity which no more make the Church One Society on earth, than the circumstance of all men having the same Creator, and being derived from the same Adam, renders the Human Race one Family. That Scripture often speaks of Christians generally under the term, " the Church," is true; but if we wish fully to understand the force of the term so applied, we need only call to mind the frequent analogous use of ordinary historical language when no such doubt occurs. Take, for example, Thucydides' *History of the Peloponnesian War*. It contains an account of the transactions of two opposed parties, each made up of many distinct communities; on the one side were Democracies, on the other Oligarchies. Yet precisely the same use is made by the historian of the terms " the Democracy" and " the Oligarchy," as we find Scripture adopting with regard to the term " the Church." No one is misled by these, so as to suppose the Community of Athens *one* with that of Corcyra, or the Theban with the Lacedæmonian. When the heathen writer speaks of "the Democracy of" or "in" the various democratical States, we naturally understand him to mean distinct Societies *formed on similar principles;* and so, doubtless, ought we to interpret the sacred writers when they, in like manner, make mention of the Church of, or in, Antioch, Rome, Ephesus, Corinth, &c.

"'But there was also an especial reason why the term Church should have been often used by the sacred writers as if it applied to One Society. God's dispensation had hitherto been limited to a single society,—the Jewish People. Until the Gospel was preached, the Church of God *was* One Society. It therefore sometimes occurs with the force of a transfer from the objects of God's *former* dispensation, to those of his *present* dispensation. In like manner, as Christians are called "the Elect," their bodies "the Temple," and their Mediator "the High Priest;" so, their condition, as the objects of God's new dispensation, is designated by the term "the Church of Christ," and "the Church."

"'The Church is *one*, then, not as consisting of One Society, but because the various societies, or Churches were then modelled, *Unity of the Church, what.* and ought still to be so, on the same principles; and because they enjoy common privileges,—one Lord, one Spirit, one baptism. Accordingly, the Holy Ghost, through his agents the Apostles, has not left any detailed account of the formation of any christian Society; but He has very distinctly marked the great principles on which all were to be founded, whatever distinctions may exist amongst them. In short, the foundation of the Church by the Apostles was not analogous to the work of Romulus, or Solon; it was not properly, the foundation of christian Societies which occupied them, but the establishment of the principles on which Christians in all ages might form societies for themselves.'—*Encyclopædia Metropolitana.* "Age of Apostolical Fathers," p. 774.

"The above account is sufficiently established even by the mere negative circumstance of the absence of all mention in the Sacred Writings of any *one* Society on earth, having a Government and officers of its own, and recognised as the Catholic or Universal Church: especially when it is considered that the frequent mention of the particular Churches at Jerusalem, Antioch, Rome, Corinth, &c.—of the seven Churches in Asia,—and of 'the care of all the Churches' which Paul had founded, would have rendered unavoidable the notice of the One Church (had there been any such) which bore rule over all the rest, either as its subjects, or as provincial departments of it.

"This negative evidence, I say, would alone be fully sufficient, considering that the whole burden of proof lies on the side of those who set up such a claim. He who appeals to the alleged decisions of a certain Community, is clearly bound, in the first place, to prove its existence. But if we proceed to historical evidence, we find on examination, that there *never was a time* when the supremacy of any one Church was acknowledged by all, or nearly all Christians. And to say they *ought* to have done so, and that as many as have refused such submission are to be regarded as schismatics and rebels, is evidently to prejudge the question.

Church-authority. "The Universal Church, then, being *one*, in reference, not to any one Government on earth, but only to our divine Head, even Christ, ruling Christians by his Spirit, which spoke to them from time to time through the Apostles while these were living, and speaks still in the words of the Christian Scriptures, it follows that each Christian is bound (as far as Church authority extends) to submit to the ordinances and decisions,—

not repugnant to Scripture, (see Art. XXXIV.) of the particular Church of which he is a member.

"If it were possible that all the Christians now in existence—suppose 250 millions—could assemble, either in person, or by deputations of their respective Clergy, in one place, to confer together; and that the votes, whether personal or by proxy, of 230 or 240 millions of these were to be at variance (as in many points they probably would be) with the decisions and practices of our own Church; we should be no more bound to acquiesce in and adopt the decision of that majority, even in matters which we do not regard as essential to the christian Faith, than we should be, to pass a law *for this realm*, because it was approved by the majority of the *human race*."[1]

Many persons are accustomed to speak as if a *majority* had some natural inherent right to control and to represent the *whole* of any Assembly or Class of persons.[2] *No natural rights in a Majority.* We are told of this or that being "held by *most* of the early Fathers;"—of the opinions or practices of "the *greater part* of the members of the early Church;"—of the "decision of the *majority* of" such and such a council, &c. No doubt, *when other points are equal*, the judgment of a greater number deserves more consideration than that of a less; but a majority has no such controlling or representing power, except by express, arbitrary, regulation and *enactment;* and regulations as to this point differ in different cases. Thus, the *decision of a Jury*, in England, is their *unanimous* decision; in Scotland, that of *two-thirds;* a decision of the House of Peers, is that of a majority of those who are (personally, or by Proxy) *present;*—of the House of Commons,—of a majority

---

[1] *Essays*, 4th Series, pp. 166—171.
[2] See *Note N.*

in a House of not less than *forty;* &c. And when there is *no* express enactment or agreement on this point, nothing can fairly be called an opinion or decision of such and such persons, except one in which they *all* concur. When they do not, we then look, not merely to the *numbers,* but also to the *characters* and circumstances of each party.

Ambiguity of the words " Authority " & " Church." Many again are misled by the twofold ambiguity in the phrase " Authority of the Catholic (or Universal) Church;" both " Authority," and " Church "[1] being often employed in more than one sense. Authority, in the sense, not of *power*, but of a claim to *attention* and to deference, (more or less as the case may be) belongs, of course, to the " Universal Church," meaning thereby, not, any *single Society*, but Christians generally throughout all regions :— the " christian World," or (in modern phraseology) " the christian Public." Whatever is, or has been, attested, or believed, or practised, by all of these, or by the greater part of them, or by several of those whom they may regard as the best and wisest among them,—is, of course, entitled to a degree of attentive and respectful consideration, greater or less according to the circumstances of each case.

It is in quite a different sense that we speak of the " Authority," for instance, of Parliament; meaning, of an *Act of Parliament*, regularly passed according to the prescribed forms, and claiming (if not at variance with the divine laws) submission—compliance—*obedience;* quite independent of any *approbation* on our part.

It is worthy of remark too, that *Power* (or Authority in that sense) in reference to *any particular act*, or decision, does not admit of *degrees*. A man may indeed have more or less power than another; that is, he may have rightful

---

[1] See *Note I.*

power to do something which another cannot: but with respect to any specified act, he either has the power, or he has it not. On the other hand, "Authority" in the sense of a *claim to deference*, admits of infinite degrees.

And yet one may find it asserted, as a matter that admits of no doubt, and is to be taken for granted, as "generally admitted, except by those trained in a modern school, that any particular Church *owes obedience* to the Universal Church, of which it is a part." *Bold assumptions of authority for supposed Catholic decisions.*

Such assertions sometimes come from men of acknowledged learning; in reality far too learned not to be themselves well aware that there *never was*, since the days of the Apostles, any such Body *existing* as *could* claim, on the plea of being the recognised representative of the whole christian World, this "obedience," from each particular Church; and hence, these bold assertions will often succeed in overawing the timid, in deceiving the ignorant and inconsiderate, and in satisfying the indolent.

The temptation, doubtless, is very strong —especially for those who would maintain doctrines or practices, that are, seemingly at least, at variance with Scripture—to make an *Awe inspired by appeals to an undefined authority.*
appeal to a standard that is inaccessible to the mass of mankind, and that is in all respects so vague; to a vast and *indefinite* number of writers, extending over a very long and *indefinite* space of time;—and to avail oneself of the awe-inspiring force of sacred names, by exhorting men, in the apparent language of Scripture[1]—(for no such passage really exists) to "hear the Church!"

---

[1] Our Lord directs his disciples, in the event of a dispute between two individuals, to refer the matter, in the last resort, to the decisions of the Congregation, Assembly, or Church (Ecclesia); and that if any one *disobey* (or "refuse to hear," as our translators render it) this, he is to be

§ 23. The readiness with which some persons acquiesce, at least profess to acquiesce, in supposed decisions of the Universal or Catholic Church, using the term in a sense in which it can even be proved that no such Community ever existed on Earth, and of General Councils such as, in fact, never met, and of Traditions several of which are such as to need proof, first, how far they are genuine, and next, how far, if admitted to be genuine, they would be binding on all Christians,—this ready acquiescence, I say, is the more extraordinary, when we consider that many of the points which are attempted to be supported by an appeal to such authority, do, in fact, stand in no need of that support, but have a firm foundation in Scripture, by virtue of the powers plainly conferred by Christ Himself on Christian communities.

Appeals to supposed decisions, &c. of the Catholic Church, as superfluous as they are unsound.

Any forms, for instance, for Public Worship, and for the ordaining of christian Ministers, which "contain" (as our Reformers maintain respecting those they sanctioned)[1] "nothing that is in itself superstitious and contrary to God's Word," are plainly binding, by Christ's own sanction, on the members of the Church that appoints them.

But some, it should seem, are not satisfied with a *justification* of their own ordinances and institutions, unless they can find a plea for condemning all those who differ from them. And this plea they seek not by endeavouring to show the superior expediency, with a view to decency, good order, and edification, of the enactments

Not only self-vindication sought, but also condemnation of others.

---

regarded "as a heathen," &c. ἐὰν τῆς ἐκκλησίας παρακούσῃ. Those who adduce this passage, would, it may be presumed, have at least preferred bringing forward, if they could have found one, some passage of Scripture which does support their views.

[1] Article xxxvi.

they would defend, but by maintaining the obligatory character of supposed apostolical traditions; and then they are driven, as I have said, to shift our own institutions from the foundation on a rock, to place them on sand.

When one sees persons not content with the advantages they enjoy, unless they can exclude others, and in the attempt to do so, " falling into the midst of the pit they have digged for another," it is hardly possible to avoid recalling to one's mind the case of Haman, and the result of his jealousy of Mordecai.

Some persons have endeavoured from time to time, to represent our Reformers as appealing to the practice of what is called the Primitive Church, and to the writings of the early Fathers, as the principal,—or as one principal—ground on which they rest the vindication of their own decisions; and as taking for their authoritative standard of rectitude and truth in religious matters, not Scripture alone, but Scripture combined and " blended with Tradition." *Reformers represented as appealing to Scripture and Tradition jointly.*

And it is very true that they do frequently refer (as it was perfectly natural they should, engaged as they were in controversy with the Romanists) to the records which their opponents appealed to, in order to show that the very authorities these last were accustomed to rely on, are in fact opposed to them. It was a fair and allowable " personal argument;"—*argumentum ad hominem*. They point out the proofs extant that many doctrines and practices which *had been made to rest on supposed ancient* tradition, were in fact comparatively modern innovations; and they vindicate themselves from the charge of *innovation* in some points by referring to ancient precedents. All this is perfectly natural, and perfectly justifiable. *Conduct of the Reformers in respect of their controversy with Romanists.*

But it is quite a different thing from acknowledging a decisive authority in early precedents, and in Tradition, either alone, or "blended with Scripture." If any man is charged with introducing an *unscriptural novelty*, and he shows, first, that it is *not unscriptural*, and then (by reference to the opinions of those who lived long ago) that it is *no novelty*, it is most unreasonable to infer that Scripture-authority would have no weight with him unless backed by the opinions of fallible men.

The maxim of "abundans cautela nocet nemini" is far from a safe one if applied without limitation. (See *Logic*, b. ii. ch. 5, § 6.)

It is sometimes imprudent (and some of our Divines have, I think, committed this imprudence) to attempt to "make assurance doubly sure" by bringing forward confirmatory reasons, which, though in themselves perfectly fair, may be interpreted unfairly, by representing them as an acknowledged *indispensable* foundation;—by assuming for instance, that any appeal to such and such of the ancient Fathers or Councils, in confirmation of some doctrine or practice, is to be understood as an admission that it would fall to the ground if *not* so confirmed.

No one would reason thus absurdly in any other case. For instance, when some bill is brought into one of the Houses of Parliament, and it is represented by its opponents as of a *novel* and unheard-of character, it is common, and natural, and allowable, for its advocates to cite instances of similar Acts formerly passed. Now, how absurd it would be thought for any one thence to infer that those who use such arguments must mean to imply that Parliament has no power to pass an Act unless it can be shown that similar Acts have been passed formerly!

If any Bishop of the present day should be convinced that such and such Theologians,—ancient or modern—have given correct and useful expositions of certain parts of Scripture, he could not but wish that the Clergy he ordained should give similar expositions; and he would probably recommend to their attentive perusal the works of those theologians. Now how monstrous it would be to represent him, on such grounds, as making those works a *standard of faith conjointly* with Scripture!

Of a like character is the very reference I have now been making to the documents put forth by those Reformers themselves. I certainly believe these to be in accordance with the principles above laid down as scriptural and reasonable: but I protest (and so probably would they) against "blending with Scripture" the writings of the Reformers, to constitute jointly a rule of faith binding on every Christian's conscience. If any one is convinced that the doctrines and practices and institutions of our Church are unscriptural, he is bound in conscience to leave it.

Reference to the writings or procedure of any persons, no proof that their authority is put forth as decisive.

Our Reformers believed, no doubt, that their institutions were, on the whole, similar to those of the earliest Churches: perhaps they may have believed this similarity to be greater than it really is: but what is the *ground* on which they rested the claim of these institutions to respectful acquiescence? On the ground of their "not being in themselves superstitious, and ungodly, and *contrary to God's Word;*"—on the ground of the "power of each particular Church to ordain, and abrogate, or alter" (though not wantonly and inconsiderately) "Church-rites and ceremonies, provided nothing be done contrary to Scripture."

Standard really laid down by the Reformers.

So also, they believed, no doubt, that the doctrines they taught, and which they commissioned others to teach, were such as had been taught by many early Fathers; and thinking this, they could not but wish that the teaching of the Clergy should coincide with that of those Fathers: but what was the *rule* laid down—the standard fixed on, for ascertaining what should be taught as a part of the Christian Religion? It was Holy Scripture: not Scripture and Tradition, jointly, and "blended together;" but the Written Word of God; nothing being allowed to be taught as an Article of faith that could not thence be proved.

Again, they doubtless believed that there were early precedents for the form of Church-government they maintained,—for the different Orders of the Ministry, and for the mode of appointing each. They believed, no doubt, as a fact, that the Apostles ordained Ministers, and these, others, and so on in succession, down to the then-existing period. But what was the basis on which they deliberately chose to rest their system? On the declared principle that "those and those only are to be accounted as lawfully-appointed Ministers who are called and sent out by *those who have authority* in the Congregation" (or Church) " to call and send labourers into the Lord's vineyard:" and though themselves deliberately adhering to episcopal Ordination, they refrain, both in the Article on the "Church" and in that on "ministering in the Church" from specifying Episcopacy, and episcopal Ordination, as among the essentials.

The Articles the Symbol embodying the deliberate decisions of our Church.

§ 24. Some *individuals* among the Reformers have in some passages used language which may be understood as implying a more strict obligation to conform to ancient precedents than is acknowledged in the Articles. But the Articles being deliberately and jointly drawn up for the very purpose of precisely determining what it was designed should be determined respecting the points they treat of, and in order to supply to the

Anglican Church their Confession of Faith on these points, it seems impossible that any man of ingenuous mind can appeal from the Articles, Liturgy, and Rubric, put forth as the authoritative *declarations of the Church*, to any other writings, whether by the same or by other authors.[1] On the contrary, the very circumstance that opinions going far beyond what the Articles express, or in other respects considerably differing from them, did exist, and were *well known and current*, in the days of our reformers, gives even the *more* force to their *deliberate omissions* of these, and their distinct declaration of what they do mean to maintain. It was not hastily and unadvisedly that they based the doctrines of their Church on "the pure Word of God," and the claim of their Church to the character of a christian Community, on its being a "Congregation of

---

[1] Articles XIX. XX. XXIII. XXXIV. XXXVI.

"XIX. *Of the Church.*—The visible Church of Christ [" ecclesia Christi visibilis est," &c. evidently *A* visible Church of Christ is *a* congregation, &c.] is a congregation of faithful men, in the which the pure word of God is preached, and the Sacraments be duly administered according to Christ's ordinance in all those things that of necessity are requisite to the same.

"As the Church of *Jerusalem, Alexandria,* and *Antioch*, have erred; so also the Church of *Rome* hath erred, not only in their living and manner of Ceremonies, but also in matters of Faith.

"XX. *Of the Authority of the Church.*—The Church hath power to decree Rites or Ceremonies, and authority in Controversies of Faith: And yet it is not lawful for the Church to ordain anything that is contrary to God's word written, neither may it so expound one place of Scripture, that it be repugnant to another. Wherefore, although the Church be a witness and a keeper of holy Writ, yet, as it ought not to decree anything *against* the same, so, *besides* the same, ought it not to enforce anything to be believed for necessity of Salvation.

"XXIII. *Of Ministering in the Congregation.*—It is not lawful for any man to take upon him the office of public preaching, or ministering the Sacraments in the Congregation, before he be lawfully called, and sent to execute the same. And those we ought to judge lawfully called and sent, which be chosen and called to this work by men who have public authority given unto them in the congregation, to call and send ministers into the Lord's vineyard.

"XXXIV. *Of the Traditions of the Church.*—It is not necessary that Traditions and Ceremonies be in all places one, and utterly like; for at all times they have been divers, and may be changed according to the di-

believers, in which that pure Word is preached, and the christian Sacraments duly administered."

Distinction between what was believed by any of the Reformers, and what was agreed on as essential.

Whatever therefore may have been the private opinion of any individuals among their number, they have declared plainly what it was they *agreed* in regarding as a safe and sufficient foundation, and as essential, and consequently requiring to be set forth and embodied in the Symbol or Creed of their Church.[1]

Explaining away the decisions of our Church.

But neither the Reformers of our Church, nor any other human Being, could frame any expressions such as not to admit of being explained away, or the consequences of them somehow evaded, by an ingenious person who should resolutely set himself to the task. And accordingly our Church

---

versities of countries, times, and men's manners, so that nothing be ordained against God's Word. Whosoever through his private judgment, willingly and purposely, doth openly break the traditions and ceremonies of the Church, which be not repugnant to the Word of God, and be ordained and approved by common authority, ought to be rebuked openly, (that others may fear to do the like,) as he that offendeth against the common order of the Church, and hurteth the authority of the Magistrate, and woundeth the consciences of the weak brethren.

"Every particular or national Church hath authority to ordain, change, and abolish, ceremonies or rites of the Church ordained only by man's authority, so that all things be done to edifying."

[It is quite evident from the context, that in this Article the expression "*the Church*," means the "particular Church" to which one belongs.]

"XXXVI. *Of Consecration of Bishops and Ministers.*— The Book of Consecration of Archbishops and Bishops, and Ordering of Priests and Deacons, lately set forth in the time of Edward the Sixth, and confirmed at the same time by authority of Parliament, doth contain all things necessary to such Consecration and Ordering: neither hath it anything, that of itself is superstitious and ungodly. And therefore whosoever are consecrated or ordered according to the Rites of that Book, since the second year of the forenamed King Edward unto this time, or hereafter shall be consecrated or ordered according to the same Rites; we decree all such to be rightly, orderly, and lawfully consecrated and ordered."

[1] See "Articles" in Eden's *Theological Dictionary*.

has been represented as resting her doctrines and her claims on Scripture and Tradition *jointly*, and "blended" together.

We have been told, for instance, of a person held up as a model of *pure Anglican Church-principles*, that he "submitted to the decisions of inspiration *wherever* it was to be found, whether in Scripture or Antiquity." And again, we have been told that " Rome differs from us as to the *authority* which she ascribes to tradition: she regards it as *co*-ordinate, our Divines as *sub*-ordinate; as to *the way in which it is to be employed*, she, as *independent* of Holy Scripture; ours, as *subservient* to, and blended with it: as *to its limits*, she supposes that the Church of Rome has the power of imposing new articles necessary to be believed for salvation; ours, that all such articles were comprised at first in the Creed, and that the Church has only the power of clearing, defining, and expounding these fixed articles."

Now whether the above description be a correct one as far as regards the tenets of the Church of Rome, I do not pretend to decide, nor does it belong to my present purpose to inquire: but the description of the tenets of the Anglican Church, is such as I feel bound to protest against. If indeed by "*us*" and "*our divines*" is to be understood certain individuals who profess adherence to the Church of England, the above description is, no doubt, very correct as far as relates to THEM: but if it be meant that such are the tenets of our Church itself, as set forth in its authoritative Confession of Faith,—the Articles, —nothing can be more utterly unfounded, and indeed more opposite to the truth. Our Church not only does *not* "blend Scripture with Tradition," but takes the most scrupulous care to *dis'inguish* from everything else the Holy Scriptures, as the sufficient and *sole* authoritative standard.

The Anglican Church does not blend Tradition with Scripture.

Grounds on which the creeds are made to rest.

Our Reformers do not merely *omit* to ascribe to any Creed or other statement of any doctrine, an *intrinsic* authority, or one derived from tradition, but, in the Article on the three Creeds,[1] they *take care distinctly to assign the ground* on which those are to be retained; viz. that "they may be *proved* by *Holy Writ.*"

Traditional transmission of Ordinances and Institutions.

It has been alleged, however, that a less amount of Scripture-proof ought to satisfy us as to the "divine appointment,"[2] and universal obligation of an *Ordinance* or *Institution,* than where the question relates to a *Doctrine;* on the ground that anything *external* might be handed down from Age to Age with far greater certainty than a doctrine. But though a doctrine is indeed more likely to be *totally forgotten* than an Ordinance or Institution, these last are quite as liable to be materially *altered* by "the insensible operations of the great innovator, Time,"[3] while the *names,* perhaps, (as is generally the case,) remain unchanged. Ages ago, England was governed by King, Lords, and Commons: and if we had not more complete and accurate histories of our own Country than we have of

---

[1] Nor, by the way, is it true that our Church has declared, in that, or in any other Article, "that all such Articles as are necessary to be believed for Salvation were comprised at first in the [Apostles'] Creed." This, in fact, is neither done, nor was intended to be done by the framers of that Creed; if at least they held—as I doubt not they did—*the doctrine of the Atonement:* for *this is not at all mentioned* in the Apostles' Creed. For though the "forgiveness of sins" was, I doubt not, connected, *in their minds,* as it is in ours, with the Atonement, this connexion is so far from being distinctly *stated* by them, that the Creed may be recited by a Socinian. The cause of the omission, I have no doubt, was, that the doctrine had not in the earliest ages been *disputed.* But at any rate, the fact is certain; that the Creed does dwell on the reality of the historical transaction only, the actual *death* of Christ, without asserting *for whom* or *for what* He suffered death.

[2] See § 17.

[3] Bacon.

many ecclesiastical transactions, some persons probably would be unaware how greatly our Constitution at the present day differs from what it was under the Henrys. Again, the "Extreme-unction" of the Church of Rome is an ordinance derived from the apostolical practice of *miraculously healing* the sick, by anointing; though it is now administered exclusively to those whose recovery is hopeless.

The *title*, again, of Bishop is retained unchanged; though the Office is so far altered from the earlier usage, that instead of being, each, the supreme Head on Earth of a distinct Church, a Bishop is, now, only one out of many officers in the same Church. The title again, of the Priests [Elders] originally appointed by the Apostles, remains; though the office has been, in most Churches,—as in our own, before the Reformation—so completely changed into that of a sacrificing [Sacerdotal, or Hieratical] minister, that the very title of *Priest* (*i. e.* Presbyter, or Elder) has come to be ordinarily transferred to the Jewish and Pagan Sacerdotal Priests; who, of old, were never called Elders, any more than the title of Hiereus was applied to the Elders ordained by the Apostles.[1] And the error thus introduced imperceptibly, as to the real character of the Christian-minister, is far from being eradicated from the minds of all, even in the Reformed Churches. And whether the Deacons spoken of by the Apostle Paul had that office (which we know modern Deacons have not) of Almoners and Stewards of the Church-property, which was exercised by those SEVEN traditionally called Deacons, and whether those "Seven" were Deacons at all, in the sense of the Apostle,[2]—these are disputed points among the learned.

---

[1] See *Discourse on the Christian Priesthood*, appended to the *Bampton Lectures*.
[2] See Bernard's *Vitringa*.

And many other instances might be adduced to show to how great a degree Institutions and Ordinances, as well as Doctrines, are liable to the uncertainties, and to the occasional corruption, of Tradition.

Distinction between traditional doctrines and institutions.

One distinction however there is between a *Doctrine* and an Institution, which ought not to be—as it often is—lost sight of: that any *doctrine* which was really taught by the Apostles, though they may not have meant to enrol it among the essentials of the Gospel, must at least be *true*, now, no less than it was originally: of any *Institution*, on the other hand, which we believe them to have sanctioned, when they have not declared its perpetual obligation, we can only know that it was the wisest and best *at a particular time* and *place;* and it is not fair to infer from this, that they designed to supersede for ever all exercise of the judgment, as to that point, of all Churches throughout the world.

But whatever conclusion we may come to as to the correctness of any traditional records, whether of a Doctrine, or of an Institution, the question still recurs, is it credible that the Apostles should have designed to *entrust to the keeping of Tradition* any of the *essentials* of Christianity?

Pretended distinction between co-ordinate and subordinate tradition.

§ 25. As for the distinction drawn between making Tradition on the one hand "an authority *co-ordinate with* Scripture, on the other hand, "*subordinate and blended with* Scripture," I cannot but think it worse than nugatory.[1] The latter doctrine I have no

---

[1] It is not meant to be implied that all persons who take this view are, themselves, disposed to join the Romish Church, or to think little of the differences between that and their own. Distinctions may be felt as important by *one* person, which may appear to *others*, and may really be,

scruple in pronouncing the worse of the two; because while it virtually comes to the same thing, it is more insidious, and less likely to alarm a mind full of devout reverence for Scripture.

For when men are told of points of faith which they are to receive on the authority of Tradition *alone,* quite independently of any Scripture-warrant, they are not unlikely to shrink from this with a doubt or a disgust, *Tradition blended with Scripture, the most dangerous.* which they are often relieved from at once, by a renunciation, in words, of such a claim; and by being assured that Scripture is the supreme Authority, and that Tradition is to be received as its handmaid only,—as not independent of it, but " subordinate and blended with it." And yet if any or every part of Scripture is to be interpreted according to a supposed authoritative Tradition, and from that interpretation there is to be *no appeal,* it is plain that, to all practical purposes, this comes to the same thing as an independent Tradition. For on this system, anything may be made out of anything. The Jews may resort whenever it suits their purpose, (and often do) to an appeal to their Scriptures INTERPRETED *according to their tradition,* in behalf of anything they are disposed to maintain. I remember conversing some years ago with an educated Jew on the subject of some of their observances, and remarking, in the course of the conversation, that their prohibition of eating butter and flesh at the same meal, rested, I supposed, not, like several other prohibitions, on the Mosaic written Laws, but on Tradition alone. No, he assured me it was prohibited in the Law. I dare say my readers would be as much at a

---

utterly insignificant. The members, for instance, (of the Russian branch at least,) of the Greek Church, are said to abhor *image-*worship, while they pay to *pictures* an adoration which Protestants would regard as equally superstitious.

loss as I was, to guess where. He referred me to Exod. xxiii. 19.

Consequences of authoritative interpretations of Scripture by Tradition.

In like manner, if an ordinary student of Scripture declares that he finds no warrant there for believing in the bodily presence of Christ in the Eucharist, and that he finds, on the contrary, our Lord Himself declaring that "it is the *Spirit* that quickeneth" (giveth life); "the *flesh profiteth nothing*," he is told that Tradition directs us to interpret literally the words "This is my body," and that he must not presume to set up his "private judgment" against the interpretation: and this, when perhaps he is assured by the same person, on similar grounds, that "the whole Bible is one great Parable!"

If again he finds the Apostles ordaining Elders, (Presbyters) and never alluding to any person, except Christ Himself, as bearing any such office in the christian Church as that of the Levitical Priest, (Hiereus) he is told, on the authority of Tradition, which he must not dispute, that Presbyter means Hiereus, a sacrificing Priest. Mahomet's application to himself of the prophecy of Jesus, that He would "send another Paraclete" or Comforter, was received by his followers on grounds not dissimilar; that is, it was an interpretation which he chose to put on the words; and woe to him who should dispute it!

If again we find the whole tenor of Scripture opposed to invocation of Saints, and Image-worship, we may be told that there is a kind of invocation of Saints which the Scriptures, as interpreted by Tradition, allow and encourage. And so on, to an indefinite extent; just as effectually, and almost as easily, as if Tradition had been set up independent of Scripture, instead of being "blended with it."[1]

"Tradition" and "Church-interpretation" are made,

---

[1] See Powell *on Tradition,* § 14—17.

according to this system, subordinate to, and dependent on Scripture, much in the same way that some parasite-plants are dependent on the trees that support them. The parasite at first clings to, and rests on the tree, which it gradually overspreads with its own foliage, till by little and little, it weakens and completely smothers it:

<blockquote>Miraturque novas frondes, et non sua poma.</blockquote>

And it may be added that the insidious character of this system is still further increased, if the principle be laid down without following it out, at once, into all the most revolting consequences that may follow, and that have followed from its adoption. For by this means a contrast is drawn between the most extravagant, and a far more moderate, system of falsehood and superstition; and it is insinuated that this favourable contrast is the result of the one being built on "co-ordinate" and the other on "subordinate" Tradition: the real difference being only that every usurped and arbitrary power is usually *exercised with comparative leniency at first*, till it has been well established. Let but the *principle* which is common to both systems be established; and the one may be easily made to answer all the purposes of the other.

Insidious character of a wrong principle not at first followed out into all its results.

Many, again, deceive both others and themselves, by a misapplication, in respect of this and of several other points, of the precepts relative to the preservation of the "golden mean," and the avoiding of *extremes*. They congratulate themselves as safe from mistake because they "do not go quite so far" as such and such a treatise, or person, or party:[1]

Mistake respecting the Via media.

---

[1] Numerous instances, in various subjects, might be given, of the tendency towards this false and inconsistent middle-course.

For example, some, who "would not go quite so far" as to punish with *death* those who hold religious errors, would yet shun what they account the

and yet perhaps the "VIA MEDIA" which they adhere to will be found on examination to be an attempt to *stop short between the premises and the conclusion ;* — a Medium between the *abandonment of a false principle,* and the adoption of *all* the consequences which legitimately follow from it. Thus, in the present case, if we once admit the principle that Church-tradition is entitled to *uninquiring acquiescence,* we have thereby virtually admitted it to be the Word of God ; and if we then hesitate to follow it whithersoever it may lead, we are only manifesting our own inconsistency, and pronouncing self-condemnation.

* Proved to whom ? *an important question.*

And all this time the advocates of this authoritative tradition may loudly proclaim that they require no assent to anything but what " may be proved by Scripture ;" that is, proved *to them ;* and which, on the ground of *their* conviction, must be implicitly received by every man. It is most important,—when the expression is used of " referring to Scripture as the infallible standard ;" and requiring assent to such points of faith only as can be thence proved, to settle clearly, in the outset, the important question, " proved *to whom ?*" If any man, or Body of men, refer us to Scripture, as the sole authoritative standard, meaning that we are not to be called on to believe anything as a necessary

---

opposite extreme, of complete toleration, and admission to civil rights ; as if the Civil-Magistrate, (supposing religious error does come within his proper province,) could have any more right to *tolerate* heresy than theft or incendiarism. [See *Appendix* to *Essay I.*] And some, again, though they "would not go so far" as to deny *all* government-grants to a College in which a theology that they disapprove is taught, yet would make it a point of conscience to keep the grant so scanty as to prevent the institution from being respectable and well-conducted.

In such, and in many similar instances, it is found that (as I have elsewhere remarked) a bad example does harm the most extensively to those who do *not* follow it ; by *lowering their standard* of propriety, and leading them to fancy themselves in the true middle course, because they do not deviate from it so glaringly as some others.

point of faith, on their word, but only on *our own* conviction that it is scriptural, then, they place our faith on the basis, not of human authority, but of divine. But if they call on *us*, as a point of conscience, to receive whatever is proved to *their* satisfaction from Scripture, even though it may appear to *us* unscriptural, then, instead of releasing us from the usurped authority of Man taking the place of God, they are placing on us two burdens instead of one. "You require us," we might reply, "to believe, first, that whatever you teach is *true;* and, secondly, besides this, to believe also, that it is a truth *contained in Scripture;* and we are to *take your word* for both!

§ 26. I can imagine persons urging, in reply to what has been said, the importance of giving the people religious instruction over and above the mere reading of Scripture,— *Alleged importance of human teaching.* the utility of explanations, and comments,—and the necessity of creeds and catechisms, &c.; and dwelling also on the reverence due to antiquity, and on the arrogance of disregarding the judgment of pious and learned men, especially of such as lived in or near the times of the Apostles.

It is almost superfluous to remark that nothing at variance with all this has been here advanced. The testimony of ancient writers as to the *facts* that such and such doctrines or practices did or did not prevail in their own times, or that such and such a sense was, in their times, conveyed by certain passages of Scripture, may often be very valuable; provided we keep clear of the mistake of inferring, either that whatever is ancient is to be supposed apostolical, or even necessarily, *in accordance* with apostolical teaching; (as if errors had not crept in, even during the lifetime[1]

---

[1] See *Note K.*

of the Apostles,) or again, that every practice and regulation that really had the sanction of the Apostles (and which, therefore, must be concluded to have been the best, *at that time*) was designed by them,—when they abstained [see § 16] from recording it in writing,—to be of universal and eternal obligation ;—in short, that they entrusted to *oral Tradition* any of the *essentials* of Christianity.[1] And, again, the opinions of any author, ancient or modern, are entitled to respectful consideration, in proportion as he may have been a sensible, pious, and learned man: provided we draw the line distinctly between the works of divine messengers inspired from above, and those of fallible men.

Paradoxes disguised as truisms. But what is the object (unless it be, to mystify the readers, and draw off their attention from the real question) of dwelling on truths which are universally admitted,[2] not only in theory

---

[1] And yet one may find persons defending this view by alleging that we have the Scriptures themselves by Tradition. Any one may be believed to be serious in urging such an argument, if it is found that he places as much confidence in the genuineness of some account that has been transmitted from *mouth to mouth by popular rumours* from one end of the kingdom to another, as in a *letter* that has been transmitted over the same space. See *Note I.*

[2] It is no uncommon practice with some writers, to shelter (as in the present instance) some paradoxical tenet, when opposed, under the guise of a *truism ;* and, when this has been admitted without suspicion, to unmask the battery as it were, and by a seemingly slight change, to convert a self-evident and insignificant truth into a dogma of fearful importance. Thus for instance, when we are sometimes told with much solemn earnestness, of the importance of holding fast "the faith of the Holy Catholic Church," this is explained as being "what has been held by *all* Christians, *always,* and *everywhere :* " [" quod semper, quod ubique, quod ab omnibus"] and of course no one can think of denying that what has always been held *universally* by all Christians as a part of their faith, must be a part of the *universal* [or Catholic] faith. There "needs no ghost to tell us that ;" as it is in fact only saying that "Catholic" means "Universal," and that what is believed is believed. But when the wooden horse has been introduced, it is found to contain armed men concealed within it. "All Christians" is explained to mean "all the orthodox ;" and the "orthodox"t to be, those in agreement with the authors who are instructing us.

but in practice, by Christians of every denomination? Catechisms, oral or written,—expositions of Scripture—religious discourses or tracts, of some kind or other, &c. are in use, more or less, among all. The utility, and indeed necessity, of human instruction, both for young Christians and adults, has never, that I know of, been denied by any christian Church or Denomination. The only important distinction is between those who do, and those who do not, permit, and invite, and encourage, their hearers to " search the Scriptures whether these things be so," which they are taught by their pastors.

It is to be observed, however, that what I am speaking of, is, a reference to Scripture, as the *sole basis* of the articles of necessary faith,—the only *decisive authority*.

Distinction between what is derived from Scripture, and what is conformable to Scripture.

Some persons, while claiming reception for such and such confessions of faith, declare continually and with much earnestness, that they are teaching nothing but what is " *conformable* to Scripture," " *agreeable* to Scripture," &c. And the unwary are often misled by not attending to the important distinction between this,—between what is, simply *agreeable* to Scripture,—and what is *derived from* Scripture,—*founded* on it, and claiming no other authority.

When it is said that the Old Testament and the New are *not at variance*, but *conformable* to each other, this is quite different from saying that either of them *derives all its authority* from the other. On the other hand, our Reformers do not maintain merely that the Creeds which they receive *are agreeable to Scripture;* but that they are to be received *because* they may be proved from Scripture.[1]

The distinction, as I have above remarked, is apparent

---

[1] See *Index* to *Tracts for the Times.* Art. " Creed," " Church," &c.

only, and not really important, between those who require the acceptance of what they teach, independently of Scripture, and those who do refer to Scripture as the ground of their *own* conviction, or at least as confirmatory of their teaching, but require *their* interpretations of Scripture to be implicitly received; denying to individuals the right and the duty[1] of judging ultimately for themselves. The real distinction is between those who do, and those who do not, recognise this right and duty. For if a certain comment is to be received implicitly and without appeal, it not only is placed, practically, as far as relates to everything except a mere question of *dignity*, on a level with Scripture,[2] but has also a strong — and as experience has abundantly proved,—an increasing tendency to supersede it. A regular and compact *system* of theology, professedly compiled from Scripture, or from " Scripture and Tradition blended together,"[3] if it be that which, after all, we must acquiesce in as infallible, whether it accord or not with what appears to *us* to be the sense of Scripture, being more compendious and methodical than the Sacred Books themselves, will naturally be preferred by the learner. And all study, properly so called, of the rest of Scripture,—(I say " the rest," because on the above supposition, such a comment would be itself a part of Scripture, infallible and divinely inspired,

---

[1] See Dr. Hawkins *on the Duty of Private Judgment.*

[2] Among the Parliamentarians at the time of the Civil War, there were many,—at first a great majority,—who professed to obey the King's commands, as *notified to them by Parliament*, and levied forces in the King's name, against his person. If any one admitted Parliament to be the sole and authoritative interpreter and expounder of the regal commands, and this, without any check from any other power, it is plain that he virtually admitted the sovereignty of that Parliament, just as much as if he had recognised their formal deposition of the King. The parallelism of this case with the one before us, is too obvious to need being dwelt on.

[3] See *Essay* (Third Series) on *Undue Reliance on Human Authority.*

as much as any other)—all lively interest in the perusal,— would be nearly superseded by such an inspired compendium of doctrine; to which alone, as being far the most convenient for that purpose, habitual reference would be made in any question that might arise. "Both would be regarded, indeed, as of divine authority; but the compendium, as the fused and purified metal; the other, as the *mine*, containing the crude ore."[1]

§ 27. The uses are so important, and the abuses so dangerous, of the instruction which may be afforded by uninspired christian teachers, that it may be worth while still further to illustrate the subject by an analogy, homely perhaps and undignified, but which appears to me perfectly apposite, and fitted by its very familiarity to answer the better its purpose of affording explanation.

Use and abuse of human instruction.

The utility of what is called paper-currency is universally acknowledged and perceived. Without possessing any intrinsic value, it is a convenient representative of coins and ingots of the precious metals. And it possesses this character, from its being known or confidently believed, that those who issue it are ready, on demand, to exchange it for those precious metals. And the occurrence from time to time, of this demand, and the constant liability to it, are the great *check* to an over-issue of the paper-money. But if paper-money be made a legal tender, and not convertible into gold and silver at the pleasure of the holder,—if persons are required to receive it in payment, by an arbitrary decree of the Government, either that paper *shall* be considered as having an intrinsic value, or again, that it shall be considered as representing

Bullion and paper-currency.

---

[1] See *Note F.*

bullion, or land,[1] or some other intrinsically valuable commodity, the existence and amount of which, and the ability of Government to produce it, are to be believed, not by the test of any one's demanding and obtaining payment, but *on the word of the very Government* that issues this inconvertible paper-currency, then, the consequences which ensue are well known. The precious metals gradually disappear, and a profusion of worthless paper alone remains.

Scripture proof to be produced on demand.

Even so it is with human teaching in religion. It is highly useful, as long as the instructors refer the People to Scripture, exhorting and assisting them to "prove all things and hold fast that which is right;"—as long as the Church "ordains nothing contrary to God's word,"—nothing, in short, beyond what a christian Community is authorized, both by the essential character of a Community, and by Christ's sanction, to enact; and requires nothing to be believed as a point of christian faith "that may not be declared"[2] (*i. e.* satisfactorily proved) to be taken from Holy Scripture. But when a Church, or any of its Pastors, ceases to make this payment on demand — if I may so speak—of Scripture-proof,[3] and requires implicit faith, on human authority, in human dogmas or interpretations, all *check* is removed to the introduction of any conceivable amount of falsehood and superstition; till human inventions may have overlaid and disfigured Gospel-truth, and Man's usurped authority have gradually superseded divine: even as was the case with the rabbinical Jews, who con-

---

[1] This was the case with the Assignats and Mandats of France.

[2] The word "declared" is likely to mislead the English reader, from its being ordinarily used in the present day in a different sense. The Latin "declarare," to which it was evidently intended to correspond, signifies "to make clear"—"to set forth plainly."

[3] See *Note L.*

tinued to profess the most devout reverence for the Mosaic Law, even at the time when we are told that "in vain they worshipped God, teaching for doctrines the commandments of men."[1]

§ 28. It is worth remarking also that the persons who make this use of Tradition, are often found distinctly advocating the deliberate suppression, in the instruction of the great mass of Christians, of a large portion of the Gospel-doctrines which are the most earnestly set forth in Scripture; as a sort of esoteric mystery, of which ordinary believers are unworthy, and which should be "reserved" as a reward for a long course of pious submission.[2] This system of "reserve" or "economy" is vindicated, by studiously confounding it with the *gradual* initiation of Christians in the knowledge of their religion, in proportion as they are "able to bear it;" *i. e.* able and willing to understand each point that is presented to their minds: and the necessity of gradual teaching,—of reading the first line of a passage before the second,—and the care requisite to avoid teaching anything, which, though true in itself, would be falsely understood by the hearers, is thus confounded with the system of withholding a portion of Gospel-truth from those *able* and *willing* to receive it;— the system of "shunning to set before men all the counsel of God," and of having one kind of religion for the initiated few, and another for the mass of the christian World. Very different was the Apostle Paul's Gospel, which he assures us, "if it was hid, was hid from them that are lost" (men on the road to destruction, ἀπολλυμένοις), "whom the god of this world hath blinded."

System of Reserve.

---

[1] See Dr. Hawkins on *Tradition*.
[2] See Dr. West's Discourse on *Reserve*. See also *Index* to the *Tracts for the Times*; Art. "Reserve."

Suppression of Gospel-truths may amount to falsification.

But the charge of teaching something different from what they inwardly believe, the advocates of this system repel, by alleging that all they do teach is agreeable to Scripture, although they withhold a part, and do not teach *all* that is to be found in Scripture: as if this did not as effectually constitute two different religions as if they had added on something of their own. For, by expunging or suppressing at pleasure, that which remains may become totally different from what the religion would have been if exhibited as a whole.[1]

It has been remarked that every statue existed in the block of marble from which it was carved; and that the Sculptor merely *discloses* it, by removing the superfluous portions;—that the Medicean Venus, for instance, has not in it a single particle which did not originally exist exactly in the same relative position as now; the artist having *added* nothing, but merely *taken away*. Yet the statue is as widely different a thing from the original block, as if something *had* been added. What should we think of a man's pleading that such an image is not contemplated in the commandment against *making* an image, because it is not "made," as if it had been moulded, or cast, out of materials *brought together* for the purpose? Should any one scruple to worship a moulded, but not a sculptured image, his scruple would not be more absurdly misplaced,

---

[1] A striking instance of this may be found in a work published a few years ago, termed *Elucidations of Dr. Hampden's Lectures;* in which by picking out a sentence here, and a half-sentence there, an impression was produced of the general tendency of the work totally different from what the work itself warranted.

Those who thus garble and misrepresent a man's expressions, in order to bring on him abhorrence and persecution from credulous bigots, may be regarded as the genuine successors of those tyrannical emperors, who used to *dress up in the skins of wild beasts* their wretched victims the ancient Christians, and then set dogs at them to worry them to death.

than if he should hold himself bound, in his teaching, not to *add on* to Scripture anything he did *not* believe to be true, but allowed to suppress any portions of Gospel-truth at his pleasure, and to exhibit to his People the remaining portions, as the whole System of their religion.

It may be added also, that as a christian teacher is not authorized either to suppress any portion of the Gospel as unfit for those disposed and able to receive it, or to inculcate as an essential portion of it, anything not revealed in Scripture, but dependent on Tradition, whether alone or "blended with Scripture," so, he ought not to insist on the acceptance, as essential, of anything which, even though it may be satisfactorily proved from Scripture, yet is so slightly hinted at there, that till attention has been called to it, and the arguments by which it is supported brought together, whole Churches, for whole generations together, may have studied Scripture without finding it. I do not say that nothing of this character *should be maintained*, and supported by arguments which may satisfactorily prove it; but it should not be *maintained as something necessary* to Salvation, unless it is *clearly* revealed to an ordinary reader of candid mind.

Doctrines not clearly revealed.

For instance, there are some who think that an intermediate state of consciousness,—and others, of unconsciousness,—between death and the resurrection,—may be proved from Scripture; but I cannot think it justifiable to represent *either* opinion as an essential *article of faith*.[1]

Again, *the call of the Gentiles* to be partakers with the Jews of the privileges of God's People, and the *termination of the Mosaic dispensation*, are *contained*, but not *clearly* revealed, in the Old Testament, and in the discourses of

---

[1] See *Lectures on a Future State*, L. 2, 3, &c.

our Lord; these doctrines are not so *obviously* contained there, as to make them an essential part of the Jewish faith, or of the faith required of our Lord's followers while He was on earth. This, therefore, was a case in which a *fresh and distinct declaration*, supported by miraculous evidence, was fairly to be expected: and *this was accordingly afforded*. A distinct miraculous revelation was made to the Apostle Peter as to this very point.[1]

Unsound reasons brought in aid of sound ones.

§ 29. In saying that the essential doctrines of Christianity are to be found in Scripture, or may be satisfactorily proved from it, and that the enactments of any Church, with a view to good government, "decency and order," derive a sufficient authority *from that very circumstance*, inasmuch as the Apostle commands us to "do all things decently and in order," and our Heavenly Master has given power to "bind and loose" in respect of such regulations, I do not mean to imply that such reasons always *will*, in fact, prove satisfactory to careless and uncandid reasoners,—to the fanciful, the wilful, and the arrogant. But nothing is in reality gained by endeavouring to add force to sound reasons by the addition of unsound ones. To seek, when men will not listen to valid arguments, for some other arguments which they *will* listen to, will, I am convinced, (to say nothing of its unfairness) be found in the end, to be unwise policy.

---

[1] According to our Lord's promise respecting the Holy Spirit:—"He shall teach you all things, and *bring all things to your remembrance*," &c. Our Lord's purpose in giving such obscure intimations as He did (in the parables, for instance, of the labourers in the Vineyard, of the Prodigal Son, &c.) of doctrines which were afterwards to be clearly revealed, was, doubtless, that the Apostles might then perceive that there was no *change of purpose;* but that the Gentiles had been, from the first, "elect according to the foreknowledge of God."

Yet I cannot but suspect that the principles I have been deprecating must have been sometimes maintained by persons, not altogether blind to the inconsistent consequences they lead to, but actuated by a desire of impressing on the minds of the multitude not only an additional confidence in the doctrines of our Church, but also that reverence, which is so often found to be deficient, for Church-institutions and enactments, and for regularly-ordained christian Ministers: and that they have been influenced by a dread of certain consequences as following from an adherence to what I have pointed out as the only sound and secure principles.[1]

For instance, it has been thought dangerous to acknowledge a power in any Body of uninspired men to depart in the smallest degree from the recorded precedents of the earliest churches: including (be it remembered by the way) those existing after the times of the

Supposed danger of a power to modify ancient regulations.

---

[1] For instance, the view taken (see *Thoughts on the Sabbath*) of the Lord's Day, as a Church-festival observed in memory of Christ's resurrection on the "first day of the week," and not in compliance with the law originally appointing the Sabbath, (whether the levitical, or, as some suppose, a patriarchal law) I have seen objected to, on the ground that "men are apt not to pay so much deference to the enactments of the Church, as to express commands of Scripture." That is to say, "although this Law be *not* really binding on Christians" (for, if it were, and the observance of the Lord's Day were a part of it, *that* would supersede all need of other arguments) "yet it is advisable to teach men that it *is*, in order that they may be the more ready to observe the Lord's Day." The Church therefore is to be represented,—and that, to men, who, by supposition, are inclined to *undervalue* Church-authority,—as having taken the liberty to *alter* a divine commandment of acknowledged obligation, by changing the *seventh* day of the week for the *first*, (besides alterations in the mode of observance) in compliance with a supposed tradition, that the Apostles sanctioned — which it is plain from Scripture they did not — this transference of the Sabbath. This is surely expecting an *unreasonable* deference for Church-authority from men who, it is supposed, are unwilling to yield to it such a deference as is *reasonable*.

Apostles, and therefore, consisting, themselves, of uninspired men. And a danger there certainly is; a danger of the misuse of any power, privilege, or liberty, entrusted to any one. The christian course is beset by dangers. They are an essential part of our trial on Earth. We are required to be on our guard against them; but we must never expect, here below, to be exempt from them. And there is nothing necessarily gained by exchanging one danger for another; the danger of erring in our own judgment, for that of following imperfect, uncertain, or corrupted traditions.

Men not always right in their use of their rights. But to maintain the right of any Community—a Church, among others—to establish, abrogate, or alter, regulations and institutions of any kind, is understood by some as amounting to an *approval* of everything that either ever *has* been done, or conceivably *might* be done, by virtue of that claim; as if a sanction were thus given to perpetual changes, the most rash, un-called for, and irrational. But what is left to men's *discretion*, is not therefore meant to be left to their *'indiscretion*. To maintain that a power exists, is not to maintain either that it matters not how it is used, or again, that it cannot possibly be abused.

The absurdity of such a mode of reasoning would be at once apparent in any other case. For instance, the Senate, Parliament, or other legislative Body of this or any other Country, has clearly a *right* to pass or to reject any proposed law that is brought before it; and has an *equal right* to do the one or the other; now no one in his senses would understand by this, that it is *equally right* to do the one or the other;—that whatever is left to the legislator's decision, must be a matter of absolute indifference; and that whatever is to be determined by his *judgment*, may fairly be determined according to his *caprice*.

A Church,—and the same may be said of a State,—may so far abuse its power, and exceed the just limits of that power, as to make enactments which a man may be bound in conscience to disobey; as for instance, if either an ecclesiastical or a civil Government should command men (as the Roman Emperors did the early Christians) to join in acts of idolatrous worship; or (as was done formerly towards the Saxon Clergy) to put away their wives. But this does not do away the truth of the general assertion that " the Powers that be are ordained of God;" —that both civil and ecclesiastical Governments have a right to make enactments that are *not* contrary to religion or morality.

Abuse of power no argument against its existence.

And again, even of these enactments,—such as a State or a Church does possess a right to make,—it is not only conceivable, but highly probable, that there will be some which may appear to many persons, and perhaps with reason, to be not the very wisest and best. In such a case, a man is bound to do his best towards the alteration of those laws:[1] but he is not, in the mean time, exempted from obedience to laws which he may not fully approve.[2] For supposing his objections to any law to be well-founded, still, as infallibility does not exist among men, all professions and precepts relative to the duty of submission to Government, would be nugatory, if that duty were to be suspended and remain in abeyance, till an unerring government should arise.

---

[1] See *Appeal in behalf of Church-Government:* (Houlston;) a very able pamphlet, since re-published in Bishop Dickinson's *Remains*.

[2] See Sermon on *Obedience to Laws*.

If any one, accordingly, is convinced that a certain Church is essentially unscriptural, either in the doctrines it inculcates, or in the ordinances and religious worship it enjoins, he cannot with a sound conscience belong to its communion. But he may consistently adhere to it, even though he should be of opinion that in some non-essential points it has adopted regulations which are not the most expedient. He may still consistently hold these to be binding, as coming from a competent authority; though he may wish, that they had been, or that they should be, settled otherwise.

Difficulty of ascertaining unbroken succession.

§ 30. But as there are some persons who are too ready to separate from any religious Community on slight grounds, or even through mere caprice, to "heap up to themselves teachers, having itching ears," it has been thought —or at least maintained,—that the only way of affording complete satisfaction and repose to the scrupulous, and of repressing schism, is to uphold, under the title of " Church-principles," the doctrine that no one is a member of Christ's Church, and an heir of the covenanted Gospel-promises, who is not under a Ministry ordained by Bishops descended in an unbroken chain from the Apostles.[1]

Now what is the degree of satisfactory assurance that is thus afforded to the scrupulous consciences of any members of an episcopal Church? If a man consider it as highly *probable* that the *particular Minister* at whose hands he receives the sacred Ordinances, is really thus apostolically descended, *this* is the very utmost point to which he can, with any semblance of reason, attain: and the more he reflects and inquires, the more cause for hesitation he will

---

[1] See Note to 14.

find. There is not a Minister in all Christendom who is able to trace up with any approach to certainty his own spiritual pedigree. The sacramental virtue (for such it is that is implied,—whether the term be used or not—in the principle I have been speaking of) dependent on the imposition of hands, with a due observance of apostolical usages, by a Bishop, himself duly consecrated, after having been in like manner baptized into the Church, and ordained Deacon and Priest,—this sacramental virtue, if a single link of the chain be faulty, must, on the above principles, be utterly nullified ever after, in respect of all the links that hang on that one. For if a Bishop has not been duly consecrated, or had not been, previously, rightly ordained, his Ordinations are null; and so are the ministrations of those ordained by him; and their Ordination of others; (supposing any of the persons ordained by him to attain to the episcopal office) and so on, without end. The poisonous taint of informality, if it once creep in undetected, will spread the infection of nullity to an indefinite and irremediable extent.

And who can undertake to pronounce that during that long period usually designated as the Dark Ages, no such taint ever was introduced? Irregularities could not have been wholly excluded without a perpetual miracle; and that no such miraculous interference existed, we have even historical proof. Amidst the numerous corruptions of doctrine and of practice, and gross superstitions, that crept in, during those Ages, we find recorded descriptions not only of the profound ignorance, and profligacy of life, of many of the Clergy, but also of the grossest irregularities in respect of discipline and form. We read of Bishops consecrated when mere children;—of men officiating who barely knew their letters;—of Prelates expelled, and others put

Informality common during the dark ages.

into their places, by violence;—of illiterate and profligate laymen, and habitual drunkards, admitted to Holy Orders; and in short, of the prevalence of every kind of disorder, and reckless disregard of the decency which the Apostle enjoins. It is inconceivable that any one even moderately acquainted with history, can feel a certainty, or any approach to certainty, that, amidst all this confusion and corruption, every requisite form was, in every instance, strictly adhered to, by men, many of them openly profane and secular, and unrestrained by public opinion, through the gross ignorance of the population among which they lived; and that no one not duly consecrated or ordained, was admitted to sacred offices.

Possibility of informality, never quite removed. Even in later and more civilized and enlightened times, the probability of an irregularity, though very greatly diminished, is yet diminished only, and not absolutely destroyed. Not many years ago, an artful impostor, pretending to be a clergyman, came over from Canada, and succeeded in deceiving many persons in England and in Ireland. He was allowed to officiate in our Churches, and he collected money for some pretended Institution in Canada. He was not detected, till, on his return to Canada, he came across some one who knew him, and exposed his fraud.

Some years before that, a pretended clergyman even obtained a curacy in Ireland, which he held for a considerable time: and it was found necessary, as I am informed, to pass a special Act of Parliament to give validity to the marriages he had celebrated.

Again, some years before this, an impostor deceived many persons in England, pretending to have lost his letters of Orders in a fire, or in a shipwreck. But in order to quiet any suspicions, he pretended to write a letter to an Archdeacon of the diocese where he professed to have been ordained. He produced a letter, signed with the Archdeacon's name, and having the proper post-mark, certifying his ordination, and containing a high eulogium on the admirable examination he had passed. This satisfied every one, except a single obstinate doubter, who, to make quite sure, wrote, himself, to the Archdeacon, and received an answer, saying that no such person had ever been heard of.

The man was afterwards transported for a forgery. And having soon obtained what is called a "ticket of leave," he was employed (being really an able man, and a scholar) as a *tutor* in the families of Settlers.

All these cases occurred not many years ago.

Now if any one of these men had succeeded in carrying out the deception, he might, conceivably, have been raised to the Episcopate, and have been the Ordainer of an indefinite number of clergymen.

But, some may say, all these impostors were *detected*. Of course they were; else, they could not have been now mentioned. Every *recorded* case of imposture, *must* be one of detected imposture. But it would be very rash to conclude that because *some* impostures have been detected, therefore none can ever have escaped detection.

Now, let any one proceed on the hypothesis that there are, suppose, but a hundred links connecting any particular minister with the Apostles; and let him even suppose that not above half of this number pass through such periods as admit of any possible irregularity; and then, placing at the lowest estimate the probability of defectiveness in respect of each of the remaining fifty, taken separately, let him consider what amount of probability will result from the *multiplying* of the whole together.[1] The ultimate conse-

---

[1] Supposing it to be one hundred to one, in each separate case, in favour of the legitimacy and regularity of the transmission, and the links to amount to fifty, (or any other number) the probability of the unbroken con-

quence must be, that any one who sincerely believes that his claim to the benefits of the Gospel-Covenant depends on his own minister's claim to the supposed sacramental virtue of true Ordination, and this again, on perfect Apostolical Succession as above described, must be involved, in proportion as he reads, and inquires, and reflects, and reasons, on the subject, in the most distressing doubt and perplexity.

It is no wonder, therefore, that the advocates of this theory studiously disparage reasoning, deprecate all exercise of the mind in reflection, decry appeals to evidence, and lament that even the power of reading should be imparted to the People. It is not without cause that they dread and lament "an Age of too much light," and wish to involve religion in "a solemn and awful gloom."[1] It is not without cause that, having removed the Christian's confidence from a rock to base it on sand, they forbid all prying curiosity to examine their foundation.

Fallacy of confounding together the apostolical succession of a Body of men and of each individual.

The fallacy, indeed, by which, according to the above principles, the Christian is taught to rest his own personal hopes of salvation, on the individual claims to "Apostolical succession" of the particular Minister he is placed under, is one so gross that few are thoughtless enough to be deceived by it in any case where Religion is not concerned;

---

tinuity of the whole chain must be computed as $\frac{99}{100}$ of $\frac{99}{100}$ of $\frac{99}{100}$, &c to the end of the whole fifty.

Of course, if different data are assumed, or a different system is adopted of computing the rate at which the uncertainty increases at each step, the ultimate result will be different as to the *degree* of uncertainty; but when once it is made apparent that a considerable and *continually-increasing* uncertainty does exist, and that the result must be, in respect of any individual case, a matter of *chance,* it can be of no great consequence to ascertain precisely what the chances are on each side. (See *Cautions for the Times,* No. 16.).

[1] Κλέπτῃ δέ τε νυκτὸς ἀμείνω.

—where, in short, a man has not been taught to make a virtue of uninquiring, unthinking, acquiescence. For the fallacy consists in confounding together the unbroken Apostolical succession of *a christian Ministry generally*, and the same succession in an unbroken line, of *this or that individual Minister*. The existence of such *an Order of men as christian Ministers*, continuously from the time of the Apostles to this day, is perhaps as complete a moral certainty, as any historical fact can be; because (independently of the various incidental notices by historians, of such a class of persons) it is plain that if, at the present day, or a century ago, or ten centuries ago, a number of men had appeared in the world, professing (as our Clergy do now) to hold a recognised office in a christian Church, to which they had been regularly appointed as successors to others, whose predecessors, in like manner, had held the same, and so on, from the times of the Apostles,—if, I say, such a pretence had been put forth by a set of men assuming an office which no one had ever heard of before,—it is plain that they would at once have been refuted and exposed. And as this will apply equally to each successive generation of christian Ministers, till we come up to the time when the institution was confessedly new,—that is, to the time when christian Ministers were appointed by the Apostles, who professed themselves eye-witnesses of the Resurrection,—we have, in the christian Ministry, (as Leslie has remarked)[1] a standing Monument of the fact of that event's having been proclaimed immediately after the time when it was said to have occurred. This therefore is fairly brought forward as an evidence of its truth.

But if each man's christian hope, is made to rest on his receiving the christian Ordinances at the hands of a Minister

---

[1] *Short Method with Deists.*

to whom the sacramental virtue that gives efficacy to those Ordinances, has been transmitted in unbroken succession from hand to hand, everything must depend on *that particular* Minister: and *his* claim is by no means established from our merely establishing the uninterrupted existence *of such a class of men as christian Ministers.* " You teach me," a man might say, " that my salvation depends on the possession by *you*—the *particular* Pastor under whom I am placed—of a certain qualification; and when I ask for the proof that you possess it, you prove to me that it is possessed *generally*, by a *certain class* of persons of whom you are one, and probably by a large majority of them!" How ridiculous it would be thought, if a man laying claim to one of the Fellowships which, in certain Colleges, are appropriated to the Founder's-kin, should, instead of establishing his own pedigree, merely allege his being one of a number of persons bearing a certain surname, of whom it was believed that *probably*, a very large *majority*, and *perhaps*, *all*, were akin to the Founder! Such a claim would, in secular matters, be derided by all; including even those who would have us stake our christian privileges on its validity.

Strained interpretation of Scripture-promise.

But some have even gone so far as to maintain that our Lord's promise of being with his Church " even to the end of the world," and of " the Gates of Hell not prevailing against it," are to be understood as implying his especial inteference to prevent any interruption of that kind of Apostolical-Succession above alluded to; and that consequently we are bound to trust that no one can ever *appear* to possess true Apostolical-Ordination who does not really possess it: and this, although we know, from the very warnings of the Apostles themselves, that, even in their own time, and even in respect of the vital truths of the Gospel, "deceitful workers" arose, "speaking perverse things, to draw away disciples after them;" and that as "Satan transforms himself into an angel of light," it is no marvel if "his ministers also" are equally transformed.

Attempt to meet the difficulties of the doctrine.
Others again maintain that, though we are bound to regard as wholly void and worthless the ministrations of any one who is not (in the above sense) a rightful successor of the Apostles, and though it is impossible in the case of *each individual* Minister to ascertain this with perfect certainty, still, any one who receives the rights of the Church at the hands of those whom he *believes*, according to the *very best judgment* and *most perfect knowledge within his reach*, to possess the requisite qualification, will have *done his best;* and may, on that ground, hope for acceptance before his Divine Judge: trusting that he shall suffer no loss through any possible mistake that was wholly unavoidable.

And certainly, if any one should, after having used all possible care and precaution, administer to a sick man a poisonous dose, he would—although the patient would die, not the less—be acquitted of all moral blame. And so also, if he were transmitting to some distant country a cargo of Bibles, which were changed, through the fraud or negligence of an agent, for a parcel of worthless or noxious books, though the people receiving them would lose the edification designed, one may hope that the divine goodness would accept, in respect of the sender, the will for the deed.

But then, it should be remembered that if no *more* is required of a man than to do his utmost, he is also required to do no *less*. One who should administer a medicine *without* due care, even though it should chance to be the right one, would be no less morally responsible than if the same want of care had happened to produce a fatal result.

Re-ordination should be sought by those holding the doctrine.

Whoever therefore puts in the plea of having *done his best* to secure the ministrations of one possessing the above qualification, ought, consistently with his own principle, to be (conditionally) *re-baptized, re-ordained, re-consecrated*, &c. again and again, as often as he has access to any fresh Ministers: just as any one, who is earnestly bent on conveying some most important intelligence to a friend in a remote part of the world, will write by *every* ship likely to touch there, in order to make sure of leaving nothing undone towards effecting his object.

We have here therefore a ready *test*, for judging whether a person who professes the above principle, and puts in the above plea, is really sincere, and heartily and practically in earnest, in his profession.

Chances of invalidity may be diminished, but never, on the above principle, done away.

It has been alleged, for instance, that the chances of any interruption of Apostolical-Succession are greatly diminished by the presence of *three* Bishops, instead of only one, at the Consecration of a new one. And this is admitted; but then it must also be admitted that the risk, how much soever *lessened*, is not, nor ever can be, *annihilated;* and moreover that it would be still *further*, and further, diminished by the presence of *four*, or five, and of any greater number, to an unlimited extent. And it is also evident that however minute the chance may ultimately be of any *actual* mistake, still, this makes no difference as to the responsibility of those who put in the plea, not, of actual avoidance of mistake, but, of having done *their very utmost* to guard against it.

Those who hold that the presence of three or more Bishops is an appointment merely for the sake of decent and solemn publicity, need suffer no anxious doubts as to the validity of any public act, performed according to the rules laid down in the Church. But one who regards the presence of the three Bishops as constituting some degree of *safeguard* against the *danger of nullity* that might result from some by-gone informality, must admit the *existence* of such danger, and also, that it would be still further diminished (though never completely done away) by resorting to the ministration of fresh and fresh Bishops without limit. And this he clearly *is* bound to resort to, if he sincerely rests his justification, not, on the extreme smallness and insignificance of the risk, but, on his having *left nothing undone* to provide against it.

§ 31. Then as to the danger of Schism, nothing can be more calculated to create or increase it, than to superadd to all the other sources of difference among Christians, those additional ones resulting from the theory we are considering. Besides all the divisions liable to arise relative to the essential *doctrines* of Scripture, and to the most important points in any *system* of Church-Government, Schisms, the most difficult to be remedied, may be created by that theory from *individual cases* of alleged irregularity.

Increased danger of Schism.

A most remarkable instance of this is furnished in the celebrated schism of the Donatists, in Africa, in the beginning of the fourth century.[1] They differed in no point of doctrine or Church-discipline from their opponents, the Orthodox, (that is, the predominant party;) but were at issue with them on the question as to an alleged irregularity in the appointment of a certain Bishop; whose ordinations consequently of other Bishops and Presbyters, they inferred, were void; and hence, the

Schism of the Donatists.

---

[1] See Waddington's *Ecclesiastical History*, &c.

baptisms administered by those ministers were also void, and their whole ministration profane; so that they re-baptized all who joined their party, (as I believe the Greek Church does, to this day) and regarded their opponents in the light of Heathen. And this schism distracted the greater part of the Eastern portion of the Church for upwards of two hundred years.

Schism of the Non-Jurors. And an attempt was made in the last century, by the Non-jurors, to introduce, in these realms, the ever-spreading canker of a similar schism. They denied the episcopal character of those who had succeeded the displaced prelates; and, consequently, regarded as invalid the Orders conferred by them; thus preparing the way for all the consequences resulting from the Donatist-schism.[1]

The sect died away before long, through a happy inconsistency on the part of its supporters; who admitted the claims of the substituted Bishops *on the death of their predecessors;* though it is hard to understand how those who were not true Bishops at first, could *become* such, through a subsequent event, without being reconsecrated; the Presbyters ordained by them, becoming at the same time true Presbyters, though their ordination *had been* invalid. It seems like maintaining that a woman, who, during her husband's life-time marries another man, and has a family,

---

[1] " Dr. George Hickes, the deprived Dean of Worcester, who was regarded as the head of the Non-juring clergy, being lately dead, [1716] the publication of his papers revealed the intentions of his party respecting the Church, whenever the Stuart line should be restored. They held that all the conforming clergy were schismatic; and pronounced the invalidity of Orders conferred by Bishops made by usurping monarchs: consequently all baptisms performed by these schismatic divines were deemed to be illegal; and it was resolved that neither the one nor the other should be acknowledged, until the parties had received fresh ordination or fresh baptism from the hands of their own part of the Church, which had never bowed the knee to Baal."—Bishop Monk's *Life of Bentley,* vol. i. p. 426.

becomes, on her real husband's death, the lawful wife of the other, and her children legitimate.

More recently still, an attempt was made of the same nature, on the occasion of the suppression (as it was called) of some of the Irish Bishoprics; that is, the *union* of them with others.[1] It has been publicly and distinctly declared that an effort was made to represent this measure as amounting to an "interruption of Apostolical succession;" though it is not very easy to say how this was to be made out, even on the above principles.[2]

In short, there is no imaginable limit to the schisms that may be introduced and kept up through the operation of these principles, advocated especially with a view to the *repression* of schism.

§ 32. Some have imagined however that since no rule is laid down in Scripture as to the *number* of persons requisite to form a christian Community, or as to the mode in which any such Community is to be set on foot, it must follow that persons left to Scripture as their sole decisive authority, will be at liberty,—all, and any of them,—to form and dissolve religious communities at their pleasure; —to join, and withdraw from, any Church, as freely as if it were a Club or other such institution; and to appoint themselves or others to any ministerial Office, as freely as

Irregular formations of christian Communities.

---

[1] I do not mean to maintain that this was seriously believed by all those —some of them men of intelligence and learning — who put it forward. It may very likely have been one of their " *exoteric* doctrines," designed only for the Multitude. But, be this as it may, they evidently meant that it should be believed by others, if not by themselves.

[2] According to this view, the Apostolical succession must have been long since lost in some parts of England, and the greatest part of Ireland. For there were many such unions existing *before* the Act in question; such as Cork and Ross, Ferns and Leighlin, and several others.

the members of any Club elect Presidents, Secretaries, and other functionaries.

And it is true that this licence has been assumed by weak and rash men: who have thus given occasion to persons of the class who " mistake reverse of wrong for right," to aim at counteracting one error by advocating another. But so far are these anarchical consequences from being a just result of the principles here maintained, that I doubt whether, on any other subject besides Religion, a man would not be reckoned insane who should so reason.

Analogous case of civil governments. To take the analogous case of civil government: hardly any one in his right mind would attempt a universal justification of rebellion, on the ground that men may be placed in circumstances which morally authorize them to do what, in totally *different* circumstances, *would* be rebellion.

Suppose, for instance, a number of emigrants, bound for some Colony, to be shipwrecked on a desert island, such as afforded them means of subsistence, but precluded all reasonable hope of their quitting it: or suppose them to have taken refuge there as fugitives from intolerable oppression, or from a conquering enemy; (no uncommon case in ancient times) or to be the sole survivors of a pestilence or earthquake which had destroyed the rest of the nation; no one would maintain that these shipwrecked emigrants or fugitives were bound, or were permitted, to remain—themselves and their posterity—in a state of anarchy, on the ground of there being no one among them who could claim hereditary or other right to govern them. It would clearly be right, and wise, and necessary, that they should regard themselves as constituted, by the very circumstance of their position, a civil Community; and should assemble to enact such laws, and appoint such magistrates, as they might judge most suitable to their circumstances. And obedience to those laws and governors, as soon as the Constitution was settled, would become a moral duty to all the members of the Community: and this, even though some of the enactments might appear, or might be, (though not at variance with the immutable laws of morality, yet) considerably short of perfection. The King, or other Magistrates thus appointed, would be legitimate rulers: and the laws framed by them, valid and binding. The precept of "submitting to every ordinance of man, for the Lord's sake," and of "rendering to all, their due," would apply in this case as completely as in respect of any Civil Community that exists.

And yet these men would have been doing what, *in ordinary circumstances*, would have been manifest rebellion. For if these same, or any other, individuals, subjects of our own, or of any existing Government, were to take upon themselves to throw off their allegiance to it, *without* any such necessity, and were to pretend to constitute themselves an independent Sovereign-State, and proceed to elect a King or Senate,—to frame a Constitution, and to enact laws, all resting on their own self-created authority, no one would doubt, that, however wise in themselves those laws might be, and however personally well-qualified the magistrates thus appointed,— they would not be legitimate governors, or valid laws: and those who had so attempted to establish them, would be manifest rebels.

Extraordinary emergencies justify what would otherwise be wrong.

A similar rule will apply to the case of ecclesiastical Communities. If any number of individuals,—not having the plea of an express revelation to the purpose, or again, of their deliberate conviction that the Church they separate from is fundamentally erroneous and unscriptural—take upon themselves to constitute a new Church, according to

Case of ecclesiastical Communities, parallel.

o

their own fancy, and to appoint themselves or others to ministerial offices, without having any recognised authority to do so, derived from the existing religious Community of which they were members, but merely on the ground of supposed personal qualifications, then, however wise in themselves the institutions, and however, in themselves, fit the persons appointed, there can be no more doubt that the guilt of Schism would be incurred in this case, than that the other, just mentioned, would be an act of rebellion.

Or again, if certain members, lay or clerical, of any Church, should think fit to meet together and constitute themselves a kind of Synod for deciding some question of orthodoxy, and should proceed to denounce publicly one of their brethren as a heretic, there can be no doubt that—whether his doctrines were right or wrong,—these, his self-appointed judges (whatever abhorrence of Schism they might express, and however strongly they might put forth their own claim to be emphatically the advocates of Church-unity) would be altogether schismatical in their procedure. If the Apostle's censure of "those that cause divisions" does not apply to this case, it may fairly be asked what meaning his words can have.

On the other hand, men placed in the situation of the supposed shipwrecked emigrants or exiles above spoken of, would be as much authorized, and bound, to aim at the advantages of a Religious, as of a Civil Community; only with this difference, arising out of the essential characters of the two respectively; that they would not be authorized in the one case, as they would, in the other, to resort to *secular coercion*.[1] Compliance with civil regulations, may, and must, be *absolutely enforced;* but not so, the profession of a particular Creed, or conformity to a particular mode of Worship.

---

[1] See *Appendix* to *Essay I.*

Another point of distinction between the formation of a Civil and an ecclesiastical Constitution arises out of this circumstance, that it was plainly the design of the Apostles that there should be as much as possible of *free intercommunion*, and facility of interchange of members, among christian Churches. *Christian Communities designed to afford facilities for intercommunion.* Consequently, when it is said, here and elsewhere, that each of these is bound to make such enactments respecting nonessentials, as its governors may judge best, it is not meant that they have to consider merely what would seem *in itself* best, and supposing *they* were the *only christian Community* existing; but they must also take care to raise up no *unnecessary barrier* of separation between the members of their own and of other—essentially pure—Churches. Any arrangements or institutions, &c. which would tend to check the free intercourse,[1] and weaken the ties of brotherhood, among all Christ's followers throughout the world, should be as much as possible avoided.

This, however, is no exception to the general rule, but an application of it. For, those enactments which should tend to defeat, without necessity, one of the objects which the Apostles proposed, would (however good in themselves) evidently *not* be the best, for that very reason.

But it would be absurd to maintain that men placed in such a situation as has been here supposed, are to be shut out, generation after generation, from the christian Ordinances, and the Gospel-covenant. Their circumstances would constitute them (as many as could be brought to agree in the essentials of faith and christian worship) a christian Community; and would *Christians bound when possible, to combine as a christian Society.*

---

[1] As, for instance, if some one Church were to change Christmas-day to another part of the year, as being nearer to a correspondence with the time of our Lord's birth.

require them to do that which, if done *without* such necessity, would be schismatical. To make regulations for the Church thus constituted, and to appoint as its ministers the fittest persons that could be found among them, and to celebrate the christian Rites, would be a proceeding not productive, as in the other case, of division, but of union. And it would be a compliance,—clearly pointed out to them by the Providence which had placed them in that situation,—with the manifest will of our Heavenly Master, that Christians should live in a religious Community, under such Officers and such Regulations as are essential to the existence of every Community.

To say that christian ministers thus appointed, would be, to all intents and purposes, real legitimate christian ministers, and that the Ordinances of such a Church would be no less valid and efficacious (supposing always that they are not in themselves superstitious and unscriptural) than those of any other Church, is merely to say in other words, that it would *be* a real christian Church; possessing, consequently, in common with *all Communities* of whatever kind, the essential rights of a Community to have Officers and Bye-laws; and possessing also, in common with all *christian* Communities, (*i.e.* Churches) the especial sanction of our Lord, and his promise of ratifying ("binding in Heaven") its enactments.[1]

It could not have been the Lord's will that men should exclude themselves from his Church.

It really does seem not only absurd, but even impious, to represent it as the Lord's will, that persons who are believers in his Gospel, should, in consequence of the circumstances in which his Providence has placed them, condemn themselves and their posterity to live as Heathens, instead of con-

---

[1] See in *Note M* a quotation from an Appeal of Luther's, in 1520, cited in D'Aubigne's *History of the Reformation*.

forming as closely as those circumstances will allow, to the institutions and directions of Christ and his Apostles, by combining themselves into a christian Society, regulated and conducted, in the best way they can, on Gospel-principles. And if such a Society does enjoy the divine blessing and favour, it follows that its proceedings, its enactments, its officers, are legitimate and *apostolical*, as long as they are conformable to the principles which the Apostles have laid down and recorded for our use: even as those (of whatever race " after the flesh ") who embraced and faithfully adhered to the Gospel, were called by the Apostle, " Abraham's seed,"[1] and " the Israel of God."[2]

The Ministers of such a Church as I have been supposing, would rightly claim " Apostolical succession" because they would *rightfully hold the same office* which the Apostles conferred on those " Elders whom they ordained in every City." And it is impossible for any one of sound mind, seriously to believe that the recognition of such claims in a case like the one here supposed, affords a fair precedent for men who should wantonly secede from the Church to which they had belonged, and take upon themselves to ordain Ministers and form a new and independent Church according to their own fancy.

Apostolical succession dependent on adherence to apostolical principles.

§ 33. I have spoken of seceding from " the Church to which they had belonged," because, in each case the presumption[3] is in favour of *that;* not, necessarily, in favour of the Church to which a man's *ancestors* may formerly have belonged,[4] or the one which

Presumption in favour of the Church to which one actually belongs.

---

[1] Rom. v. 16.
[2] Gal. vi. 16.
[3] See *Rhetoric*, Part i. ch. 3, § 2.

[4] Accordingly, if we suppose the case of the Romish Church reforming all its errors, and returning to the

can boast the greatest *antiquity*, or, which is *established* by the Civil Government. The Church, whatever it is, in which each man was originally enrolled a member, has the first claim to his allegiance, supposing there is nothing in its doctrines or practice which he is convinced is unscriptural and wrong. He is of course bound, in deference to the higher authority of Christ and the Apostles, to renounce its communion, if he does feel such a conviction; but not, from motives of mere fancy, or worldly advantage.

All separation, either a duty or a sin.

All separation, in short, must be *either* a duty, or a sin.[1]

Obligation to conform to the ordinances of a Church, not dependent on the regularity of its original formation.

And the Christian's obligation to submit to the (not unscriptural) Laws and Officers of his Church, being founded on the principles above explained, is independent of all considerations of the regularity or irregularity of the original formation of that Church: else indeed, no one could be certain what were his duties as a member of a certain Church, without entering on long and difficult researches into ecclesiastical history; such as are far beyond the reach of

---

state of its greatest purity, although we should with joy "give the right hand of fellowship" to its members, it would be utterly unjustifiable for any member of our Church to throw off his allegiance to it and go over to the Church of Rome, on the ground of his *ancestors* having belonged to that; nor would such a reform confer on the Bishop of Rome any power over the Anglican Church.

[1] It may be necessary perhaps here to remind the reader that I am speaking of *separating* from, and *renouncing*, some Church; not, of merely *joining* and becoming a member of some other. This latter does not imply the former, except when there is some *essential point of difference* between the two Churches. When there is none, a man's becoming a member of another Church on changing his residence,—as, for instance, a member of the Anglican Church, on going to reside in Scotland or America, where Churches essentially in agreement with ours exist—this is the very closest conformity to the principles and practice of the Apostles. In their days (and it would have been the same, always, and everywhere, had their principles been universally adhered to) a Christian of the Church of Corinth for instance, on taking up his abode, suppose, at Ephesus, where there was a christian Church,—differing perhaps in some non-essential customs and forms, but agreeing in essentials,—

ninety-nine persons in the hundred. A certain Church may, suppose, have originated in a rash separation from another Church, on insufficient grounds; but for an individual to separate from it *merely for that reason*, would be not escaping, but incurring, the guilt of Schism.[1]

It may indeed often be very desirable to attempt the re-union of Christian Communities that had been separated on insufficient grounds: but no individual is justified in renouncing, from motives of mere taste or convenience, the communion of the Church he belongs to, if he can remain in it with a safe conscience.

As for the question, what are, and what are not, to be accounted essential points,—what will, and what will not, justify, and require, separation,—it would be foreign from the present purpose to discuss it. The differences between two Churches may appear essential, and non-essential, to two persons equally conscientious, and equally careful in forming a judgment. All I am insisting on is, that the matter is one which does call for that careful and conscientious judgment. A man should, deliberately, and with a sense of deep responsibility, make up his mind, as to what is, or is not, to the best of his judgment, essential, before he resolves on taking, or not taking, a step which must in every case be either a duty or a sin.

§ 34. It may be said however that it is superfluous to enter at all on the consideration of what *would* be allowable and right under some *supposed* circumstances, which are not our own; and to decide beforehand for some

Apprehension of what is called unsettling men's minds.

---

was received into that Church as a brother; and this was so far from implying his *separation* from the former, that he would be received into the Ephesian Church only on letters of recommendation ['Επιστολαὶ συστα- tικαί. See 2 Cor.] from the Corinthian.

[1] For some very sensible and valuable remarks on this subject, see Hinds's *History of the Rise and Early Progress of Christianity*, vol. ii. p. 42.

imaginary emergency that may never occur ; at least never to ourselves.

It may be represented as an empty and speculative question to inquire whether our Ministry derive their authority from the Church, or the Church from them, as long as the rights *both* of the Church and its Ministers, are but acknowledged. And if any one is satisfied both that our Ministers are ordained by persons descended in an unbroken series of episcopal Ordination from the Apostles, and also that they are the regularly-appointed and recognised Officers of a christian Community constituted on apostolical principles, it may be represented as impertinent to trouble him with questions as to *which* of these two things it is that gives them the rightful claim to that deference which, as it is, he is willing to pay to them.

It is in this way that the attempt is often made, and not seldom with success, to evade the discussion of important general principles ; and thus to secure an uninquiring acquiescence in false assumptions which will not stand the test of examination, and which when once admitted will lead to very important and very mischievous practical results. Why should we unsettle men's minds—one may hear it said—by speculations on any imaginary or impossible case, when they are satisfied as they are? As long as any one will but believe and do what he ought, what matters it whether his reasons for acquiescence are the most valid, or not? And then, when, in this way, men's minds have been "settled" in false notions, some of them are likely to follow out a wrong principle into the pernicious consequences to which it fairly leads ; and others again become most dangerously, and perhaps incurably, *un*settled, when the sandy foundation they have been taught to build on happens to be washed away.

If, as has been above remarked, a man is taught that view of apostolical succession which makes every thing depend on the unbroken series between the Apostles and the *individual* minister from whom each man receives the Sacraments, or the individual bishop conferring Ordination,—a fact which never can be ascertained with certainty—and he is then presented with proofs, *not* of *this*, but of a different fact instead,—the apostolical succession, generally, of the great Body of the ministers of his Church;—and if he is taught to acquiesce with consolatory confidence in the regulations and ordinances of the Church, not on such grounds as have been above laid down, but on the ground of their exact conformity to the model of the "ancient Church," which exact conformity is, in many cases, more than can be satisfactorily proved, and in some, can be easily *dis*proved, the result of the attempt so to settle men's minds, must be, with many, the most distressing doubt and perplexity.

Real danger of unsettling men's minds.

And others again, when taught to "blend with Scripture," as a portion of Revelation, the traditions of the first three, or first four, or first seven, or fifteen centuries, may find it difficult to understand, when, and where, and why, they are to stop short abruptly in the application of the principles they have received:—why, if *one* general Council is to be admitted as having divine authority, to bind the conscience, and supersede private judgment, *another* is to be rejected by private judgment: and that too, by the judgment of men who are not agreed with each other, or even with themselves, whether the council of Trent, for instance, is to be regarded as the beginning of the Romish Apostasy, or as a promising omen of improvement in the Church of Rome. That man must be strangely constituted who can find consolatory security for his faith in such a guide:—who can derive satisfactory confidence from the oracles of a Proteus!

Supposed case, neither an impossible one, nor useless even if it were.

§ 35. Moreover, the supposed case of Christians deprived of a regular succession of Episcopally-ordained Ministers, and left to determine what course they ought, under such circumstances, to take, is *not* inconceivable, or impossible, or unprecedented; nor again, *even if it were*, would the consideration of such a question be necessarily an unprofitable speculation; because it will often happen that by putting a supposed case (even when such as could not possibly occur) we can the most easily and most clearly ascertain on what *principle* a person is acting. Thus when Plato[1] puts the impossible case of your possessing the ring of Gyges,[2] which, according to the legend, could make the bearer invisible, and demands how you would then act, he applies a kind of test, which *decomposes*, as the chemists say, the complex mass of motives that may influence a man, and calls on you to consider whether you abstain from bad actions through fear of the censure of the world, or from abhorrence of evil in itself.

So again—to take another instance—if any one is asked how men ought to act when living under a Government professing, and enforcing under penalties, a false religion,

---

[1] "Atque hoc loco, philosophi quidam, minime mali illi quidem, sed non satis acuti, fictam et commentitiam fabulam prolatam dicunt a Platone: quasi vero ille, aut factum id esse, aut fieri potuisse defendat. Hæc est vis hujus annuli et hujus exempli, si nemo sciturus, nemo ne suspicaturus quidem sit, cum aliquid, divitiarum, potentiæ dominationis, libidinis, causâ feceris,— si id diis hominibusque futurum sit semper ignotum, sisne facturus. Negant id fieri posse. Quanquam potest id quidem; sed quæro, quod negant posse, id si posset, quidnam facerent? Urgent rustice sane: negant enim posse, et in eo perstant. Hoc verbum quid valeat, non vident. Cum enim quærimus, si possint celare, quid facturi sint, non quærimus, possintne celare," &c.—*Cic. de Off.* b. iii. c. 9.

[2] *Rhetoric*, pt. i. c. 2, § 8.

and requiring of its subjects idolatrous worship, and other practices contrary to Scripture, if he should object to the question, on the ground that there is no prospect of *his* being so circumstanced, and that he is living, and may calculate on continuing to live, under a Government which inculcates a true religion, it would be justly inferred that he was conscious of something unsound in his principles, from his evading a test that goes to ascertain whether he regards religious truth and the command of God, as things to be adhered to at all events, or merely, when coinciding with the requisitions of Government.

So also, in the present case: when a Church possesses Ministers who are the regularly appointed officers of a christian Community constituted on evangelical principles, and who are also ordained by persons descended in an unbroken series from those ordained by the Apostles, the two circumstances *coincide*, on which, according to the two different principles, respectively, above treated of, the legitimacy and apostolical commission of christian Ministers may be made to depend. Now in order to judge fairly, and to state clearly the decision *which* foundation we resolve to rest on, it is requisite to propose a case (even supposing—which is very far from being the fact —that it could not actually occur) in which these two circumstances do *not* come together; and then to pronounce which it is that we regard as essential.

Case of coincidence in the conclusions resulting from different principles.

§ 36. As a matter of fact, there can be no reasonable doubt that the Apostles did "ordain Elders in every city." Even if there had been no record of their doing so, we might have inferred it from the very fact of their instituting christian Societies; since every Society must have Officers;

Cases of a moral necessity for separation.

and the founder of a Society will naturally take upon him to nominate the first Officers; as well as to "set in order the rest" of the appointments.[1] And those Officers, acting in the name and on the behalf of the Community, would, of course, appoint others to aid, and to succeed them; and so on, from generation to generation. As long as every thing went on correctly in each Church, and its doctrines and practices remained sound, there would be nothing to interrupt this orderly course of things. But whenever it happened that the Rulers of any Church departed from the christian faith and practice which it is their business to preserve,—when, for instance, they corrupted their worship with superstitions, made a traffic of "indulgences," and "taught for doctrines the commandments of men," by "blending" human traditions with Scripture, and making them, either wholly or in part, the substitute, as a rule of faith, for the records of inspiration,—in any such case, it became the duty of all those who perceived the inroads of such errors, to aim at the reformation of them; and, when all or any of the spiritual Pastors of such a Church obstinately stood out against reform, to throw off their subjection to persons so abusing their sacred office, and, at all events, reform themselves as they best could.[2] It is as plain a duty for men so circumstanced to obey their Heavenly Master, and forsake those who have apostatized from Him, as it would be for the loyal portion of a garrison of soldiers to revolt from a general who had turned traitor to his King, and was betraying the city into the enemy's

---

[1] 1 Cor.

[2] It may be worth while to observe that a person who disapproves of persecution, is *not*, on that ground alone, justified in separating from a Church *in behalf of which* persecution has been employed; for on such a principle he would be required to renounce Christianity itself. It is for him to protest against it, and to endeavour to prevent it; and if, for so doing, his Church should excommunicate him, the act would then be entirely theirs and not his.

hands. So far from being rebellious subjects in *thus* revolting, they would be guilty of rebellion if they did not.

In like manner, the very circumstances in which such a Body of reformers, as I have been alluding to, are placed, confer on them hat independence which they would have been unjustifiable in assuming wantonly. *Independence conferred by circumstances.* The right is bestowed, and the duty imposed on them, of separation from the unreformed, which, under opposite circumstances, would have been schismatical. They are authorized, and bound, by the very nature of their situation, either to subsist as a distinct Community, or to join some other Church;[1] even as the vitality which Nature has conferred on a scion of a tree, enables it, *when cut off* from the parent-stock, either to push forth fresh roots of its own, or to unite, as a graft, with the stock of some kindred tree.

It is for men so circumstanced to do their best according to their own deliberate judgment, to meet their difficulties, to supply their deficiences, and to avail themselves of *Conduct suitable for conscientious seceders.* whatever advantages may lie within their reach. If they have among their number christian Ministers of several Orders, or of One Order,—if they can obtain a supply of such from some other sound Church,—or if they can unite themselves to such a Church with advantage to the great ultimate objects for which Churches were originally instituted,—all these are advantages not to be lightly thrown

---

[1] An instance of this was very recently afforded by the people of Zillerthal, in the Austrian dominions; who, being deliberately convinced of the errors of the Church in which they had been brought up, underwent, in consequence of their refusal of compliance, a long series of vexatious persecution, and ultimately forsook their home, and found refuge and freedom of conscience in the territory of Prussia.

away. But the unavoidable absence of any of these advantages, not only is not to be imputed to them as a matter of blame, but, by imposing the *necessity*, creates the *right*, and the *duty*, of supplying their deficiencies as they best can. Much as they may regret being driven to the alternative, they ought not to hesitate in their decision, when their choice lies between adherence to the human Governors of a Church, and to its divine Master;—between " the form of godliness, and the power thereof;"—between the means and the end;—between unbroken apostolical succession of individuals, and uncorrupted Gospel-principles.

Mistakes to be guarded against by Reformers when compelled to separation.

§ 37. Persons so situated ought to be on their guard against two opposite mistakes: the one is, to underrate the privileges of a christian Community, by holding themselves altogether debarred from the exercise of such powers as naturally and essentially belong to every Community; the other mistake is to imagine that whatever they have an undoubted *right* to do, they would necessarily be *right* in doing. In no other subject perhaps would such a confusion of thought be likely to arise, as is implied by the confounding together of things so different as these two. Although the legislature (as I have above remarked) has an undoubted right to pass, or to reject, any Bill, a man would be deemed insane who should thence infer that they are *equally right* in doing either the one or the other. So also the Governors of a Church are left, in respect of ordinances and regulations not prescribed or forbidden in Scripture, to their own judgment; but they are bound to act according to the *best* of their judgment. What is left to their discretion is not therefore left to their caprice; nor are they to regard every point that is not *absolutely essential*, as therefore *absolutely indifferent*.

They have an undoubted right, according to the principles I have been endeavouring to establish, to appoint such Orders of christian Ministers, and to allot to each such functions, as they judge most conducive to the great ends of the Society; they may assign to the *whole*, or to a *portion* of these, the office of ordaining others as their successors; they may appoint one superintendent of the rest, or *several;* under the title of Patriarch, Archbishop, Bishop, Moderator, or any other that they may prefer; they may make the appointment of them for life, or for a limited period,—by election, or by rotation,—with a greater, or a less extensive, jurisdiction; and they have a similar discretionary power with respect to Liturgies, Festivals, Ceremonies, and whatever else is left at large in the Scriptures.[1]

Now to infer that all possible determinations of all these and similar points, would be equally expedient, and equally wise, and good, would be an absurdity so gross that in no other case, not connected with religion, would men need even to be warned against it. In fact, it would go to do away the very existence of any such attributes as "wisdom,"—"prudence,"—"discretion,"—"judgment," &c. altogether: for there is evidently no room for the exercise of them in matters *not* left to our *choice,* and in which the course we are to pursue is decided *for* us, and distinctly marked out, by a higher Authority; nor again is there any room for them in matters where there is

Province of discretion.

---

[1] In a Discourse delivered before the Curates-Fund-Society, and published at their desire, I have briefly noticed some of the evils likely to result from the Systems which tend, more or less, to give to each Congregation a control over their Minister, and thus to change what the Apostle calls "those who are placed OVER you" into "those who are placed UNDER you."

Still, though I should recommend members of such congregations to do their best towards changing the system, I should never think of pronouncing them excluded from the Gospel-covenant.

not a right and a wrong,—a better and a worse; and where the decision is a matter of total indifference; as in the choice between two similar sheets of paper to begin writing on, when both are lying within one's reach. The *sole* province of prudent and cautious deliberation is in cases which *are* left to our decision, and in which we may make a *better or a worse* decision.

And yet I should not wonder if some persons were to take for granted that any one who does not presume at once to exclude from the Gospel-covenant all professed Christians who do not strictly conform to what we regard as the purest primitive practice, and to deny altogether the validity of all their Ordinances, must, as a matter of course, place *exactly on a level* a system founded on the most diligent, sober, and deliberate inquiry after ancient and well-tried models, and the most rash, ill-advised, and fanciful innovations that ever were devised by ignorance or presumption. As well might one infer from the Apostle's declaration that " the Powers that be are ordained of God," his complete approval of the Constitution of the Roman Empire, of its laws, and of the mode of appointing Emperors; or his total indifference as to the best or the worst system of civil Government. If all laws were equally good, or if wise laws and unwise were a matter of indifference, or if it did not rest with each Government to make either wise or unwise enactments, what room could there be for political *wisdom?*

Instances of the above mistakes. The mistakes, however, which I have been alluding to, have been not unfrequently made in what relates to the powers possessed by christian Communities, and the mode of exercising these powers. For instance, at the time of the great Reformation, some Bodies of Christians found themselves without any Bishop among their number; and formed what are called Presbyterian Churches. Some members accordingly of these Churches have felt themselves called upon in self-defence to decry Episcopacy, as a form of Government not instituted by the Apostles, and *consequently*, as one which all Christians are *bound to reject*. Erroneous as, I am convinced, their premiss was, they were, on the above principles, still more erroneous in drawing that conclusion from it. Others of them again lamented their want of Episcopacy; considering that form of government as *having* the apostolical sanction, and *consequently*, as *obligatory* and *indispensable* to be retained, when possible; but to them, *unattainable*, from the interruption of episcopal succession. And while some presume to exclude all Presbyterians from the pale of Christ's universal Church—professing at the same time, in words, what they virtually nullify by their interpretations, that "Holy Scripture contains all things *necessary to salvation*,"—others again compassionate and sympathize with the supposed *unavoidable* deficiency in the Presbyterian Churches.

Now that all these parties are mistaken in their views (though a mere mistake, when not accompanied with a want of charity, is not deserving of severe censure) must be evident to any one who embraces the principles which in the outset I endeavoured to establish. It follows from those principles, that the Bodies of Christians we have been speaking of, *had* full power to retain, or to restore, or to originate, whatever form of Church-government they, in their deliberate and cautious judgment, might deem best for the time, and country, and persons, they had to deal with; whether exactly similar, or not, to those introduced by the Apostles; provided nothing were done contrary to Gospel-precepts and principles. They were, therefore, perfectly at liberty to appoint Bishops, *even if they had none* that had joined in the reformation; or to discontinue the appointment, *even if they had:* whichever they were convinced was the most conducive, under existing circumstances, to the great objects of all Church-government. And though their decision of this point ought to have been very greatly influenced by their belief as to what were the forms adopted by the Apostles (which must have been not only wise, but the very wisest, *for those times and persons*) they had no reason to hold themselves *absolutely bound* to adhere, always, and everywhere, to those original models.

Instances of departure from the apostolical model.

Indeed, to so considerable a degree have all Churches judged themselves at liberty to depart from the exact model of the earliest institutions—especially (as I formerly remarked) in respect of that important change introduced,—whether wisely or unwisely,—by, I believe, all of what are called episcopal Churches;—that of having several bishops in one Church, instead of making each Diocese (as appears to have been the apostolical system) an entire and distinct Church;[1]—so considerable, I say, is the liberty in this respect, that has been assumed by all Churches, that those who speak of all Christians being strictly bound to conform in every point to the exact pattern of the primitive institutions, can hardly wonder if

---

[1] Some who agree with me in not regarding a strict adherence to the earliest models as absolutely *essential*, yet would have *preferred*, in this point, a closer conformity to it. They believe, and not, I think, without reason, —that if each Diocese had been left, as at first, a distinct Church, dissensions among Christians, and disagreements in essentials, and corruptions of Christianity, would have been not increased by such a system, but rather, in some degree prevented.

Be this however as it may, it does seem strange to find those who would have *preferred* a closer adherence to the apostolical model, — though not holding it to be imperatively *necessary*, —*censured* for their tenets by some who are *content* to live under a different kind of episcopal government; —one that *departs* from that precedent which they blame the others for not regarding as of universal and absolute obligation!

they find imputed to them either great want of knowledge, or of reflection, in themselves, or else, a design to take advantage of the ignorance or inattention of others.

§ 38. I have specified the want of "attentive reflection" in applying rightly in practice the knowledge men do possess, as tending to foster erroneous notions; because it is probably both a more common and more dangerous defect than mere want of sufficient *knowledge*. And it may be added, that it arises not so often from original deficiency in the mental powers, as from neglect to exercise them. There are many who inadvertently, and not a few who advisedly and designedly, resign themselves, in all matters pertaining to morals or religion, to the impressions produced on their imagination and feelings; and rather applaud than reproach themselves for not awaiting the decisions of calm judgment, or for allowing their judgment to be biassed. To such persons, there is, it must be acknowledged, something very captivating and seductive in the notions I have been censuring; and not the less, from their being somewhat vague, and dimly apprehended, incapable of abiding the test of sober examination, and invested with some of that "mysterious and solemn gloom" which has been put forth expressly by some of their advocates, as a recommendation. There is something to many minds awfully and mystically sublime in the idea of the "decisions of the Catholic Church," and of "Catholic Councils, convened in the name of Christ, and whose deliberations are overruled, and their decrees authoritative." There is something imposing in the idea of the "Sacramental character of Ordination," conferred by persons who have derived a mystical virtue from the successive imposition of hands up to the times of the Apostles:—and of the "priestly" or

Erroneous views seductive to the feelings and imagination.

"sacerdotal" character, (that of Hiereus) thus imparted, and the "Sacrifices" offered at an "altar;"—of a "primitive doctrine always to be found somewhere in the Catholic traditions," &c. And such feelings are strengthened when these matters are treated of in solemn and imposing language, of that peculiar kind of dazzling mistiness whose effect is, to convey, *at first*, to ordinary readers, a striking impression, with an appearance of being perfectly intelligible at the first glance, but to become more obscure and doubtful at the *second* glance, and more and more so, the more attentively it is studied by a reader of clear understanding; so as to leave him utterly in doubt, at the last, which of several meanings it is meant to convey, or whether any at all.[1]

The rule of "omne ignotum pro mirifico," applies most emphatically to such doctrines treated of in such language. The very simplicity and plainness of the reasoning by which, in the foregoing pages, the divine authority of a christian Church, and consequently of its regulations and its ministers, are deduced direct from the sanction given by Christ Himself as interpreted by his Apostles, is likely to be, to some minds, no recommendation, but the contrary.

Views likely to mislead the Clergy. And as men are of course less likely to exercise a clear and unbiassed judgment in respect of any theory which tends especially to exalt their own persons, and invest them with mysterious powers and awful dignity, the *Clergy* accordingly are under a peculiar temptation[2] to lean too favourably, and with too

---

[1] See Index to the *Tracts for the Times*.

[2] The minds of many persons among the Laity are so constituted as to make the same temptation very little less powerful to them, than to the Priesthood; for reasons set forth in the Essay (3rd Series) on *Vicarious Religion*. See also a *Lecture delivered at the Dublin Law-Institute, on the Moral and Intellectual Influence of the Professions;* since reprinted in the *Elements of Rhetoric.*

little of rigorous examination, towards a system which confers the more elevation and grandeur on *them*, in proportion as it detracts from the claims of the entire Community. It is not the most flattering to them to be urged to say continually, not only in words, but by their conduct, " We preach not ourselves, but Christ Jesus the Lord, and us, your Servants for Jesus' sake ;"—to be taught and to teach that they are merely the Functionaries of the particular Church of which they are members,—that it is in that capacity only that they derive their station and power from Christ, by virtue of the sanction given by Him to christian Communities ;—that their authority therefore comes direct from the Society so constituted; in whose name and behalf they act, as its representatives, just to that extent to which it has empowered and directed them to act. These views do indeed leave them a most awfully important and dignified office, as Servants in " the House of God,"—(the " Temple of the Holy Ghost,")—as Stewards (*i.e.* dispensers; οἰκονόμοι) of divine truth to his People, and as Messengers from Christ, (so far as they " set forth his true and lively Word, and duly administer his Holy Sacraments,") as having been appointed conformably to his will. But although their title is thus placed on the secure basis of a clear divine sanction given, once for all, to *every* regularly-appointed Minister of any christian Community constituted on Gospel-principles, instead of being made to depend on a long chain, the soundness of many of whose links cannot be ascertained, yet this last is a system more flattering to human weakness; inasmuch as it represents the Priesthood as comparatively independent of each particular Church, and derives their Church's authority rather from *them*, than theirs, from it.

And accordingly so strong is the prejudice in the minds of many persons in favour of this system, that to rest the

Claims of christian Ministry based on those of a christian Church. claims of a christian *Ministry* on the basis of the *divinely-sanctioned* institution of a christian *Church*, would appear to them to be making the Ministry altogether a *human* ordinance; though in truth, its claim to be a divine Ordinance rests on that very sanction: so completely do they lose sight of the whole character of a *Church*, and of a *Community*. I remember seeing a censure passed on some one who had presumed to appoint another as a Bishop: not on the ground (which would have been a very just one) of his having no authority from any Church to make the appointment, but on the ground of his not being *himself* a Bishop; for how—it was urged—can a spring rise above the level of its source? how can an individual appoint another to an ecclesiastical office higher than he himself holds? How indeed,—it might have been added —can *any* individual, whether Bishop or not, appoint another to *any* office,—high or low—unless *authorized* by the *Community* to do so? For an individual to pretend to create another a King, or a Magistrate of any other description, or the humblest civil Functionary,—even though he were himself a King,—*without lawful authority from the Community to make such appointment*, would be regarded as a most extravagant and absurd assumption. On the other hand, a *Community*, and consequently those acting under its sanction, *may* appoint a man to an office higher than is possessed by any of the individuals who perform that act; as is the case, for instance, in the election of a *member of Parliament*. And, in the case of the supposed shipwrecked emigrants above adverted to, no reasonable man could doubt their right to elect one of their number as their King. But in the case of *ecclesiastical* Communities, many persons are found to advocate that fanciful and groundless system which goes to deprive *these* of all the rights which Christ's sanction of such a Community confers.

For, according to this system, the sacramental virtue of Holy Orders, which is indispensable for all the christian Ordinances and means of Grace, is inherent indefeasibly in each individual, who has derived it, in no degree from any particular Community, but solely from the Bishop whose hands were laid on him; who derived *his* power to administer this sacrament, altogether from Consecration by another Bishop—not necessarily a member of the same particular Church, but obtaining his power again from another Bishop; and so on, up to the apostolic times. On this system the Church is made a sort of appendage to the Priesthood; not, the Ministry, to the Church.[1] A people separated from their Ministers by some incurable disagreement as to christian doctrine, even supposing these last to have occasioned it by an utter apostasy from Gospel-truth,—would be left (supposing they could not obtain other ministers qualified by the same kind of transmission of sacramental virtue,) totally and finally shut out from the pale of Christ's universal Church, and from his "covenanted mercies;" while the Ministers, on the contrary, though they might be prohibited by civil authority, or prevented by physical force, from exercising their functions within a particular district, would still, even though

Error of making the authority of a Church emanate from that of its Ministers.

---

[1] That pernicious popular error, which confounds the Church with the *Clergy*, (see note to § 33,) as if the spiritual Community consisted only of its officers, is partly kept up perhaps by men's neglecting to notice one peculiarity belonging to Christ's kingdom, at its first *establishment;* viz. that it did, then, consist of Ministers only; though it was by no means designed so to continue. *All* the Disciples who constituted the infant Church were those destined to be employed in various offices therein: so that an inattentive reader is liable to confound together what our Lord said to them *as Ministers,* and what as *Members;*— as Rulers of a Church, and as the Church itself.

antichristian in doctrine and in life, retain their office and dignity unimpaired,—the sacramental virtue conferred on them by Ordination, and the consequent efficacy of their acts, undiminished.

Case of deposed Bishops and Presbyters.

§ 89. And this is not merely an inference fairly deducible from the principles of the system. One may even find persons who acknowledge that, if a Bishop, of our own Church for instance, who had been, for some crime, removed and degraded by regular process, should think proper afterwards to ordain men Priests or Deacons, though he, and they, would be legally punishable, still, his Ordinations would be valid, and these men consequently (however morally unfit) real Clergymen, capable of exercising the spiritual functions. This is to recognise a fearful power, and that, placed in the very worst hands, of producing and keeping up schism with something of an apparent divine sanction to give it strength.[1] For on this principle, a Bishop of some other church—the Roman-catholic for instance, or the Greek—who should have been ejected from his Diocese, might take upon him to ordain men according to the rites of *our* Church; and we should be bound to recognise his Ordinations as valid.

I need hardly remark, that, according to the principles I have been endeavouring to maintain, a Bishop when removed from his Diocese, (whether for any crime, or otherwise) and not appointed to any other, though he may continue a member of the episcopal *Order*, (unless regularly removed from it by competent authority,[2]) ceases altogether,

---

[1] See above, § 32.

[2] For, it is evident that as, in respect of Church-regulations, the powers of "binding" and of "loosing" have, equally, the divine sanction, so, the power of any christian Church to *admit* any one (either simply into the number of its *Members*, or) into any particular *Order* or Office, implies a power to *remove* him from either, when the case shall be such as to call for its removal.

ipso facto, to be a Bishop, in respect of episcopal *functions;* and has no more right to ordain, or to perform any other act, in the capacity of a Bishop, than a Layman would have: that is, till the same, or some other christian Church shall think proper to receive him in that capacity.[1]

If indeed any Church should be so very unwise as to recognise as Clergymen persons ordained by a deprived Bishop, these would undoubtedly be ministers of that Church; because *that* recognition would constitute them such; and a christian Community has power (though in that case there would be a gross abuse of its power) to determine who shall be its Officers. But what I am contending against, is, the notion of an inherent, indefeasible, sacramental virtue conveyed by the imposition of hands, and giving validity to the official acts, regular or irregular, of the persons possessing it. And this does seem to me a most pernicious as well as groundless tenet, tending to destroy the rightful authority of a *Church*, by unduly exalting the pretended privileges of its Functionaries.

On the same principle which has been now set forth in respect of Bishops, the acts of a Presbyter, or Deacon, or other Minister, of any Church, cease to be valid, as soon as ever the christian Community in which he was appointed, withdraws its sanction from his acts. If another Church think fit to receive him as a Minister, they have an undoubted right to do so; and he then becomes a minister of that Church. So he does also, when *not* expelled from the Society to which he originally belonged, supposing the Church to which he transfers himself *thinks fit to recognise*

---

[1] For, a Bishop, it should be observed, does not, in becoming such, enter on a new *Profession*, (as he did on taking Orders) but only on a new description of *Office* in his profession. A person may indeed, as I have said, continue to belong to a certain *Order* of Clergy, though with suspended functions; but the important point to be insisted on is, that no *official acts* have any validity but what is *derived from the Community* to which, in each case, the Officer belongs.

the Ordinations of the other; which they may do, or refuse to do, entirely at their own discretion. This is a point which every Church has a full right to determine according to its own judgment.

Conditions of Ordination imposed by a Church.

And as for the individual himself who is regularly deprived by his Church, if, on becoming a Clergyman, he engaged (as is required by, I believe, most existing Churches) that he would follow *no other* profession,[1] of course he cannot absolve himself from that engagement; but must continue so far a Clergyman, though with suspended functions. Moreover a Church has a *right*,—though I think such a regulation a very unwise one,—to recognise as valid the acts of a degraded Minister; (while subjecting him nevertheless to penalties for performing such acts) or of a Layman.

Confusion of the questions, what a Church may do, ought to do, and has done.

Concerning several points of this class,— such as the validity of lay-baptism, or of baptism by heretics or schismatics, &c. questions have been often raised, which have been involved in much unnecessary perplexity, from its being common to mix up together what are in fact *several distinct questions*, though relating to the *same subject*. For instance, in respect of the validity of Lay-baptism, three important and perfectly distinct questions may be raised; no one of which is answered by the answering, either way, of the others: viz. 1st. What has a Church the *right* to determine as to this point? 2dly.

---

[1] It would be, I am convinced, very advantageous that this rule should be modified as regards *Deacons*. We might avail ourselves of the services of some very useful assistants, if we would admit to this subordinate office some who could not maintain themselves wholly, without resorting (as the Apostle Paul did) to some secular employment. That some such distinction was in the view of the framers of our *Ordination-services* for Deacons and for Priests will, I think, appear probable to any one who attentively examines those Services, in reference to this point.

What is the *wisest* and best determination it can make? and, 3dly. What *has* this or that particular Church *actually* determined? Now persons who are agreed concerning the answer to one of these questions, may yet differ concerning the others; and *vice versâ*.[1]

§ 40. But to return to the consideration, generally, of the whole system of what is called "Catholic tradition," &c. which I have been censuring; it is calculated, as has been said, to produce at the first glance a striking and imposing effect, and to recommend itself strongly to the imagination and the feelings of some persons: but will not stand the test of a close examination. The advocates of these doctrines, accordingly, either from a consciousness of this, or else from indistinctness in their own conception, often set them forth with something of oracular obscurity and ambiguity, half concealed behind a veil, as it were, of mystery; as something of which the full import and complete proof were to be reserved for a chosen few. And when clear evidence is demanded of a sufficient foundation for the high pretensions put forth, and the implicit submission demanded, we are sometimes met by a rebuke of the "pride of human intellect," and of the presumptuous expectation of having every thing that we are to believe made perfectly level to our understanding, and satisfactorily explained.[2]

System of traditionists incapable of being supported by clear arguments.

No one, it may be said, would believe in a God, if he were to insist on first obtaining a clear and full comprehension of the nature and attributes of such a Being; an explanation,—such as no man of sense would think

What things one may, and may not, demand to have explained.

---

[1] See *Note N.* Hooker, in his 5th Book, maintains at great length the validity of Baptism by laymen and women.
[2] See Professor Powell's *Tradition Unveiled.*

of giving, or of seeking,—of the divine attributes, brought down to the capacity of such a Being as Man. Nor would any one believe in the christian Revelation, if he were to require, previously, to have a clear and full comprehension of the mysteries of the Incarnation, of the Redemption, of the Trinity, and of every thing else appertaining to the Gospel-scheme. We must content ourselves, therefore, we are told, with faint, indistinct, and imperfect notions on religious subjects, unless we would incur deserved censure for want of faith.

Clear or faint apprehension of the evidence, and of the subject of it, not to be confounded.

How often and how successfully the fallacy here sketched out has been employed, is really wonderful, considering how totally different and entirely unconnected are the two things which are thus confounded together; the clear or indistinct notion of the *subject-matter* itself,—of the fact or proposition—that is before us; and, the clear or indistinct notion of the *evidence* of it,—of the reasons for believing it. A moment's reflection is sufficient for any one to perceive the difference between the two; and yet, in the loose language of careless or sophistical argument, they are continually confused together, and spoken of indiscriminately, as if they were the same thing.

Every one, whether possessing christian faith or not, believes firmly,—and must believe,—and that, on the clearest evidence,—in the existence of many things concerning which he has but a very imperfect knowledge, and can form but indistinct and confused ideas of their nature; while to believe in whatever is proposed to us without any *clear proof* that it is *true*,—with an imperfect and indistinct apprehension of any *reason* for believing it,—is usually regarded as a mark of credulous weakness. And on the other hand, some description, narrative, or statement, may be, in itself, perfectly clear and intelligible, and yet may be very doubtful as to its truth, or may be wholly undeserving of credit.

For instance, there is, I suppose, no one who seriously doubts the existence of something which we call Soul—or Mind—be it Substance or Attribute, material or immaterial —and of the mutual connexion between it and the Body. Yet how very faint and imperfect a notion it is that we can form of it, and of many of its phenomena that are of daily occurrence! The partial suspension of mental and bodily functions during Sleep,—the effects of opium and other drugs, on both body and mind;—the influence again exercised by volition, and by various mental emotions, on the muscles, and on other parts of the bodily frame, and many other of these phenomena, have exercised for ages the ingenuity of the ablest men to find even any approximation towards but an imperfect explanation of them. Yet the *evidence on which we believe in the reality* of these and of many other things no less dimly and partially understood, is perfect.

On the other hand, the characters, transactions, &c. represented by dramatic writers, or described by historians, are often as *clearly intelligible* as it is possible for any thing to be; yet from the total want of evidence, or from the want of clear and decisive evidence, as to their *reality*, we regard them as either entire fictions, or mixtures of fable and truth, or as more or less likely to have actually existed.[1] The character and conduct of Lear, for instance, or Othello, of Hamlet, and Macbeth, are perfectly intelligible; though it is very doubtful how far the tales which suggested to Shakspeare the idea of most of his dramas had any foundation in fact, or were originally fictitious. Many again of

---

[1] See *Rhetoric*, part i. c. 2, § 2. "On the plausible and the historically probable."

the Orations recorded by the ancient Greek and Roman historians are as easily and plainly to be understood as any that are reported in our own times; but in what degree each of these is a faithful record of what was actually spoken, is a point on which we have, in some cases, a slight and imperfect evidence; and in others, none that deserves the name.

Fallacies resorted to on religious subjects.

§ 41. In all subjects where religion is not concerned, no one of ordinary good sense ever confounds together two things so dissimilar and unconnected as those I have been speaking of. But in what pertains to religion, the fallacy is, as I have said, often introduced. Yet Religion does not, in this respect, really differ from other subjects.

Character of Christ's religion imperfectly understood: evidence of it, clear.

Our Saviour's character and his teaching were matter of wondering perplexity to all around Him; even in a far greater degree than after the establishment of his Kingdom, on his personal ministry being completed; both because the Jews were full of the expectation of a totally different kind of Deliverer, and because great part of his discourses were not even designed to be fully intelligible, at the time, to his own disciples; but to be explained afterwards by the occurrence of the events He alluded to. Some of his followers, accordingly, "went back and walked no more with Him," on the occasion of one of these discourses. But the Apostles, who adhered to Him, did so, neither from having any clearer notions concerning his revelations, (for we often find it recorded that "they understood not this saying," &c.) nor again, from being satisfied to believe without any clear proof of his high pretensions; but because they "believed, and were sure that He was the Christ, the Son of the living God," on such evidence as He had Himself appealed to: "the works that I do in my Father's name, they bear witness of me." Dim, and indistinct, and imperfect as were still their notions (as, to a great degree, ours must be also) concerning "the Son of God," it was no indistinct or imperfect evidence on which they believed that He *was* so.

A converse case is that of the several false Christs who afterwards arose. "I am come," says our Lord, "in my Father's name," (with such manifestations of divine power as testified his coming from God) "and ye receive me not; if another shall come in his own name," *Character and pretensions of the false-Christs, readily understood: evidence wanting.* (*viz.* requiring acceptance on his own bare word, without any miraculous credentials) "him ye will receive."[1] *Their* teaching, their pretensions, and promises were as clearly intelligible to the greater part of the Jews,—because falling in with the prevailing belief and expectations,—as those of Jesus had been (even to his own disciples) obscure, perplexing, or unintelligible. Accordingly, vast multitudes followed these pretenders, without requiring any clear and sufficient evidence of the *truth* of their pretensions: and they followed them to their own and their Country's ruin.

The very history of our religion, therefore, supplies us here with an illustration of the distinction I have been speaking of. On the one side we have a revelation, itself dimly and partially understood, and doubtful, in great part, as to its *meaning*, but with clear *evidence* that it really came from God: on the other, a pretended revelation, containing, to those it was proposed to, no doubts or difficulties as to its sense and its design, but supported by no evidence that could satisfy an unprejudiced mind, bent on the attainment of truth.

---

[1] See Sermon on the *Name Emmanuel:* and also Cruden's *Concordance* on the word "Name."

§ 42. However plausible then the system I have been objecting to may appear to any one,— however imposing and mysteriously sublime,—however gratifying and consolatory to the feelings, let him not thence neglect to inquire for the proofs by which its high pretensions are to be sustained; but rather examine with more care the foundation on which so vast a superstructure is made to rest. Let no one be deterred from this by fierce denunciations against the presumptuousness of all inquiry, and the profaneness of all use of private judgment in religious matters; and by eulogies on the virtue of faith; but let him remember that the "*faith*" thus recommended is precisely that *want of faith* for which those Jews just mentioned were so severely condemned. They refused to listen to good evidence, and assented to that which was worthless.

False views of what is faith.

And let no one allow himself to be persuaded that he is evincing an humble piety, acceptable to the "*jealous* God," in hastily giving credence to the pretensions to divine authority put forth in behalf of uninspired men, (not producing the miraculous "Signs of an Apostle") by those who are for blending "Tradition with Scripture," and "following the dictates of inspiration wherever found, whether in Scripture or Antiquity;" and to pronounce according to their own arbitrary choice, what are, and what are not, the general Councils whose "deliberations were overruled by the Holy Spirit, and their decrees consequently authoritative."

Danger of misdirected piety.

"If any of these entice thee secretly, saying, Let us go after other Gods, thou shalt not hearken unto him." And those who speak in the name of Jehovah, saying, "Thus saith the Lord; when the Lord hath not spoken," are no more exempt from the guilt of enticing to idolatry, than the worshippers of Baal.

The more disposed any one is to submissive veneration, the greater the importance of guarding him against misdirected veneration ;— against false piety ;—against reverencing as divine, what in reality is human.[1] And the more awfully important any question is, the greater is the call for a rigid investigation of what may be urged on both sides ; that the decision may be made on sound, rational, and scriptural grounds, and not according to the dictates of excited feelings and imagination.

And in these times especially, and in respect of this subject, men need to be warned against a mistake which at all times is not uncommon ;—that of allowing themselves to be misled by names and professions, which are often—apparently by designed choice,—the most opposite to the things really intended. *Use of terms opposite to the things designated.* Thus, for instance, the term "Apostolical" is perpetually in the mouths of some who the most completely set at nought the principles which the Apostles have laid down for our guidance in the inspired Writings; and who virtually nullify these, by blending with them the traditions of uninspired men. None more loudly censure the "pride of human intellect," and inculcate "pious humility," than those who are guilty of the profane presumption of exalting fallible Man to a level with God's inspired messengers, and of deciding how far they shall impart, or "reserve," the truths which God has revealed.[2] The evils of "schism" again, are especially dwelt on by some who maintain principles the tendency of which has been shown to be to generate and perpetuate schism. To satisfy and "settle men's minds," is the profession of some, whose principles lead (as has been above remarked) in proportion as each man has the most tender conscience, and

---

[1] See *Essay I.* Third Series.   [2] See *Note O.*

the greatest anxiety about religious truth, to perplex and torment him with incurable doubts and scruples. "Church-principles" again is a favourite phrase with some who are, in fact, lowering the just dignity and impairing the divinely conferred rights of a Church. By none is a professed veneration for the " episcopal Office" carried to a more extravagant height than by some who are the most daring in usurping for themselves the government of the Church, and who set at nought with the greatest contumely every Bishop who ventures to disagree with them.[1] And none more loudly profess devoted and submissive admiration for the "Anglican Church," than many of those who are emphatically opposed, in some of the most important points, to the principles on which our Reformers proceeded, and the spirit which actuated them throughout.

Those hostile to the principles of the Church, ought to withdraw from it.

If any one is deliberately convinced that those their fundamental principles are erroneous, and that they rested the doctrines and institutions of our Church on a wrong basis, he deserves credit at least for honest consistency in leaving its communion. But I know not how any one can escape the imputation of very lax notions of morality, who continues to retain his position in our Church, and speaks with bitterness of those not in communion with it, while he opposes the principles, and even vilifies the characters, of our Reformers.

Principles of the Anglican Reformers.

§ 43. To me it does appear, that—without attributing to those Reformers an infallibility which they expressly disclaim—we may justly give them credit for such sound views, and such resolute adherence to evangelical truth, combined with such

---

[1] See a *Letter to the Bishop of Oxford*, by the Rev. Mr. Goode.

moderation and discretion, as were—considering the difficult circumstances they were placed in,—truly wonderful; and such as are, in all times, and not least in the present, well worthy of imitation. It was their "wisdom, to keep the mean" (as is expressed in the preface to the Book of Common Prayer) "between the two extremes, of too much stiffness in refusing, and too much easiness in admitting, any variation." It was "their wisdom" also to "keep the mean" between the claims—never conflicting, except when misunderstood—of Scripture, and of a Church. It was "their wisdom" to keep the mean between a slavish bondage to ancient precedents on the one hand, and a wanton and arrogant disregard of them, on the other. It was "their wisdom"—their pious and Christian wisdom—to keep the mean between rash and uncharitable judgment of other Churches, and equally rash carelessness, or fondness for innovation, in the regulations of their own. They conformed as closely as, in their judgment, circumstances would warrant, to the examples of the earliest Churches, without for an instant abandoning the rightful claims of their own; and yet without arrogantly pronouncing censure on those whose circumstances had led *them* to depart farther from those ancient precedents. Their "Faith" they drew from the Scriptures; their "Hope" they based on the Scriptures; their "Charity" they learned from the Scriptures.

A member of the Anglican Church,—I mean a sincere and thoroughly consistent member of it—ought to feel a full conviction—and surely there are good grounds for that conviction,—both that the reforms they introduced were no more than were loudly called for by a regard for Gospel-truth, and that the Church, as constituted by them, does possess, in its regulations and its officers, "Apostolical succession," in the sense in which it is essential that a christian Community *should* possess it; viz.:—in being a regularly-constituted christian Society, framed in accordance with the fundamental principles taught us by the Apostles and their great Master.

Successors of the Apostles. Successors, in the Apostolic office, the Apostles have none. As *personal attendants* on the Lord Jesus, and *witnesses* of his *Resurrection*,[1] as *Dispensers* of *miraculous* gifts,—as inspired *Oracles* of divine *Revelation*,—they have no successors. But as *Members*,—as *Ministers*,—as *Governors*—of christian Communities, their successors are the regularly-admitted Members,—the lawfully-ordained Ministers,—the regular and recognised Governors,— of a regularly-subsisting christian Church; especially of a Church which, conforming in fundamentals,—as I am persuaded ours does,—to Gospel-principles, claims and exercises no rights beyond those which have the clear sanction of our great Master, as being essentially implied in the very character of a Community.

Duty of members of our Church. May the members of a Church which our Reformers cleansed of so much corruption, and placed on its true basis, have the grace to profit by their example, and follow out their fundamental principles; labouring to be apostolical "not in mere words and in tongue, but in deed and truth;" actuated by the same spirit which was found in those great and good men, so far as they decreed what is agreeable to God's word, and to the " pure and peaceable wisdom that is from above." And especially, may all who profess Church-principles be careful to guard themselves and others against the two most prevailing errors of these days;—the two kinds of encroachments on the legitimate rights of a Church; on the

---

[1] "Last of all, He was seen of me also," says Paul (1 Cor. xv. 8), probably at the time referred to in Acts, xxii. 17; which was most likely when sent from Antioch to Jerusalem (Acts, xi. 8) just before his ordination as Apostle. See *Note B*.

one side by presumptuous and self-sufficient irregularities, and defiance of lawful authority; and by the pretensions of supposed "Antiquity" and "Tradition," on the other; that they may be enabled, under the divine blessing, to carry into effect more and more fully, and to bring to completion "all the holy desires, all the good counsels, and all the just works," of our Reformers, and of all other our predecessors, as many as have endeavoured, in simplicity and truth, to conform to the instructions of our divine Master and his Apostles.

NOTES TO ESSAY II.

Note A, pp. 31, 80.

"THAT no society can exist without some rules, and without some means of enforcing obedience to those rules, is obvious. When therefore it is asked, whether Christ or the Holy Spirit left any ecclesiastical laws, or vested anywhere power to enforce those laws? if the question is put with a view to ascertain whether Church-government be of divine origin, it is idle; inasmuch as the very institution of the ecclesiastica lsociety, the Church, implies the design that rules should be established, and means provided to enforce them.

" But another object may be intended by the question. It may be put with the view of ascertaining what those rules are, whereby this society, the Church, is designed to be governed. For, it may be said, and plausibly enough, that granting the intention of the Church's Founder to have laws established to be ever so apparent, how are we to know *what kind of government* he intended?

" On one point the inquirer must satisfy himself. If, from the nature of the Church, and from existing circumstances, the members were already possessed of the means of acquiring this knowledge, in that case neither Christ nor the Holy Spirit would be likely to leave any code of ecclesiastical laws; on precisely the same principle, as no code of ethics was left.

" Now, is there anything in the nature of the Church to guide us, as to what are ecclesiastical offences? Undoubtedly there is. In every society there must be such a principle; and by reference to it in each, are formed laws for the government of each. Every society recognises peculiar offences, arising out of, and depending solely on, the peculiar nature of the society; so that, in proportion as this latter is understood, the former are defined. Much mischievous confusion in some instances arises from a want of attention to this connexion; and the attention is frequently diverted from it by the accidental circumstance, that the same act often becomes an offence against many societies. Thus, theft is at once an offence against the supreme Ruler of the Universe,—against the political body to which the thief is attached,—against some certain class of society, perhaps, in which he moves, and so on. The act being one, it is only by reflection that we are enabled to separate the different views which render it in each case an offence, and in each of a different magnitude. Again, what becomes a crime because violating the principle of one society, may be none in another; if, namely, it does not interfere with the object proposed in the formation and preservation of that other society. Thus, the violation of the academical rules of our Universities does not render the offending member amenable to the laws of the land. Thus, too, the very conduct which recommends a smuggler or a robber to his confederacy, becomes an offence against the political body with which he is associated.

"In order, therefore, to ascertain what are inherent offences or crimes in any society, it is necessary that we should know with what object or objects such society is formed. If information of this kind then be found in the sacred record, respecting the Christian society, ecclesiastical law by revelation was no more to be expected, than a code of ethics to tell men what their own consciences were already constituted by God to declare.

"It is certain, however, that if the question need not be answered in the affirmative, in order either to establish the divine origin of ecclesiastical government, or to determine what offences come under its cognizance, there is yet a third object which may be proposed in urging it. What *punishments* are authorized, in order to check those offences? Ought not these to have been specified? and, not having been specified, does the nature of the case here also supersede the necessity of a revelation, and enable us to know what coercion is, and what is not, agreeable to the Divine will? The inquiry, too, seems to be the more reasonable, because in looking to the methods by which various societies are upheld, we find the punishment even in similar societies by no means the same. Military discipline, for instance, in different countries, and at different periods, has been enforced by penalties unlike in degree and in kind. In different countries and ages, the social tie between the master and the slave has been differently maintained. All this is true, but still, in looking at the question so, we take only a partial view, and lose one important feature in the establishment of coercion,—the right.

"Now, this right is either inherent in the society, or conventional, or both, as is the case in most confederate bodies. When the right is limited to what the society exercises as inherent and indispensable,—inherent in its nature, and indispensable to its existence,—the extreme punishment is, *exclusion;* and the various degrees and modifications of punishment, are only degrees and modifications of exclusion. When the right is conventional, also, (as far as it is so,) the punishment is determined by arbitrary enactment, proceeding from some authority acknowledged by all parties, (whether that authority be lodged in the parties themselves or in competent representatives, or in other delegated persons,) and therefore styled conventional. Few societies have ever existed without a large portion of these latter. Hence the anomaly above alluded to, and hence too the vulgar impression, that all punishments are arbitrary, and depend solely on the caprice and judgment of the government. What is popularly and emphatically termed *society*, affords a good instance of the first ; that is, of a social union regulated and maintained only by a right inherent. In this, excessive ill manners and the gross display of ungentlemanly feelings are punished by absolute exclusion. According as the offence is less, the party offending is for a time excluded from some select *portion* of good society, or from certain meetings and the like, in which more particularly the spirit and genuine character of gentility are to be cherished. All its lawful and appropriate punishments are a system of exclusion, in various shapes and degrees."—*Encyclopædia Metropolitana*, (Historical Division,) vol. ii. pp. 744, 745.

It may be added that we ought carefully to keep in mind the distinction between *punishment*, strictly so called, and *exclusion* from a society; which, in the case of ecclesiastical societies, is called "excommunication." The exclusion from membership in any society, of those who will not, or cannot, conform to its rules, (which is essential to every society,) may often be attended, *incidentally*, with much pain and mortification to the feelings of the person excluded : but "the *designed* infliction of suffering, for the purpose of *deterring* others from offending," which is the essential characteristic of "punishment," is, here, absent.[1] And if, because

---

[1] See the articles "Penalty," &c. in Eden's *Theological Dictionary*.

punishment occasions suffering, everything that occasions suffering were to be called a punishment, there would be no end to the confusion which such an innovation in language would introduce. For instance, a voyager, coming from a place suspected of infection, is confined for weeks performing Quarantine in a comfortless lazzaretto; which he would probably be glad to commute for a considerable fine. He *may* even incur by this means not only inconvenience, but heavy loss. Yet it would be absurd to talk of his being *punished* for having come from a place suspected of Plague. Every one would say, that the suffering inflicted being *incidental* and unavoidable, not designed, there was no punishment in the case. The same reasoning would apply to the case of a father's refusing his consent to his daughter's marriage with a man whose property and prospects seemed insufficient; to the great discomfort, perhaps, of both parties, but without any idea of inflicting what can be properly called punishment. And the same with innumerable similar cases.

It is to be observed, however, that of those sufferings and privations which are not properly reckoned " punishments," as not being *designed* to influence men's *conduct*, there are some which do, and others which do not, *operate* as punishments; that is, incidentally exercise such influence. For instance, on the one hand, the exclusion from certain privileges of some race of men on account of the colour of their skin, how much soever they may feel aggrieved, cannot *operate* as a *punishment*, because they cannot " by taking thought make one hair black or white." On the other hand, to exclude from office those of a certain creed,—though the object be merely their *exclusion* and not their *conversion*—is likely to operate as a punishment; *i. e.* to influence their conduct by holding out to them a temptation to profess what they do not believe. To influence their conduct in this way, is so far from being, in general, the object *sought* by legislators, that it is what they would rather deprecate. Such an exclusion therefore, much as it is at variance with the principles of the Gospel,[1] is not properly a punishment. But we should not overlook its tendency to *operate* as a punishment, and thus to produce, in addition to the immediate hardship, a distinct class of evils besides. Still, we ought also to be careful not to confound with punishment, properly so called, any kind of incidental suffering or privation.

---

[1] See *Essays*, 4th Series, Appendix, on *Monopoly of Civil Rights*.

Indeed the distinction is so obvious when pointed out, as to appear a self-evident truism. Such unauthorized innovations in language, however, as this, (oftener probably the result of inadvertency than of sophistical design,) are apt to escape the notice both of the writer and the reader, if not habitually on their guard against laxity in the use of terms; and much confusion of thought will usually ensue. For instance, in the present case, the right naturally inherent in a Church to determine who shall be members of it, is liable in this way to be confounded with the right to inflict punishment with a view to coerce men into conformity; that is, to make Christ's kingdom a "kingdom of this world."

NOTE B, pp. 82, 94, 228.

"HEREUPON doth the Apostle lay a divine directory before him, concerning their manner of praying, choosing and ordaining of ministers, approving deacons, admitting widows, and regulating the people—that nothing could be wanting to the healthful temper of that church, if they receive and embrace these applications; in the most of which prescriptions, he useth exceeding much of their synagogue-language, that he may be the better understood; and reflecteth upon divers of their own laws and customs, that what he prescribeth, may imprint upon them with the more conviction. He calleth the minister 'Episcopus,' from the common and known title 'the chazan' or 'overseer' in the synagogue : he prescribeth rules and qualifications for his choice, in most things suitable to their own cautions in choosing of an elder: he speaketh of 'elders ruling only, and elders ruling and labouring in the word and doctrine;' meaning, in this distinction, that same that he had spoken of in chap. iii. 'bishops and deacons.' Both these in the common language, then best known, were called 'elders,' and both owned as 'rulers.' Yea, the very title, that they usually termed, 'deacons,' (Parnasin,) was the common word that was used to signify, 'a ruler.' The Jerusalem Talmud, speaking of the three 'Parnasin,' or 'deacons,' that were in every synagogue, hath these two passages, which may be some illustration to two passages in this epistle :—'They appoint not less than three Parnasin in the congregation : for if matters of money were judged by three, matters of life much more require three to manage them.' Observe that the deacon's office was accounted as an office that concerned life; namely, in taking care for the existence of the poor. According to this, may that in chap. iii. 12, be understood: ' For they that have used the office of a deacon well, purchase to themselves a good degree:' a good degree towards being entrusted with souls, when they have been faithful in the discharge of their trust concerning the life of the body."—*Lightfoot's Harmony of the New Testament. Edited by the Rev. John Pitman.* Vol. iii. p. 257

" The Apostles at Jerusalem, hearing the glad tidings of the conversion of Samaria, send down Peter and John; and why these two rather than any other of the twelve, is not so easy to resolve, as it is ready to observe, that if, in this employment, there was any sign of primacy, John was sharer of it as well as Peter. Being come, they pray, and lay their hands upon them, and they receive the Holy Ghost. Here episcopacy thinketh it hath an undeniable argument for proof of its hierarchy, and of the strange rite of confirmation. For thus pleadeth Baronius for the former: ' From hence (saith he) it may be seen, that the hierarchical order was instituted in the church of God, even in this time; for Philip doth so baptize those that believe, that yet he usurpeth not the apostolical privilege,—namely, the imposition of hands granted to the Apostles.' And thus the Rhemists both for it, and for the latter, in their notes on Acts vii. 17 :—
' If this Philip had been an Apostle, (saith St. Bede,) he might have imposed his hands, that they might have received the Holy Ghost; but this none can do, saving bishops. For though priests may baptize and anoint the baptized also with chrism consecrated by a bishop,—yet can he not sign his forehead with the same holy oil; because that belongeth only to bishops, when they give the Holy Ghost to the baptized.' And after this testimony of Bede, they subjoin their inference: ' This imposition therefore of hands, together with the prayer here specified (which no doubt was the very same that the church useth to that purpose) was the ministration of the sacrament of confirmation.'

" Now let the reader, with indifferency and seriousness, but ruminate upon these two queries, and then judge of these two inferences :—

" First, whether apostleship were not an Order for ever inimitable in the church: for besides the reason given to prove that it was, upon the chusing of Matthias, others may be added to make it more clear:—as, 1. The end of their election was peculiar, the like to which was not to be in the church again; for they were chosen to be with Christ, Mark iii. 14; to be eye-witnesses of his resurrection, Acts i. 22, ii. 32, and x. 41; as they had been of his actions and passion, Luke i. 2. And, therefore, Paul pleading for his apostleship, that 'he had seen the Lord,' 1 Cor. ix. 1; and in the relation or story of his calling, this particular is singularly added, that 'he saw that Just One, and heard the voice of his mouth,' Acts xxii. 14.

"Secondly, the name of 'Apostles' keepeth itself unmixed or confounded with any other order. It is true, indeed, that the significancy of the word would agree to other ministers that are to preach; but there is a peculiar propriety in the sense, that hath confined the title to the twelve and Paul:[1] as any indifferent eye will judge and censure upon the weighing of it in the New Testament.

"Thirdly, when Paul reckoneth the several kinds of ministry, that Christ Jesus left in the church at his ascension, Eph. iv. 11, and 1 Cor. xii. 28,—there is none that can think them all to be perpetuated, or that they should continue successively in the like order from time to time. For within a hundred years after our

---

[1] I know not why the author, while specifying Paul, omits Barnabas, who was equally an Apostle, and appointed at the very same time.

The word "Apostolos" denoting originally any *Emissary*, is sometimes so applied, in that, its "first-intention," to a person deputed by some church to transact some business in its behalf; as for instance, to Epaphroditus, the bearer of contributions from the Philippians to Paul, and thence styled by him their [Apostle] "messenger:" see Phil. ii. 25, and iv. 18. But in the "second-intention" it is applied, emphatically, to those whose title at full length (and occasionally so expressed) was "Apostles *of Jesus Christ;*" and whose qualifications and office were manifestly peculiar.

Of these Apostles strictly so called, there were in all fifteen, though never at any one time more than thirteen: Matthias being appointed after the removal of Iscariot; and Saul, along with Joseph Barnabas (who was most likely, as is remarked in Hinds's *History*, the very "Joseph Barsabas" formerly put into nomination along with Matthias,) after James, the brother of John, had been slain by Herod.

Saviour's birth, where were either prophets or evangelists, miracles or healings? And if these extraordinary kinds of ministration were ordained but for a time, and for special occasion, and were not to be imitated in the church unto succeeding times; much more, or at the least as much, were the Apostles, an Order much more, at least, as much extraordinary, as they.

"Fourthly, the constant and undeniable parallel, which is made betwixt the twelve Patriarchs, the fathers of the twelve tribes, and the twelve Apostles, not only by the number itself, but also by the New Testament, in the four-and-twenty Elders, Rev. iv. 4,—and in the gates and foundations of the New Jerusalem, Rev. xxi. 12, 14,—doth argue and prove the latter order as inimitable as the first. These things well considered, if there were no more, it will show, how improbable and unconsonant the first inference is, that is alleged, that because there was a subordination betwixt the Apostles and Philip, therefore, the like is to be reputed betwixt bishops and other ministers, and that bishops in the church are in the place of the Apostles."—*Lightfoot's Commentary on the Acts*, vol. viii. p. 125.

"1. Here beginneth 'the kingdom of heaven;' when the Gentiles are received to favour and to the Gospel, who had been so long cast off, and lain in ignorance and idolatry; and when no difference is made betwixt them and the Jews any longer,—but, of every nation, they that fear God and work righteousness are accepted of him, as well as Israel. This is the very first beginning or dawning to the kingdom of heaven; and so it grew on more and more, till Jerusalem was destroyed; and then was the perfect day, when the Gentiles only were become the church of Christ: and no church or commonwealth of Israel to be had at all, but they destroyed and ruined.

"2. Here 'Peter hath the keys of the kingdom,' and unlocked the door for the Gentiles to come in to the faith and gospel, which, till now, had been shut, and they kept out. And Peter only had the keys, and none of the apostles or disciples but he, for though they from henceforward brought in Gentiles daily into the kingdom of heaven, by converting them to the Gospel,—yet it was he that first and only opened the door; and the door, being once opened, was never shut, nor never shall be to the end of the world. And this was all the priority that Peter had before the other apostles, if it were any priority; and how little this concerneth Rome, or the Papacy, as to be any foundation of it, a child may observe.

"3. Peter here looseth the greatest strictness, and what was the straitest bound up of anything that was in all the policy of Moses and customs of the Jews,—and that was, the difference of clean and unclean, in the legal sense. And this he looseth on earth, and it is loosed in heaven; for from heaven had he an immediate warrant to dissolve it. And this he doth, first declaratively, showing that nothing henceforward is to be called common or unclean, and showing his authority for this doctrine; and then practically conforming himself to this doctrine that he taught, by going in unto the uncircumcised, and eating with them. 'Binding and loosing,' in our Saviour's sense, and in the Jews' sense, from whose use he taketh the phrase, is 'of things and not of persons; for Christ saith to Peter, ὃ ἐὰν δήσῃς, and ὃ ἐὰν λύσῃς; ὃ and not ὅν; 'whatsoever' thou bindest, and not 'whomsoever;' and to the other apostles, ὅσα ἐὰν δήσητε, Matt. xviii. 18, ὅσα and not ὅσους, 'whatsoever *things*,' and not 'whatsoever *persons;*' so that, though it be true and indeed, that Jews and Gentiles are loosed henceforward one to the communion of another,—yet the proper object of this loosing, that is loosed by Peter, was that law or doctrine that tied them up. And so concerning the eating of those things that had been prohibited,—it is true, indeed, that the Jews were let loose henceforward to the use of them in diet, and to eat what they thought good; but this loosing was not so properly of the men, as the loosing of that prohibition that had bound them before. And this could be no way but doctrinally, by teaching that christian liberty that was given by the gospel.

"Now, though Peter only, and none but he, had 'the keys of the kingdom' of heaven, yet had all the apostles the 'power of binding and loosing,' as well as he; and so have all the ministers of the gospel as well as they; and all in the same sense, namely, doctrinally to teach what is bound and loose, or lawful and unlawful; but not in the same kind: for the apostles having the constant and unerring assistance of the Holy Ghost, did nullify, by their doctrine, some part of Moses's law, as to the use of it, as circumcision, sacrifices, purifyings, and other legal rites,—which could not have been done by men, that had not had such a

Spirit; for there must be the same Spirit of prophecy to abrogate a law which had set it in force."—P. 219.

" Besides these there was 'the public minister of the synagogue,' who prayed publicly, and took care about the reading of the law, and sometimes preached, if there were not some other to discharge this office. This person was called, ' The Angel of the Church,' and ' the Chazan or Bishop of the Congregation.' The public minister of the synagogue himself read not the law publicly; but, every sabbath, he called out seven of the synagogue (on other days, fewer) whom he judged fit to read. He stood by him that read, with great care observing, that he read nothing either falsely, or improperly,—and calling him back, and correcting him, if he had failed in any thing. And hence he was called Ἐπίσκοπος, or 'Overseer.' Certainly, the signification of the word ' Bishop,' and ' Angel of the Church,' had been determined with less noise, if recourse had been made to the proper fountains, —and men had not vainly disputed about the signification of words, taken I know not whence. The service and worship of the temple being abolished, as being ceremonial, God transplanted the worship and public adoration of God used in the synagogues, which was moral, into the Christian church; to wit, the public ministry, public prayers, reading God's word, and preaching, &c. Hence the names of the ministers of the gospel were the very same, 'The Angel of the Church,' and ' The Bishop,'—which belonged to the ministers in the synagogues."—*Hebrew and Talmudical Exercitations upon the Gospels of St. Matthew and St. Mark*, vol. xi. p. 88.

Ver. 19: Καὶ δώσω σοι τὰς κλεῖς τῆς βασιλείας τῶν οὐρανῶν. 'And I will give thee the keys of the kingdom of heaven.' That is, 'Thou shalt first open the door of faith to the Gentiles.' He had said, that he would build his church to endure for ever, against which 'the gates of hell should not prevail,' which had prevailed against the Jewish church: and 'To thee, O Peter (saith he), I will give the keys of the kingdom of heaven; that thou mayest open a door for the bringing in of the gospel to that church.' Which was performed by Peter in that remarkable story concerning Cornelius, Acts x. And I make no doubt, that those words of Peter respect these words of Christ, Acts xv. 7;

'Ἀφ' ἡμερῶν ἀρχαίων ὁ Θεὸς ἐν ἡμῖν ἐξελέξατο διὰ τοῦ στόματός μου ἀχοῦσαι τὰ ἔθνη τὸν λόγον τοῦ Εὐαγγελίου, καὶ πιστεῦσαι. 'A good while ago God made choice among us, that the Gentiles should hear the word of the Gospel by my mouth, and believe.'

" Καὶ ὃ ἐὰν δήσῃς ἐπὶ τῆς γῆς, &c. '*And whatsoever thou shalt bind on earth*, &c.' Καὶ ὃ ἐὰν λύσῃς ἐπὶ τῆς γῆς, &c. '*And whatsoever thou shalt loose on earth*,' &c.

" I. We believe the keys were committed to Peter alone, but the power of binding and loosing to the other apostles also, chap. xxviii. 18.

" II. It is necessary to suppose, that Christ here spake according to the common people,—or he could not be understood without a particular commentary, which is nowhere to be found.

" III. But now ' to bind and loose,' a very usual phrase in the Jewish schools, was spoken of things, not of persons; which is here also to be observed in the articles, ὃ and ὅσα, 'what,' and ' whatsoever,' chap. xviii.—*Lightfoot*, p. 226.

Note C, pp. 93, 94.

" It was indeed not at all to be expected that the Gospels, the Acts, and those Epistles which have come down to us, should have been, considering the circumstance in which they were written, anything different from what they are: but the question still recurs, why should not the Apostles or their followers have *also* committed to paper, what we are sure must have been perpetually in their mouths, regular instruction to Catechumens, Articles of Faith, Prayers, and directions as to Public Worship, and administration of the Sacraments?

" Supposing that the other avocations of the Apostles would not allow any of *them* leisure for such compositions,—though we know that some of them did find time for writing, two of them, not a little,—even this supposition does not at all explain the difficulty; for the Acts, and two of the Gospels, were written by men who were only attendants on the Apostles. Nor would such writings as I am speaking of have required an *inspired* penman; only, one who had *access* to persons thus gifted. We know with what care the Apostolic Epistles were preserved, first by the

Churches to which they were respectively sent, and afterwards, by the others also, as soon as they received copies. How comes it then that no one of the Elders (Presbyters) of any of these Churches should have written down, and afterwards submitted to the revision of an Apostle, that outline of catechetical instruction —that elementary introduction to the Christian faith—which they must have received at first from that Apostle's mouth, and have afterwards employed in the instruction of their own converts? Why did none of them record any of the Prayers, of which they must have heard so many from an Apostle's mouth, both in the ordinary devotional assemblies, in the administration of the Sacraments, and in the 'laying on of hands,' by which they themselves had been ordained?

"Paul, after having given the most general exhortations to the Corinthians for the preservation of decent regularity in their religious meetings, adds, 'the rest will I set in order when I come.' And so doubtless he did; and so he must have done, by verbal directions, in all the other churches also; is it not strange then that these verbal directions should nowhere have been committed to writing? This would have seemed a most obvious and effectual mode of precluding all future disorders and disputes: as also the drawing up of a compendious statement of Christian doctrines, would have seemed a safeguard against the still more important evil of heretical error. Yet if any such statements and formulas *had* been drawn up, with the sanction and under the revision of an Apostle, we may be sure they would have been preserved and transmitted to posterity, with the most scrupulous and reverential care. The conclusion therefore seems inevitable, that either no one of the numerous Elders and Catechists ever thought of doing this, or else, that they were forbidden by the Apostles to execute any such design; and each of these alternatives seems to me alike inexplicable by natural causes.

"For it should be remembered that, when other points are equal, it is much more difficult to explain a *negative* than a *positive* circumstance in our Scriptures. There is something, suppose, in the New Testament, which the first promulgators of Christianity,—considered as mere unassisted men,—were not likely to write; and there is something else, which they were, we will suppose, equally unlikely to *omit* writing: now these two difficulties are by no means equal. For, with respect to the former, if we can make out that *any one* of these men might have been, by nature or by circumstance, qualified and induced to write it, the phenomenon is solved. To point out even a single individual able and likely to write it, would account for its being written. But it is not so with respect to the other case, that of omission. Here, we have to *prove a negative ;*—to show, not merely that this or that man was likely not to write what we find omitted, but, that *no one was* likely to write it." * * * *

"Although however we cannot pretend, in every case, to perceive the reasons for what God has appointed, it is not in the present case difficult to discern the superhuman wisdom of the course adopted. If the Hymns and forms of Prayer,—the Catechisms,—the Confessions of faith,—and the Ecclesiastical regulations, which the Apostles employed, had been recorded, these would all have been regarded as parts of *Scripture :* and even had they been accompanied by the most express declarations of the lawfulness of altering or laying aside any of them, we cannot doubt that they would have been in practice most scrupulously retained, even when changes of manners, tastes, and local and temporary circumstances of every kind, rendered them no longer the most suitable. The Jewish ritual, designed for one Nation and Country, and intended to be of temporary duration, was fixed and accurately prescribed : the same Divine Wisdom from which both dispensations proceeded, having designed Christianity for all Nations and Ages, left Christians at large in respect of those points in which variation might be desirable. But I think no *human* wisdom would have foreseen and provided for this. That a number of *Jews,* accustomed from their infancy to so strict a ritual, should, in introducing Christianity as the second part of the same dispensation, have abstained not only from accurately prescribing for the use of all Christian Churches for ever, the mode of divine worship, but even from recording what was actually in use under their own directions, does seem to me utterly incredible, unless we suppose them to have been restrained from doing this by a special admonition of the divine Spirit.

"And we may be sure, as I have said, that if they *had* recorded the particulars of their own worship, the very words they wrote would have been invested, in our minds, with so much sanctity, that it would have been thought presumptuous to vary or to omit them, however inappropriate they might become. The Lord's Prayer, the only one of general application that is recorded in the Scriptures, though so framed as to be suitable in all Ages and Countries, has yet been subjected to much superstitious abuse." *   *   *   *   *   *

"Each Church, therefore, was left, through the wise foresight of Him who alone 'knew what is in Man,' to provide for its own wants as they should arise;—to steer its own course by the Chart and Compass which his holy Word supplies, regulating for itself the Sails and Rudder, according to the winds and currents it may meet with.

"'The Apostles had begun and established precedents, which, of course, would be naturally adopted by their uninspired successors. But still, as these were only the formal means of grace, and not the blessing itself, it was equally to be expected that the Church should assume a discretionary power whenever the means established became impracticable, or clearly unsuitable; and either substitute others, or even altogether abolish such as existed. . . .

"'It might seem at first that the apostolical precedents were literally binding on all ages; but this cannot have been intended; and for this reason, that the greater portion of the apostolical practices have been transmitted to us, not on apostolical authority, but on the authority of the uninspired Church: which has handed them down with an uncertain mixture of its own appointments. How are we to know the enactments of the inspired rulers from those of the uninspired? and if there be no certain clue, we must either bring down the authority of apostolical usage to that of the uninspired church, or raise that of the uninspired church to that of the apostolical. Now the former is, doubtless, what was, to a certain extent, intended by the Apostles themselves, as will appear from a line of distinction by which they have carefully partitioned off such of their appointments as are designed to be perpetual, from such as are left to share the possibility of change, with the institutions of uninspired wisdom.

"'If then we look to the account of the Christian usages contained in Scripture, nothing can be more unquestionable, than that while some are specified, others are passed over in silence. It is not even left so as to make us imagine that those mentioned may be all: but while some are noted specifically, the establishment of others is implied, without the particular mode of observance being given. Thus, we are equally sure from Scripture, that Christian ministers were ordained by a certain form, and that

Christians assembled in prayer; but while the precise process of laying on of hands is mentioned in the former institution, no account is given of the precise method of church service, or even of any regular forms of prayer, beyond the Lord's Prayer. Even the record of the Ordination Service itself admits of the same distinction. It is quite as certain that, in it, some prayer was used, as that some outward form accompanied the prayer; but the form is specified, the prayer left unrecorded.

"'What now is the obvious interpretation of the holy Dispenser's meaning in this mode of record? Clearly it is, that the Apostles regulated, under His guidance, the forms and practices of the church, so as was best calculated to convey grace to the church *at that time*. Nevertheless, part of its institutions were of a nature which, although formal, would never require a change; and these therefore were left recorded in the Scriptures, to mark this distinction of character. The others were not, indeed, to be capriciously abandoned, nor except when there should be manifest cause for so doing; but as such a case was supposable, these were left to mingle with the uninspired precedents; the claims of which, as precedents, would be increased by this uncertain admixture, and the authority of the whole rendered so far binding, and so far subject to the discretion of the Church. They might not be altered unless sufficient grounds should appear; but the settling of this point was left to the discretion of the Church.'[1]

"The Apostles themselves, however, and their numerous fellow-labourers, would not, I think, have been, if left to themselves, so far-sighted as to perceive (all, and each of them, without a single exception) the expediency of this procedure. Most likely, many of them, but according to all human probability, some of them, would have left us, as parts of Scripture, compositions such as I have been speaking of; and these, there can be no doubt, would have been scrupulously retained for ever. They would have left us Catechisms, which would have been like precise directions for the cultivation of some plant, admirably adapted to a particular soil and climate, but inapplicable in those of a contrary description: their Symbols would have stood like ancient sea-walls, built to repel the encroachments of the waves, and still scrupulously

---

[1] Hinds's *History*, vol. ii. pp. 113—115.

kept in repair, when perhaps the sea had retired from them many miles, and was encroaching on some different part of the coast.

"There are multitudes, even as it is, who do not, even now, perceive the expediency of the omission; there are not a few who even complain of it as a defect, or even make it a ground of objection. That in that day, the reasons for the procedure actually adopted, should have occurred, and occurred to *all* the first Christians, supposing them mere unassisted men, and men too brought up in Judaism, is utterly incredible."—*Essay on Omissions*, pp. 15—19; 24—27; 30—34.

NOTE D, p. 107.

"IT is not, I think, unlikely that some hasty and superficial reasoners may have found an objection to Christianity in the omission of which I have been speaking. It is certain that there are not a few who are accustomed to pronounce this or that supposition improbable, as soon as they perceive that it involves great difficulties; without staying to examine whether there are more or fewer on the *other side* of the alternative; as if a traveller when he had the choice of two roads, should, immediately on perceiving that there were impediments in the one, decide on taking the other, before he had ascertained whether it were even passable. I can conceive some such reasoners exclaiming, in the present case, 'Surely, if the Apostles had really been inspired by an allwise God, they would never have omitted so essential a provision as that of a clear systematic statement of the doctrines to be believed, and the worship to be offered, so as to cut off, as far as can be done, all occasions of heresy and schism. If the Deity had really bestowed a revelation on his creatures, He would have provided rules of faith and of practice so precise and so obvious, as not to be overlooked or mistaken; instead of leaving men, whether pretending to infallibility, as the Romanists, or interpreting Scripture by the light of reason, as the Protestants, to elicit by a laborious search, and comparison of passages, what doctrines and duties are, in their judgment, agreeable to the Divine Will.'

"You think it was to be expected (one might reply) that God

would have proceeded in this manner; and is it not at least as much to be expected *that Man would?* It is very unlikely, you say, that the Apostles would have omitted these systematic instructions, if they had really been inspired: but if they were *not*, they must have been impostors or enthusiasts; does then that hypothesis remove the difficulty! Is it not at least as unlikely, on that supposition, that no one of them, or of their numerous followers, should have taken a step so natural and obvious? All reasonable conjecture, and all experience show, that any men, but especially *Jews*, when engaged in the propagation and establishment of a religion, and acting, whether sincerely or insincerely, on their own judgment as to what was most expedient, would have done what no Christian writer during the age of (supposed) inspiration *has* done. One would even have expected indeed, that, as we have four distinct Gospels, so, several different writers would have left us copies of the Catechisms, &c. which they were in the habit of using orally. This or that individual might have been prevented from doing so by accidental circumstances; but that every one of some hundreds should have been so prevented, amounts to a complete moral impossibility.

"We have here, then, it may be said, a choice of difficulties: if the Christian religion came from God, it is (we will suppose) very strange, and contrary to all we should have expected from the Deity, that He should have permitted in the Scriptures the omission I am speaking of; if, again, it is the contrivance of men, it is strange, and contrary to all we could have expected from *men*, that *they* should have made the omission. And now, which do we know the more of, God, or Man? Of whose character and designs are we the more competent judges, and the better able to decide what may reasonably be expected of each, the Creator, or our fellow-creatures? And as there can be no doubt about the answer to this question, so, the conclusion which follows from that answer is obvious. If the alternative were presented to me, that either something has been done by persons with whose characters I am intimately acquainted, utterly at variance with their nature, and unaccountable, or else that some man to whom I am personally a stranger, (though after all, the nature of every human Being must be better known to us, than, by the light of reason, that of the Deity can be,) had done something which to me is entirely inexplicable, I should be thought void of sense, if I did not embrace, as the less improbable, the latter side of the alternative.

"And such is the state of the present case, to one who finds this peculiarity in the Christian Scriptures quite unaccountable on either supposition. The argument is complete, whether we are able, or not, to perceive any wise reasons for the procedure adopted. Since no one of the first promulgators of Christianity did that which they must, some of them at least, have been *naturally* led to do, it follows that they must have been *supernaturally* withheld from it; how little soever we may be able even to conjecture the object of the prohibition. For in respect of this, and several other (humanly speaking, unaccountable) circumstances in our religion, especially that treated of in the Fourth of the *Essays* above referred to, it is important to observe, that the argument does not turn on the supposed *wisdom* of this or that appointment, which we conceive to be worthy of the Deity, and thence infer that the religion must have proceeded from Him; but, on the utter improbability of its *having proceeded from Man;* which leaves its divine origin the only alternative. The Christian Scriptures considered in this point of view, present to us a standing Miracle; at least, a Monument of a Miracle; since they are in several points such as we may be sure, according to all natural causes, they would *not* have been. Even though the character which these writings do in fact exhibit, be such as we cannot clearly account for on *any* hypothesis, still, if they are such as we can clearly perceive no false pretenders would have composed, the evidence is complete, though the difficulty may remain unexplained."—*Essay on Omissions*, pp. 19—24.

NOTE E, p. 108.

"THE three great principles then, on which every Church, or Christian society, was formed by the apostles, were SPIRITUALITY, UNIVERSALITY, and UNITY. Out of these arose one important limit to the discretionary powers of the uninspired Church, when deprived of extraordinary authority. It is of the last importance that this fact should be borne in mind, in every appeal to the practice and authority of the primitive Church. There is (even among protestant divines) a vague method of citing the authority of the early Churches in matters of discipline and practice, without any distinct view of the exact weight of that authority. In quoting doctrinal statements we are generally more accurate in our estimate; but it is undeniable, that the practices and discipline of the primitive Churches, are subject to the same kind of check from Scripture, as are their opinions and faith; and are in no instance to be received as if they were matters left altogether to their discretion. The *principles*, although not the specific rules, are given in the New Testament: and this is, perhaps, nearly all that is done in the case of the doctrines themselves. Only the elements, out of which these are to be composed, are furnished by Scripture. So far from being stated in a formal way, some of the abstract terms for these doctrines are not found in the Scriptures; such a statement and enunciation of them being left to the discretion of the Church. So, too, the principles of the Church-establishment were given, and were put in practice for illustration; and the application of these principles was all that was left to the discretion of its uninspired rulers. In short, every Church, in all ages, holds Scripture in its hand, as its warrant for its usages as well as for its doctrines; and had the immediate successors and companions of the apostles, from the very first, corrupted the government and constitution of the Church, *we* should be enabled to condemn them, from the New Testament; and to this test it is the duty of all ages to bring them. Their management of those matters which are said to be left indeterminate, has only the authority of an experiment; it is a practical illustration of Scriptural principles. Whenever they have been successful in this experiment, it would, indeed, generally be unwise and presumptuous in us to hazard a different mode of attaining the same result; but even here, any deviation is authorized by difference of circumstances; the same principle which guided them being kept in view by us. But in whatever stage of ecclesiastical history the principle itself has been forgotten,—it matters not how far back the practice may be traced,—it has no authority as a precedent. The Bible is our only attested rule; and we must appeal to it with the boldness recommended by the apostle to his converts; and though an angel from heaven preach unto us any other rule than that we have received, let him be accursed.

"This boundary line to the discretionary powers of the Church would be quite clear, supposing the ecclesiastical principles to have been left only as above considered, in the form of abstract instruction, whether formally enunciated, or certainly deducible from the Scriptures. But far more than this was done. On these very principles the apostles actually formed and regulated societies of Christians; so as to leave them not merely abstractedly propounded, but practically proved. This proceeding, while it lightened the difficulty of the uninspired Church, (especially of those who first received the guidance of it from the apostles, and who most needed it,) proportionably contracted the discretionary powers with which they were invested. If only abstract principles had been left, uninspired authorities would have been justified in regarding solely these, and regulating the means of conformity to them by their own unbiassed judgment. But the apostolical precedents created a new restriction. Rulers of infallible judgment had not only taught the principle, but the precise method by which that principle was best preserved had been practised by them, and set forth, apparently for the guidance of their less enlightened successors.

"Was the Church of all ages bound to follow their track without any deviations? If so, where was any room for discretionary power? If not, on what authority was the deviation to be made, and how far was it authorized? Here the most accurate view of the character and object of the Christian's sacred record is necessary in order to remove all obscurity from the question. That record, as far as the agency of human ministers is its object, is partly historical, partly legislative. The two terms are not, perhaps, quite expressive of the distinction intended; but, by Scripture being partly legislative, is meant, that it is partly concerned in conveying the rules and principles of religion—the revealed will, in short, of God. It is also partly historical; and of the historical portion no inconsiderable share is solely or principally a practical illustration of these rules. History and legislation are indeed both blended; and it is because they are thus connected: but the respective uses of them, as distinct portions of Scripture, are here, as in other questions of a similar nature, very important. When the historical incidents, the *facts* recorded, are recorded as specimens of the fulfilment of God's will, their only authority, as precedents and examples, arises from their conformity to the principle which they illustrate. Now it is conceivable and likely, that a change of circumstances may render a practice inconsistent with such a principle, which originally was most accordant with it, and *vice versâ*. The principle is the fixed point, and the course which has first attained it may become as unsuitable to another who pursues it, as the same line of direction would be for two voyagers who should be steering for the same landmark at different seasons, and with different winds. Still, as in this latter case, the first successful attempt would be, to a certain extent, a guide to those which follow; and this, exactly in proportion to the skill of the forerunner. The apostles were known to be infallible guides; and those who immediately succeeded them, and all subsequent ages, are quite sure that they must have pursued that which was, under the existing circumstances, the most direct line to their object,—that situated as Christianity was in their hands, all their regulations were the best possible for preserving the principles of the Church-establishment and government. The uninspired Church was therefore bound to follow them, until any apostolical practice should be found inadequate to accomplish its original purpose. Here commence the discretion and responsibility; the first obligation being to maintain the principle according to the best of their judgment, as the prudent steersman alters his track and deviates from the course marked out in his chart, when wind or tide compels him to the deviation.

"And thus we shall be at no loss for the precise difference of authority between the precedents of the apostolical and of the primitive uninspired Church. In matters which admit of appeal to the usage of the apostolical Church, we are sure, not only that the measure was wise, but the very wisest; and accordingly, the only question is, whether its suitableness has been affected by any change of circumstances. On the other hand, in a similar reference to the uninspired Church of any age, the measure is first of all pronounced wise or unwise—lawful or unlawful, as it conduces or not to the maintenance of the revealed principles of ecclesiastical society. And supposing the measure under consideration be proved to have been so conducive, still it is not at once certain, as in the former case, that it was the wisest and most judicious measure which the existing circumstances required or admitted. It emanated from fallible wisdom. Accordingly, in canvassing

Note F. 251

the authority of such a precedent, we are authorized and bound to institute two inquiries;—Was the measure the most accordant with ecclesiastical principles *then ?* Is it so *now ?* Whereas, in the former appeal to apostolic usage, the only question is, whether it is convenient, now?"—*Encyclopædia Metropolitana*, (Historical Division,) vol. ii. pp. 775, 776.

NOTE F, pp. 121, 171.

"SUPPOSING such a summary of Gospel-truths had been drawn up, and could have been contrived with such exquisite skill as to be sufficient and well adapted for all, of every age and country, what would have been the probable result? It would have commanded the unhesitating assent of all Christians, who would, with deep veneration, have stored up the very words of it in their memory, without any need of laboriously searching the rest of the Scriptures, to ascertain its agreement with them; which is what we do (at least are evidently *called on* to do) with a *human* exposition of the faith; and the absence of this labour, together with the tranquil security as to the correctness of their belief which would have been thus generated, would have ended in a careless and contented apathy. There would have been no room for doubt,—no call for vigilant attention in the investigation of truth,—none of that effort of mind which is now requisite, in comparing one passage with another, and collecting instruction from the scattered, oblique, and incidental references to various doctrines in the existing Scriptures; and, in consequence, none of that excitement of the best feelings, and that improvement of the heart, which are the natural, and doubtless the designed result of an humble, diligent, and sincere study of the christian Scriptures.

" In fact, all study, properly so called, of the rest of Scripture, —all lively interest in its perusal,—would have been nearly superseded by such an inspired compendium of doctrine; to which alone, as far the most convenient for that purpose, habitual reference would have been made, in any questions that might arise. Both would have been regarded, indeed, as of divine authority; but the Compendium, as the fused and purified metal; the other, as the mine containing the crude ore. And the Compendium itself, being not, like the existing Scriptures, that *from which* the faith is to be learned, but *the very thing to be learned*, would have come to be regarded by most with an indolent, unthinking veneration, which would have exercised little or no influence on the character. Their orthodoxy would have been, as it were, petrified, like the bodies of those animals we read of incrusted in the ice of the polar regions; firm-fixed, indeed, and preserved unchangeable, but cold, motionless, lifeless. It is only when our energies are roused, and our faculties exercised, and our attention kept awake, by an ardent pursuit of truth, and anxious watchfulness against error,—when, in short, we feel ourselves to be doing something towards acquiring, or retaining, or improving our knowledge,—it is then only, that that knowledge makes the requisite practical impression on the heart and on the conduct."—*Essay on Omissions*, pp. 34—37.

Note G, p. 131.

MANY persons are so accustomed to hear "the tradition of the primitive Church" spoken of as "designed to be the *interpreter of Scripture*," that they insensibly lose sight of the well-known facts of early christian History. Conformably with those facts it would be much more correct to speak of *Scripture* as having been designed to be the *interpreter of Tradition*. For, the first Churches did not, it should be remembered, receive their religion from the christian *Scriptures*, (as the Israelites did theirs from the books of Moses) but from *oral* teaching.

To guard against the errors, and doubts, and defects, and corruptions, to which oral Tradition must ever be liable, the sacred books,—*all of them addressed to persons who were already Christians*—were provided as a lasting, pure, and authoritative record; "that they might know the certainty of those things wherein they had been instructed."

We find accordingly, as might have been expected, the references to Scripture in the works of the early Fathers, less and less frequent and exact, the higher we go back towards the days of the Apostles; *i. e.* towards the time when the Churches had received christian history and doctrines by oral instruction *only*.

The scattered notices however in the works of the Early Fathers, of facts and doctrines substantially the same as we find in the Sacred Books, and also of those books themselves, is a most valuable evidence, that (as Paley remarks) the Gospel which Christians have now is the same as Christians had then. This evidence has been well compared to that afforded by the fossil remains of antediluvian animals which Geologists have examined, and which prove that Elephants, for instance, and such and such other animals, inhabited the earth at a certain remote period.

And it may be added, that Naturalists are accustomed, in examining fossil remains,—often mere fragments of skeletons,— to compare them with such existing animals as appear to be of kindred nature; *interpreting*, if we may so speak, the less known by the better known, and thus forming reasonable conjectures as to the general appearance and character of the fossil animal as it formerly existed. But no one would think of *reversing* this process, and taking the fossil Elephant, for instance, as a standard by which to correct and modify the description and delineation of the animal now existing among us.

Even so, when we meet with anything in the Ancient Fathers which was likely to have been derived by tradition from the Apostles, the obviously rational procedure is, to expound and *interpret* this by the *writings* of the Apostles that have come down to us.

NOTE H, p. 141.

" IT is manifest that the *concurrent* testimony, positive or negative, of several witnesses, when there can have been no concert, and especially when there is any rivalry or hostility between them, carries with it a weight independent of that which may belong to each of them considered separately. For though, in such a case, each of the witnesses should be even considered as wholly undeserving of credit, still the chances might be incalculable against their all agreeing in the *same* falsehood. It is on this kind of testimony that the generality of mankind believe in the motions of the earth, and of the heavenly bodies, &c. Their belief is not the result of their own observations and calculations: nor yet again of their implicit reliance on the skill and the good faith of any one or more astronomers; but it rests on the agreement of many independent and rival astronomers; who want neither the ability nor the will to detect and expose each other's errors. It is on similar grounds, as Dr. Hinds has justly observed, that all men, except about two or three in a million, believe in the existence and in the genuineness of manuscripts of ancient books, such as the Scriptures. It is not that they have themselves examined these; or again, (as some represent) that they rely implicitly on the good-faith of those who profess to have done so; but they rely on the *concurrent* and *uncontradicted* testimony of all who have made, or who *might make*, the examination; both unbelievers, and believers of various hostile sects; any one of whom would be sure to seize any opportunity to expose the forgeries or errors of his opponents.

"This observation is the more important, because many persons are liable to be startled and dismayed on its being pointed out to them that they have been believing something—as they are led to suppose—on very insufficient reasons; when the truth is perhaps that they have been mis-stating their reasons."—*Rhetoric*, part I. ch. 2, § 4.

" Some one may perhaps ask you, how you can know, except by taking the word of the learned for it, that there *are* these Greek and Hebrew Originals which have been handed down from ancient times? or how you can be sure that our translations of them are faithful, except by trusting to the translators? So that an unlearned Christian must, after all, (some people will tell you,) be at the mercy of the learned, in what relates to the very foundations of his faith. He must take their word (it will be said) for the very existence of the Bible in the original languages, and for the meaning of what is written in it; and, therefore, he may as well at once take their word for everything, and believe in his religion on their assurance.

" And this is what many persons do. But others will be apt to say, 'How can we tell that the learned have not deceived us? The Mohammedans take the word of the learned men among them; and the Pagans do the same; and if the people have been imposed upon by their teachers in Mohammedan and Pagan countries, how can we tell that it is not the same in christian countries? What ground have we for trusting with such perfect confidence in our christian teachers, that they are men who would not deceive us?'

" The truth is, however, that an unlearned Christian may have very good grounds for being a believer, without placing this entire confidence in any man. He may have reason to believe that there are ancient Greek manuscripts of the New Testament, though he never saw one, nor could read it if he did. And he may be convinced that an English Bible gives the meaning of the original, though he may not trust completely to any one's word. In fact, he may have the same sort of evidence in this case, which every one trusts to in many other cases, where none but a madman would have any doubt at all.

" For instance, there is no one tolerably educated who does not know that there is such a country as France, though he may never have been there himself. Who is there that doubts whether there are such cities as London, and Paris, and Rome, though he may never have visited them? Most people are fully convinced that the world is round, though there are but few who have sailed round it. There are many persons living in the inland parts of these islands who never saw the sea; and yet none of them, even the most ignorant clowns, have any doubt that there is such a thing as the sea. We believe all these, and many other such things, because we have been told them.

" Now suppose any one should say, 'How do you know that travellers have not imposed upon you in all these matters; as it is well known travellers are apt to do? Is there any traveller you can so fully trust in, as to be quite sure he would not deceive you?' What would you answer? I suppose you would say, *one* traveller might, perhaps, deceive us; or even two or three might possibly combine to propagate a false story, in some case where hardly any one would have the opportunity to detect them: but in these matters there are hundreds and thousands who would be sure to contradict the accounts if they were not true; and travellers are often glad of an opportunity of detecting each other's mistakes. Many of them disagree with each other in several particulars respecting the cities of Paris and Rome; and if it had been false that there are any such cities at all, it is impossible but that the falsehood should have been speedily contradicted. And it is the same with the existence of the sea,—the roundness of the world,—and the other things that were mentioned.

"It is in the same manner that we believe, on the word of astronomers, that the earth turns round every twenty-four hours, though we are insensible of the motion; and that the sun, which seems as if you could cover it with your hat, is immensely larger than the earth we inhabit; though there is not one person in ten thousand that has ever gone through the mathematical proof of this. And yet we have very good reason for believing it; not from any strong confidence in the honesty of any particular astronomer, but because the same things are attested by many different astronomers; who are so far from combining together in a false account, that many of them rejoice in any opportunity of detecting each other's mistakes.

"Now an unlearned man has just the same sort of reason for believing that there are ancient copies, in Hebrew and Greek, of the christian sacred books, and of the works of other ancient authors, who mention some things connected with the origin of Christianity. There is no need for him to place full confidence in any particular man's honesty. For if any book were forged by some learned men in these days, and put forth as a translation from an ancient book, there are many other learned men, of this, and of various other countries, and of different religions, who would be eager to make an inquiry, and examine the question, and would be sure to detect any forgery, especially on an important subject.

"And it is the same with translators. Many of these are at variance with each other as to the precise sense of some particular passage; and many of them are very much opposed to each other, as to the doctrines which they believe to be taught in Scripture. But all the different versions of the Bible agree as to the main outline of the history, and of the discourses recorded: and therefore an unlearned Christian may be as sure of the general sense of the original as if he understood the language of it, and could examine it for himself; because he is sure that unbelievers, who are opposed to all Christians, or different sects of Christians, who are opposed to each other, would not fail to point out any errors in the translations made by their opponents. Scholars have an opportunity to examine and inquire into the meaning of the original works; and therefore the very bitterness with which they dispute against each other, proves that where they all agree they must be right.

"All these ancient books, in short, and all the translations of them, are in the condition of witnesses placed in a witness-box, in a court of justice; examined and cross-examined by friends and enemies, and brought face to face with each other, so as to make it certain that any falsehood or mistake will be brought to light."—*Easy Lessons on Christian Evidences*, pp. 23—27.

NOTE I, pp. 150, 168.

I WILL take the liberty of here inserting extracts from the articles "Authority" and "Church," in the Appendix (on Ambiguous Terms) to the *Elements of Logic*.

"*Authority*.—This word is sometimes employed in its primary sense, when we refer to any one's example, testimony or judgment: as when, *e. g.* we speak of correcting a reading in some book, on the authority of an ancient MS.—giving a statement of some fact, on the authority of such and such historians, &c.

"In this sense the word answers pretty nearly to the Latin 'Auctoritas.'

"Sometimes again it is employed as equivalent to 'Potestas,' Power: as when we speak of the Authority of a Magistrate, &c.

"Many instances may be found in which writers have unconsciously slid from one sense of the word to another, so as to blend confusedly in their minds the two ideas. In no case perhaps has this more frequently happened than when we are speaking of the Authority of the Church: in which the ambiguity of the latter word (see the article 'Church') comes in aid of that of the former. The Authority (in the primary sense) of the Catholic, *i. e.* Universal Church, at any particular period, is often appealed to, in support of this or that doctrine or practice: and it is, justly, supposed that the opinion of the great body of the Christian World affords a presumption (though only a presumption) in favour of the correctness of any interpretation of Scripture, or the expediency, at the time, of any ceremony, regulation, &c.

s

". " On the other hand, each *particular* Church has authority in the other sense, *viz.* Power, over its own members, (as long as they chuse to remain members) to enforce anything not contrary to God's Word. But the *Catholic or Universal* Church, not being one religious community on earth, can have no authority in the sense of *Power;* since it is notorious there never was a time when the power of the Pope, of a Council, or of any other human Governors, over *all* Christians, was in fact admitted, or could be proved to have any just claim to be admitted."—Pp. 349, 350.

" *Church* is sometimes employed to signify *the* Church, *i. e.* the Universal or Catholic Church,—comprehending in it all Christians; who are 'Members one of another,' and who compose the Body, of which Christ is the Head; which, collectively taken, has no visible supreme Head or earthly governor, either individual, or council; and which is *one*, only in reference to its One invisible Governor and Paraclete, the Spirit of Christ, dwelling in it,—to the one common faith, and character, which ought to be found in all Christians,—and the common principles on which all Christian societies should be constituted. See Hinds's *History of the Rise of Christianity.*

" Sometimes again it is employed to signify *a* Church; *i. e.* any one Society, constituted on these general principles; having governors on earth, and existing as a community possessing a certain power over its own members; in which sense we read of the ' Seven Churches in Asia ;'—of Paul's having ' the care of all the Churches,' &c."—P. 353.

The two senses of the word " Authority " are in most cases so easily and completely distinguished, even by persons of no more than ordinary accuracy in the use of language, that many would be disposed, at the first glance, to wonder how any confusion ever could arise from the ambiguity. Men receive, for instance, on the " authority " of certain experienced Physicians the description of the symptoms of the Plague or some other disease, and their method of treating it; and on the " authority " of astronomers, statements and theories relative to the heavenly bodies. So also, it is on the authority of the ancient Romans,—not of the Roman *State*, but the Roman Public,—that we acknowledge the works of Cicero and Horace, and other classical authors. In all these and innumerable similar cases, no such idea as *coercive power* or claim of submission as a matter of *obligation*, is ever suggested to the mind by the word "authority." But it often happens that the *judgment* is even much more influenced by authority in this sense, than it would have been by a formal *decree* of some regularly constituted Body. For instance, if any one happened to have conversed on some subject with all, or nearly all, the individual members of the House of Commons separately and independently, and had found them all to concur in respect of some fact or opinion, this concurrence, though destitute of all *legal* force, would doubtless have more weight with its judgment than a regular *vote* of the House, if carried by a bare majority, (in a House consisting, perhaps, of not one-fifth of the whole number of members,) and perhaps opposed by the most judicious and best informed of them. And even so, if the Roman senate, or some regularly constituted academy at Rome, had formerly pronounced on the genuineness of the *Æneid*, our conviction would not certainly have been stronger, and would most likely have been much weaker, than now that it is based on the independent, spontaneous, and undisputed belief of all who took an interest in the subject.

The authority on which we rest our conviction of the genuineness of the New Testament Scriptures, is of the same *kind*, though incomparably *stronger in degree*. For it is not to the Roman world in its widest acceptation, but to the *literary* portion of it, that we appeal, in respect of any volume of the Classics. On the contrary, the christian Scriptures were addressed to all classes; (the doctrine of what is called " Reserve "—of putting the light of the Gospel under a bushel—being no part of the apostolic system) so that probably for one reader of Cicero or Livy there were more than fifty persons,—even in a very early period of the Church,—anxious to possess copies of the New Testament Scriptures, and careful, in proportion to the high importance of the subject, as to the genuineness and accuracy of what they read. On this point I will take the liberty of citing the words of an eminent writer,[1] from an unpublished discourse delivered a good many years ago at Oxford in a course of lectures. . . . " Nothing is more remarkable in Christianity than the care and anxiety with which the early Christians examined the pretensions of any writing to be received as the work of an Apostle. This will also account for

---

[1] The late Bishop Copleston.

the interval of time which elapsed before all the books of the Canon became generally received. It does not indeed appear that the genuineness of any of the four Gospels was ever doubted; but the Epistles, being addressed to particular Churches, and at various times, it must have required for one of these some interval before its communication could take place throughout every country in which the Gospel was preached, accompanied by such evidence as should be satisfactory to every other Church. . . . As soon as can be supposed possible the Christians of all countries remarkably agreed in receiving them as canonical; while the hesitation of a few proves only that this agreement was not a hasty or careless assent, but a deliberate and unbiassed judgment. . . . . It cannot be too strongly pressed upon your attention that the credit of a canon thus composed is infinitely greater than if it had rested *on the authority of some general Council.* For the decision of a Council is the decision of a majority only : whereas this is ratified by the voice of every separate church. It is moreover the decision not of one meeting, or of one age, but the uncontradicted *belief* of *all* the first churches, spreading gradually and naturally as the Gospel spread :—a belief which was not imposed *by authority,* but was the result of their own cautious and independent examination."

I have dwelt thus fully on this subject because I believe there are not a few who being accustomed to hear the authority of the Primitive Church spoken of as that on which we receive the New Testament Scriptures, are led to fancy it the authority of *some one society acting collectively,* and in its corporate capacity : and thus they lose sight of the very circumstance on which the chief force of this testimony depends; namely, that there never was a decree or decision of any *one* Society, but—what has far more weight— the concurring, independent convictions of a great number of distinct Churches in various regions of the world.

NOTE K, p. 167.

"WE are often too much disposed, perhaps, not indeed to lay it down, but tacitly to assume, that those who sat at the feet of Apostles must be secure from error. It is more probable that they would hold substantial truth not unmixed with subordinate deviations from it. It was so even during the lifetime of the Apostles; and why not after their decease? If indeed the good providence of God had not directed the Apostles themselves to bequeath to the Church their own instructions in writing, and we had to gather them only from the writings of their successors, then it might have been hoped that such very important witnesses, as the Apostolical Fathers would have thus become, would have been secured from every mistake, from every error at least which could seriously mislead us. But as it is, there was no more need of a perpetual miracle to give such an immunity from error to the immediate successors of the Apostles, than to us. Moreover, we have an unhappy advantage over them, in that we know by sad experience the fatal consequences which by degrees resulted from even slight deviations from the language and sentiments of Inspiration; such as a sacrificial character gradually ascribed to the Eucharist, or an improper exaltation of the christian ministry, or praise allotted upon unscriptural grounds to celibacy or asceticism. If Antiquity, 'quo propius aberat ab ortu et divinâ progenie, hoc melius ea fortasse, quæ erant vera, cernebat,' she may have been for that very reason,—knowing what was true, and meaning what was right,—the less suspicious of the effect of slight deviations from the exact truth of Holy Scripture. We may lament, indeed, but we cannot be surprised, that uninspired men, holding the truth substantially both as to doctrine and discipline, should slide into error here and there in tone, or sentiment, or subordinate opinion. Doubtless their errors should be our warning. Only let us be careful to detect the seeds of error even in the writings of good and holy men in primitive times, not in order to censure *them*, but to secure ourselves; to counteract our natural tendency to confound the uninspired with the inspired, and to make us doubly grateful that God has blessed his Church with the unerring records, written by inspired Apostles, of Gospel-truth."—*Hawkins's Sermon on the Ministry of Men,* pp. 41, 42.

Note L, p. 172.

"'But are we then,' (all Romanists and some Protestants would ask) 'to be perpetually waving and hesitating in our faith?—never satisfied of our own orthodoxy?—always supposing or suspecting that there is something unscriptural in our Creed or in our worship? We could but be in this condition, if Christ had *not* promised to be with his Church, " always, even to the end of the world;"—had *not* declared by his Apostle, that his "Spirit helpeth our infirmities;" had *not* taught us to expect that where we are "gathered together in his Name, there is He in the midst of us." Are we to explain away all that Scripture says of spiritual help and guidance? Or are we to look for a certain *partial and limited* help;—that the Holy Spirit will secure us from *some* errors, but lead us, or leave us, to fall into others?'

"Such is the statement, the most plausible I can give in a small compass, of the Romish (but not exclusively Romish) argument, which goes to leave no medium between a claim to infallibility on the one hand, and universal hesitation,—absolute Scepticism, on the other. An appeal to the common sense which every one, Romanist or Protestant, exercises on *all but religious* subjects, might be sufficient to prove, from the practice of those very men who use such reasoning, not only its absurdity, but their own conviction of its absurdity. In all matters which do not admit of absolute demonstration, all men, except a few of extravagant self-conceit, are accustomed to regard themselves or those under whose guidance they act, as fallible; and yet act, on many occasions,—after they have taken due pains to understand the subject, to ascertain their own competency, and to investigate the particular case before them,—without any distressing hesitation. There are questions in Medicine, in Agriculture, in Navigation, &c. which sensible men, well versed in their respective arts, would decide with sufficient confidence for all practical purposes; yet without holding themselves to be infallible, but on the contrary always keeping themselves *open* to conviction,—always *on the watch* against error,—attentive to the lessons which observation furnishes,—ready to stand corrected if any argument shall be adduced (however little they may anticipate this) which will convict them of mistake.

"'Yes,' (it may be replied,) 'all this holds good in worldly matters; but in the far more important case of religious concerns, God has graciously promised us spiritual assistance, to "lead us into all truth."'

"It is most true that He has. Christ has declared, 'If any man keep my saying, my Father will love him, and we wil come unto him, and make our abode with him:'—'without Me ye can do nothing:' for 'if any man have not the Spirit of Christ, he is none of his;' and 'as many as are led by the Spirit of God, they are the sons of God.'

"But some distinction there must be, between the spiritual guidance granted to the Apostles, which was accompanied by *sensible miracles*, and all that has ever been bestowed since the cessation of miracles. I do not mean a difference as to the *evidence for the existence* of each; for both are equally to be believed, if we have faith in the divine promises: but there must be a difference in the character of the divine assistance in the two cases, arising out of the presence, in the one, and the absence in the other, of sensibly-miraculous attestation. And this difference evidently is, that, in the one case, the divine agency is in each individual instance, *known*; in the other, *unknown*. If an Apostle adopted any measure, or formed a decision on any doctrine, in consequence of a perceptible admonition from Heaven, he *knew* that he was, in this point, infallibly right. A sincere Christian, in the present day, may be no less truly guided by the same Spirit to adopt a right measure or form a correct decision; but he never can *know* this with certainty, before the day of judgment. It is not that spiritual aid is now *withdrawn*, but that it is *imperceptible;* as indeed its ordinary sanctifying influence *always was*. It is to be known only by its fruits; of which we must judge by a diligent and candid examination of Scripture, and a careful, humble, self-distrusting exercise of our own fallible judgment.

"It is conceivable, therefore, that an individual or a Church, may be, in fact, *free* from error; but none can ever be (either at the present moment, or in future) *secure* from error. We are not bound to believe, or to suspect, that any of the doctrines we hold, are erroneous; but we are bound never to feel such a confidence in their correctness, as to shut the door against objection, and to dispense with a perpetual and vigilant examination. Even the fullest conviction that a complete perfection in soundness of doctrine is attainable, has in it nothing of arrogance,—nothing of a presumptuous claim to infallibility, as long as we steadily keep in view, that even one who should have attained this, never can, in this life, be *certain* of it. We are taught, I think, in Scripture, to expect that the pious and diligent student will be assisted by the divine guidance; and that in proportion as he is humble, patient, sincere, and watchfully on his guard against that unseen current of passions and prejudices which is ever tending to drive him out of the right course, in the same degree will he succeed in attaining all necessary religious truths. But how far he *has* exercised these virtues, or how far he may have been deceiving himself, he never can be certain, till the great day of account. In the mean time he must *act* on his convictions, as if he were certain of their being correct; he must *examine* and re-examine the grounds of them as if he suspected them of being erroneous.

" In this it is that great part of our trial in the present life consists: and it is precisely analogous to what takes place in the greater part of temporal concerns. The skilful and cautious navigator keeps his reckoning with care, but yet never so far trusts to that as not to 'keep a look out,' as it is termed, and to take 'an observation,' when opportunity offers. There is no risk incurred, from his strongly hoping that his computations will prove correct; provided he never resigns himself to such an indolent reliance on them as to neglect any opportunity of verifying them. The belief, again, whether true or false, that it is possible for a time-keeper to go with perfect exactness, can never mislead any one who is careful to make allowance for the possibility of error in his own, and to compare it, whenever he has opportunity, with the Dial which receives the light from heaven." *Essay on Omissions*, pp. 43—49.

NOTE M, p. 196.

" IT has been said that the Pope, the Bishops, the Priests, and those that dwell in convents, form the spiritual, or ecclesiastical State; and that the princes, nobles, citizens, and peasants, form the secular state or laity. This is a fine story, truly. Let no

one, however, be alarmed at it. *All* Christians belong to the spiritual State; and there is no other difference between them than that of the functions they discharge.   *   *   *   *
*   *   *   If any pious laymen were banished to a desert, and having no regularly consecrated priest among them, were to agree to choose for that office one of their number, married or unmarried, this man would be as truly as priest a if he had been consecrated by all the bishops in the world. Augustine, Ambrose, and Cyprian, were chosen in this manner. Hence it follows that laity and priests, princes and bishops, or, as they say, the Clergy and the Laity, have, in reality, nothing to distinguish them but their *functions*. They all belong to the same Estate; but all have not the same work to perform," &c.—*Luth. Opp.* l. xvii. f. 457, et seq.

It may be needful to add, that if in a Church thus constituted, or in any other, the *Laity* are admitted to a share in the government of it, and to ecclesiastical offices, this would be, not only allowable, but wise and right. That laymen,—that is, those who hold no *spiritual* office—should take part in legislating for the Church, and should hold *ecclesiastical* offices, as in the Scotch Kirk, and in the American Episcopalian Church, (always supposing, however, that they are MEMBERS of the Church; not, as in this country, belonging to other Communions) is far better than that the whole government should be in the hands of men of one Profession, the clerical.

That this has nothing of an *Erastian* character, it would be unnecessary to mention, but that I have seen the observation—in itself perfectly true—made in such a manner as to imply what is not true; *i. e.* so as to imply that some persons do, or may, maintain that there is something of Erastianism in such an arrangement. But who ever heard of any such charge being brought? Who, for instance, ever taxed the Scotch Kirk, or the American Episcopalian, with being Erastian, on account of their having Lay Elders? Erastianism[1] has always been considered as consisting in making the *State as* such,—the Civil *Magistrate by virtue of his office*,—prescribe to the People what they shall believe, and how worship God.

---

[1] I use this term in what I apprehend to be its ordinary sense, without at all pronouncing as to what were the precise opinions actually taught by Erastus himself.

Note N, pp. 149, 219.

With respect to the first question (in reference to lay-baptism) it is plain that, according to the above principles, a Church has a right to admit, or refuse to admit, Members. This right it possesses as a *Society:* as a *Christian* Society, sanctioned by our Heavenly Master, it has a right to administer his Sacraments; and it has a right to decide who shall or shall not exercise certain functions, and under what circumstances. If it permit Laymen (that is, those who are excluded from *other* spiritual functions) to baptize, it does, by that permission, *constitute* them its functionaries, in respect of that particular point. And this it has a right to do, or to refuse to do. If a Church refuse to recognise as valid any baptism not administered by such and such officers, then, the pretended administration of it by any one else, is of course null and void, as wanting that sanction of a Christian Church, which alone can confer validity.

With respect to the second question, it does appear to me extremely unadvisable,—derogatory to the dignity of the ordinance,—and tending both to superstition and to profaneness, that the admission, through a divinely-instituted Rite, of members into the Society, should be in any case entrusted to persons not expressly chosen and solemnly appointed to any office in that Society.

Nearly similar reasoning will apply, I think, to the case of Ordinations. What appears to me the wisest course, would be that each Church should require a distinct appointment *by that Church* itself, to any ministerial office to be exercised therein; whether the person so appointed had been formerly ordained or not, to any such office in *another* Church. But the form of this appointment need not be such as to cast any stigma on a former Ordination, by implying that the person in question had *not* been a real and regular minister of *another* distinct Society. For any Church has a fair right to demand that (unless reason be shown to the contrary) its acts should be regarded as valid within the pale of that Church itself: but no Church can reasonably claim a right to ordain ministers for *another* Church.

As for the remaining question,—What is the actual determination as to this point,—*this* is of course a distinct question in reference to each Church.

On this point it is only necessary to remark how important it is, with a view to good order and peace, that *some* determination should be made, and should be clearly set forth, by any Church, as to this and other like practical questions; and that they should not be left in such a state of uncertainty as to furnish occasion for disputes and scruples.[1] Many points of *doctrine*, indeed, that may fairly be regarded as non-essential, it may be both allowable and wise for a Church to leave at large, and pronounce no decision on them; allowing each Minister, if he thinks fit, to put forth his own exposition *as* the result of his own judgment, and not as a decision of the Church. But it is not so, in matters even intrinsically indifferent, where Church-*discipline* is concerned. A Minister ought to be as seldom as possible left in the predicament of *not knowing what he ought to do* in a case that comes before him. And though it is too much to expect from a Church composed of fallible men that its decisions on every point should be such as to obtain universal *approbation* as the very best, it is but fair to require that it should at least *give* decisions, according to the best judgment of its Legislators, on points which, in each particular case that arises, *must* be decided in one way or another.

That so many points of this character should in our own Church be left in a doubtful state, is one out of the many evils resulting from the want of a Legislative Government for the Church: which for more than a century has had none,[2] except the Civil Legislature; a Body as unwilling, as it is unfitted, to exercise any such functions. Such certainly was not the state of things designed or contemplated by our Reformers; and I cannot well understand the consistency of those who are perpetually eulogizing the Reformers, their principles and proceedings, and yet so completely run counter to them in a most fundamental point, as to endeavour to prevent, or not endeavour to promote, the establishment of a Church-government; which no one can doubt *they* at least regarded as a thing essential to the well-being, if not to the permanent existence, of a Church.[3]

---

[1] See *Appeal on behalf of Church-government*, reprinted in Bishop Dickinson's *Remains*.

[2] See *Case of Occasional Days and Prayers*, by John Johnson, A.M. Vicar of Cranbrook, in the Diocese of Canterbury.

[3] See *Speech on presenting a Petition from the Diocese of Kildare, with Appendix*, reprinted in a volume of *Charges and other Tracts*.

Some however have urged "the paucity of *new enactments* by Convocation, as a proof of the inutility of a Church-government.

"The constitution, or the proceedings, of the Convocation, I will not undertake to vindicate. But it certainly is a great mistake to suppose that the proper business of a Legislative body is *to make laws.* Its business is, to judge whether there be or be not, in each case, any *need* for a new enactment; and to make such enactments, then, and then only, when there *is* such need; and to frame them as far as possible in such a manner that there shall very seldom be a fresh necessity for alteration.

" Most persons I conceive would regard Parliament not a less but a more-efficient Legislature if it passed much fewer Acts than it does, and framed them with so much more care that there should not be (as now) a necessity for fresh legislation on the same points every Session ;—for ' An Act to amend an Act,' &c. in a most perplexing series.

"The occasions for the exercise of a certain power may be very few, and yet the existence of the power not the less important; because when such an occasion does arise, (and it is the *more likely* to arise, if there be no provision to meet the emergency) the consequences of not being prepared for it may be most disastrous. If any one should be so wearied with the monotonous ' all's well' of the nightly guardians of a Camp, hour after hour, and night after night, as to conclude that their service was superfluous, and accordingly to dismiss them, how much real danger, and how much unnecessary apprehension would be the result!

" It is to be observed however, that, in almost every department of life, the want of government, or of good government, where such want has *very long* existed, will often be less clearly perceived and less complained of, than in proportion to the actual extent of the evil. When indeed the business of a State, or a Diocese, or a Parish has been for some time efficiently conducted, and then negligence succeeds to activity and care, every one is struck with the amount of business left undone, or imperfectly done, and complaints are likely to arise. But where neglect has *long* existed, business seems, as it were, to dispose of itself, and wear away spontaneously; like a stream whose regular channel is choked, and which accordingly diffuses itself around till it forms a stagnant marsh, without any outlet but evaporation.

"If you look to any department of Government, or to any Parish or Diocese, that has long been left to the management of apathetic or inefficient persons, you will usually find that there are few or no complaints; because complaints having long since been found vain, will have long since ceased to be made: there will be no great arrears of business undone, and of applications unanswered; because business will not have been brought before those who it is known will not transact it; nor applications made, to which no answer can be hoped for: abuses, and defects, and evils of various kinds, which ought to have been prevented or remedied, men will have learned to submit to as to visitations of Providence; having been left without redress till they have at length forgotten that any redress is due, or is possible: and this stagnation will have come to be regarded as the natural state of things.

"Hence, it will often happen that in a Parish for instance, where for a long time very little has been done, it will appear at first sight as if there were in fact very little to do: the spiritual wants of members of the Church not appearing to be unattended to, because many persons will have *ceased* to be members of the Church, and many others will be unconscious that they have any spiritual wants.

" And in a Church accordingly that has been long without an efficient government, the want of such government will often be very inadequately perceived, from its not even occurring to men to consider whether the enormous increase of Dissent, of internal discord, and of indifference to the Church, are evils which it comes within the province of a government in any degree to prevent or mitigate."[1]

" With those who maintain that the present is *not the best* time,—on account of the violence of contending parties—for the restoration of a Church-government, I so far agree, that I am convinced it would have been *much better* to have taken the step eleven years ago; before the excitement caused by one of those parties had arisen; and yet better, some years earlier still, when the removal of religious disabilities first left the Church destitute of any Legislature consisting exclusively of its own members: and that again, a still earlier period would have been preferable, when

---

[1] This, and another passage in this Note, are extracted from *Thoughts on Church-government*.

considerable attention was for a time attracted to a work on the subject, by a person, then, and now, holding the office of Archdeacon.

"But it is far from being sufficient,—as seems to be the notion of some persons—to show that the present is not the *fittest conceivable* occasion for taking a certain step. Besides this, it is requisite to show,—not merely that a better occasion may be *imagined*,—or that a better occasion is *past ;*—that the Sybilline Books might have been purchased cheaper *some time ago ;*—but that a more suitable occasion is likely to arise *hereafter :* and *how soon;* and also, that the mischief which may be *going on during the interval* will be more than compensated by the superior suitableness of that future occasion ; in short, that it will have been worth waiting for. And in addition to all this, it is requisite to show also the probability that when this golden opportunity shall arise, men will be more *disposed to take advantage* of it than they have heretofore appeared to be ;—that they will not again fall into apathetic security and fondness for indefinite procrastination.

"This last point is as needful to be established as any; for it is remarkable that those who deprecate taking any step *just now,* in these times of extraordinary excitement, did not, on those former occasions, come forward to propose taking advantage of a comparatively calmer state of things. They neither made any call, nor responded to the call made by others.

"And indeed all experience seems to show—comparing the apathy on the subject which was so general at those periods, with the altered state of feeling now existing,—that a great and pressing emergency, and *nothing else,* will induce men to take any step in this matter; and that a period of dissension and perplexing difficulty, is, though not, *in itself,* the most suitable occasion for such a step, yet—constituted as human nature is,—the best, because the *only* occasion on which one can hope that it will be taken.

"When the valley of Martigny in Switzerland was threatened (about twenty-five years ago) with a frightful deluge from the bursting of a lake formed by a glacier which had dammed up a river, the inhabitants were for some time not sufficiently alarmed to take steps for averting the danger, by cutting channels to let off the water. They cannot therefore be said to have chosen *the best time* for commencing their operations; for had they begun earlier,—as soon as ever the dam was formed—the work would have been much easier, and probably all damage would have been prevented. As it was, they had to encounter much difficulty, and after all were but partially successful; for the undrained portion of the lake did at length burst the barrier, and considerable damage ensued; perhaps a fourth part of what *would* have taken place had things been left to themselves. But they were wise in not deferring their operations yet longer, in the hope that matters would mend spontaneously, when they saw that the evil was daily increasing. And after having mitigated in a great degree the calamity that did ensue, they took measures to provide against the like in future.

"Still however we must expect to be told by many, that, sooner or later, matters will come right spontaneously if left untouched;—that, *in time*, though we cannot tell how soon, a period of extraordinary excitement is sure to be succeeded by one of comparative calm. In the meantime it is forgotten at *what cost* such spontaneous restoration of tranquillity is usually purchased—how much the fire will have consumed before it shall have burnt out of itself. The case is very similar to what takes place in the natural body: the anguish of acute inflammation, when left to itself, is succeeded by the calm of a mortification: a limb is amputated, or drops off; and the body—but no longer the whole body—is restored to a temporary ease, at the expense of a mutilation. Who can say that a large proportion of those who are now irrecoverably alienated from the Church, might not have been at this moment sound members of it, had timely steps been taken, not, by any departure from the principles of our Reformers, but by following more closely the track they marked out for us?

"If the ultimate result of the present state of things should be—as there seems reason to apprehend—that a considerable number of persons fall away to the Church of Rome,—a far greater number, to infidelity or indifference,—and again, a great number to some dissenting sects,—we shall be told, I suppose, that the Church—that is, what remains of it—has regained tranquillity."—Ubi SOLITUDINEM faciunt, PACEM appellant.

Again, I have heard alleged the apprehension that such a Church-government as would be probably appointed would be likely to be *objectionable ;*—would probably be a *bad* one. I have no doubt of this; if by "bad" be meant *faulty.* In this sense, I am convinced that no government, civil or ecclesiastical, ever existed, or will exist, that is not "*bad.*" All governments being formed and administered by fallible men, it would be absurd to look for any that shall be exempt from errors, both in plan and in execution.[1] But the important question, and that which alone is really to the present purpose, is, whether it is likely a Government should be established that is *worse* than the absence of government.

As for the specific objections entertained against a Church-government, I believe the particular evils most commonly apprehended from the establishment of one, are these two : the conferring of an excessive power on the *Clergy,* who, it is hastily assumed, are to be sole Governors of the Church; and the predominance, in any Assembly to which the supreme power might be entrusted, of some one of the exclusive and violent parties existing in the Church ; who would accordingly, it is concluded, establish and enforce such regulations as would drive out of its Communion a large portion of its members.

The former of the above objections will disappear, I think, on a very moderate degree of reflection. The idea that all ecclesiastical government must of course be vested in the Clergy, arises, partly perhaps, from the common error of using the terms "Church" and "Clergy" as synonymous, partly, from men's recollecting that the *Convocation* (of which the shadow still remains) consisted of clergy, and forgetting that it had not the government of the Church *solely,* but conjointly with the King and the Parliament ;—that Parliament consisted of *members* indeed, but not of *ministers* of the Church ; and that the Prayer-book does not rest on the sole authority of Convocation, but is part and parcel of an Act of Parliament. And whether we look to the actual condition of our own Church, in which the appointment to all the Bishoprics, and to most of the Parishes, is in lay-hands, or to the off-shoot of our Church in the United States, which is governed partly by lay-members, we cannot consider it as anything unprecedented that the Laity should have a share in Ecclesiastical government.

---

[1] "Erunt vitia, donec homines."

In truth, nothing can be more unlikely than that either the Clergy should think of excluding the Laity, or the Laity, themselves, from all voice in ecclesiastical regulations.

The other apprehension,—that of a complete preponderance of some extreme party,—arises, I conceive, from not taking into account the influence which, in every Assembly, and every Society, is always exercised,—except in some few cases of very extraordinary excitement, and almost of temporary disorganization, by those who are in a *minority*. It might appear at first sight—and such is usually the expectation of a child of ordinary intelligence, and of all those who are deficient in an intelligent study of history, or observation of what is passing in the world,—that whatever Party might in any meeting or in any Community, obtain a *majority*, or in whatever other way, a *superiority*, would be certain to carry out their own principles to the utmost, with a total disregard of all the rest; so that in a Senate for instance, consisting, suppose, of 100 members, a majority, whether of 51 to 49, or of 70 to 30, or of 95 to 5, would proceed in all respects as if the others had no existence: and that no *mutual concessions* or compromises could take place except between parties exactly balanced. In like manner a person wholly ignorant of Mechanics might suppose that a body acted on by several unequal forces in different directions would obey altogether the strongest, and would move in the direction of that; instead of moving, as we know it ordinarily does, in a direction not coinciding with any one of them.

And experience shows that in human affairs as well as in Mechanics, such expectations are not well founded. If no tolerably wise and good measures were ever carried except in an Assembly where there was a complete predominance of men sufficiently enlightened and public-spirited to have a decided preference for those measures above all others, the world would, I conceive, be much worse governed than it really is.

No doubt, the larger the proportion of judicious and patriotic individuals, the better for the Community; but it seems to be the appointment of Providence that the prejudices, and passions, and interests of different men should be so various as not only to keep one another somewhat in check, but often to bring about, or greatly help to bring about, *mixed* results, often far preferable to anything devised or aimed at by *any* of the parties.

The British Constitution, for instance, no intelligent reader of history would regard as wholly or chiefly the work of men fully sensible of the advantages of a government so mixed and balanced. It was in great measure the result of the efforts, partially neutralizing each other, of men who leaned, more or less, some of them towards pure Monarchy, and others towards Republicanism. And again, though no one can doubt how great an advance (it is as yet only an *advance*) in the principles of religious *toleration*, and of making a final appeal to *Scripture alone*, is due to the Reformation, yet the Reformers were slow in embracing these principles. They were at first nearly as much disposed as their opponents to force their own interpretations of Scripture on every one, and to call in the Magistrate to suppress heresy by force. But not being able to agree among themselves *whose* interpretation of Scripture should be received as authoritative, and *who* should be entrusted with the Sword that was to extirpate heresy, compromises and mutual concessions gradually led more and more to the *practical* adoption of principles whose theoretical truth and justice is, even yet, not universally perceived.[1]

And similar instances may be found in every part of History. Without entering into a detailed examination of the particular mode in which, on each occasion, a superior party is influenced by those opposed to them,—either from reluctance to drive them to desperation, or otherwise,—certain it is, that, looking only to the results,—the practical working of any Government,—in the long run and in the general course of its measures,—we do find something corresponding to the composition of forces in Mechanics; and we find oftener than not, that the course actually pursued is better (however faulty) than could have been calculated from the character of the greater part of those who administer the Government. The wisest and most moderate, even when they form but a small minority, are often enabled amidst the conflict of those in opposite extremes, to bring about decisions, less wise and just indeed than they themselves would have desired, but far better than those of either of the extreme parties.

Of course we are not to expect the same exact uniformity of effects in human affairs as in Mechanics. It is not meant that each decision of every Assembly or Body of men will necessarily be the precise "resultant" (as it is called in Natural Philosophy)

---

[1] See *Appendix* to *Essay I.*

of the several forces operating,—the various parties existing in the Assembly. Some one or two votes will occasionally be passed, by a majority—perhaps by no very large majority—in utter defiance of the sentiments of the rest. But in the long run,—in any *course* of enactments or proceedings—some degree of influence will seldom fail to be exercised by those who are in a minority. This influence, again, will not always correspond, in kind, and in degree, with what takes place in Mechanics. For instance, in the material world, the impulses which keep a body *motionless* must be exactly *opposite*, and exactly *balanced*: but in human affairs, it will often happen that there may be a considerable majority in favour of taking some step, or making some enactment, yet a disagreement as to some details will give a preponderance to a smaller party who are against any such step. When the majority, for example, of a Garrison are disposed to make an attack on the besiegers, but are not agreed as to the time and mode of it, the decision may be on the side of a minority who deem it better to remain on the defensive. Accordingly, it is matter of common remark that a "Council of War" rarely ends in a resolution to fight a battle.

The results of this cause are sometimes evil, and sometimes, —perhaps more frequently—good. Many troublesome and pernicious restrictions and enactments, as well as some beneficial ones, are in this way prevented.

And again the *delay* and *discussion* which ensue when powerful parties are at all nearly balanced, afford an opening for arguments: and this, on the whole, and in the long run, gives an advantage—more or less, according to the state of intellectual culture and civilization—to the most wise and moderate,—in short, to those (even though but a small portion, numerically, of the Assembly) who have the best arguments on their side. Some, in each of the opposed parties, may thus be influenced by reason, who would not have *waited* to *listen* to reason, but for the check they receive from each other. And thus it will sometimes happen that a result may ensue even better than could have been calculated from the mere mechanical computation of the acting forces.

The above views are the more important, because any one who does not embrace them, will be likely, on contemplating any wise institution or enactment of *former times*, to be thrown into

T 2

indolent despondency, if he find, as he often will, that the majority of those around us do not seem to come up to the standard which those institutions and enactments appear to him to imply. He takes for granted that the whole, or the chief part, of the members of those Assemblies, &c., in which such and such measures were carried, must have been men of a corresponding degree of good sense, and moderation, and public spirit: and perceiving, (as he thinks) that an Assembly of such men could not now be found, he concludes that wisdom and goodness (in Governments at least) must have died with our ancestors; or at least that no good is *at present* to be hoped from any Government. And yet perhaps the truth will be that the greater part of the very Assemblies whose measures he is admiring may have consisted of men of several parties, each of which would, *if left entirely to itself*, have made a much worse decision than the one actually adopted; and *that one* may have been such, as, though not actually to coincide with, yet most nearly to approach to the opinions of the wisest and best members of the Assembly, though those may have been but a small minority. And it may be therefore, that he may have around him the materials of an Assembly not at all inferior in probity or intelligence to that which he is contemplating with despairing admiration.

To apply what has been said to the case now before us; it does seem to me that in a Church-Government established on any tolerably fair and natural principles, though we must calculate on such imperfections as must attend every thing wherein imperfect man is concerned, there would be no reason to apprehend *more* imperfections than the best *civil* Government is liable to, (which every one admits to be on the whole a most important benefit) or than are to be found in the Ecclesiastical Government of the American Episcopalians; which though administered by fallible mortals like ourselves, is found, on the whole, to work very satisfactorily.

To expect that any extreme party would exercise such uncontrolled sway as materially to corrupt or subvert the Church, would be against all experience.

Suppose for instance that the principal legislative power of some Church were lodged in some Body of men the majority of whom were attached, more or less, to two or more Parties, entertaining extreme views: one, suppose, leaning a good deal towards the system of the Greek and Romish Churches, another towards that of the Puritans, &c. It would argue, I think, great ignorance of the lessons of History to conclude that one or other of these parties must carry out their own views in the most unmitigated excess, and that the only question would be, *which* of the Parties would succeed in completely crushing the other, and would thenceforward domineer over, and rigidly coerce, or expel all other Members of the Church. The conclusion warranted by analogy would, I think, be that the opposite extremes would temper and partially neutralize each other;—that the moderate and judicious portion of the Assembly, and who were themselves the most exempt from party bias, would persuade the least *immoderate* of each party to make some concessions for the sake of peace, and to forego some of the most unreasonable of their requisitions;—that these mediators, by supporting what was right, and opposing what was wrong, in each party (for almost every party has something of each) would go a good way towards ultimately rejecting the worst part, and retaining the best part, of each proposal:—and that the final result would be, that many points would be left at large, which would have most probably been determined in an objectionable way by either party if left wholly unchecked; and that other points, (such as require to be determined one way or another in order to avoid future dissension) would be determined on wiser and better principles than the greater part of the Assembly would, in the first instance, have adopted; while an opening would remain for continual progress in the removal of such defects, and the adoption of such improvements, as experience and reflection might point out.

And it may be added—what is, in practice, a very important consideration—that in any *new* enactment or institution, whatever defects and errors may exist, men readily discover and willingly set themselves to remedy. The evils, on the other hand, or imperfections, of any state of things which people have been *long accustomed* to, even when amounting to the most crying abuses and grossest absurdities, they are slow to perceive, still slower to acknowledge, and slowest of all to remedy. As I have elsewhere observed, though "it is commonly and truly said, when any *new and untried* measure is proposed, that we cannot fully estimate the inconveniences it may lead to in practice; this is, we may be assured, even still more the case with any system which has *long been in operation*. The evils to which it may contribute, and the obstacles it may present to the attainment of any good, are partly overlooked or lightly regarded, on account of their familiarity, partly attributed to such other causes as perhaps really do co-operate in producing the same effects, and ranked along with the unavoidable alloys of human happiness, the inconveniences from which no human policy can entirely exempt us. In some remote and unimproved districts, if you complain of the streets of a town being dirty and dark, as those of London were for many ages, the inhabitants tell you that the nights are cloudy and the weather rainy: as for their streets, they are just *such as they have long been ;* and the expedient of paving and lighting has occurred to nobody. The ancient Romans had, probably, no idea that a civilized community could exist without slaves. That the same work can be done much better and cheaper by freemen, and that their odious system contained the seeds of the destruction of their empire, were truths which, familiarized as they were to the then existing state of society, they were not likely to suspect. 'If you allow of no plundering,' said an astonished Mahratta chief to some English officers, 'how is it possible for you to maintain such fine armies as you bring into the field?' He and his ancestors, time out of mind, had doubtless been *following their own footsteps* in the established routine; and had accordingly never dreamed that pillage is inexpedient as a source of revenue, or even one that can possibly be dispensed with. *Recent* experiment, indeed, may bring to light and often exaggerate the defects of a new system; but *long familiarity* blinds us to those very defects."[1]

"But it is quite otherwise with anything recently introduced. As we find men tolerating, in houses they have long inhabited, the inconvenience of some ill-placed door, or window, or passage, when the remedy would be easy, though, in a newly-built house, if any like inconvenience were found, an alteration would be made instantly, so it is in legislation, and in all human affairs. While the most inconvenient and absurd laws are suffered to remain unchanged for successive generations, hardly an Act is passed, that any defects in it are not met by 'Acts to amend' it, in the next, and in succeeding Sessions."

---

[1] *First Letter to Earl Grey,* pp. 55, 56.

The practical inference,—and it is a highly important one—is, that when any existing law or institution that is in itself bad, is remedied, even in a mode that is far from satisfactory, we ought not to be disheartened, but to look forward with cheering hope to a *remedy of the remedy*,—a removal of the newly-introduced evils,—as a change far more easily to be brought about than the *first* change.

Those who remember the University of Oxford at the commencement of this century, when in fact it hardly deserved the name of a University,—who remember with what difficulty, and after what long delay, the first statute for Degree-Examinations was introduced—how palpable were the defects of that Statute, and how imperfectly it worked,—and lastly, how easily in comparison these defects were, one by one, remedied, and successive improvements from time to time introduced,—such persons must have profited little by experience, if they deprecate the application of any remedy to such a gross and glaring evil as the want of a Church-government, for fear the remedy should not be such, in the first essay, as to meet their wishes.

The same may be said in respect of the appointment of any *new kinds* of Functionaries, as compared with those whose offices have long existed. As civilization advances, public opinion requires more and more of purity and regard to the public good in the appointment of public Functionaries, and in the conduct of those appointed. But this is incomparably more seen in the case of offices which are themselves of recent institution. Assistant-Commissioners under the New Poor-Law,—Superintendents and other Officers of National Education—and the like,—are expected to be appointed purely on the ground of superior fitness. The least shadow of a suspicion of favouritism, in the appointment even of a person confessedly *fit*, if there be a doubt whether one might not have been found still *more* fit, raises the greatest alarm and clamour, even in those who, in disposing of Livings, Bishopricks, or other long-established situations, however important, never so much as think of waiving—nor are by the Public expected to waive,—all personal and political considerations; and who take merit to themselves if the persons they appoint are not absolutely *un*fit.

"I have seen reproaches full of scornful exultation cast on

Protestants for having recourse, when treating of the subject of Church-government, to reasonings drawn from general views of Human Nature, and to illustrations from secular affairs: and for calculating what are likely to be the decisions of a Synod so and so constituted, without adverting to the promises of divine presence and protection to the Church, and without expressing confidence of providential interpositions to secure it from discord, error, and other evils.

"This kind of language has, at the first glance, a plausible air; and is well-calculated,—one cannot but think, designed—to impose on pious and well-intentioned but ignorant, weak, and unreflecting minds among the multitude. But a sober examination will show it to be either wholly irrelevant to the matter in hand, or else a mere groundless pretence.

"It is indeed true that the Lord has promised to be with his People 'even unto the end of the world,' and that 'the Gates of Hell' (*i. e.* death) 'shall not prevail against his Church;' that is, that Christianity shall never become extinct. And his 'Spirit which helpeth our infirmities' will doubtless be granted to such as sincerely exert themselves in his cause: though not necessarily so as to crown those exertions with such complete success, as, we know, was not granted to the Apostles themselves. Our efforts, however, in that cause, whether He in his unsearchable wisdom shall see fit to make them a greater or a less bene t) others, will doubtless, as far as regards ourselves, be accepted by Him. And a pious confidence in whatever God has really promised, Protestants do not fail to inculcate on suitable occasions.

"But when the question is as to the probable results of such and such a procedure in a Synod, and as to the measures likely to be adopted by a Government so and so constituted, it would manifestly be irrelevant to dwell on those general promises of the divine blessing. If there were a question what means should be used to protect a certain district from hurtful inundations, no one would think of cutting short the discussion by a reference to the promise made to Noah, that the whole Earth should never again be laid waste by a deluge. It is evident therefore that the reproaches I have alluded to must be understood as having reference to (that which alone is pertinent to the present question) confidence in a promise of supernatural interference to secure the Church for ever from strife, schism, and corruption.

"And certainly if we *had* received any such promise, all apprehensions, all calculations of probabilities,—all reasonings from the analogy of other human transactions, would be superseded; and we should have only to 'stand still and see the salvation of God.'

"But every one, except the grossly ignorant and unthinking, must be well aware that no such promise has ever been *fulfilled*, and consequently (if the Scriptures are to be taken as a record of divine truth) that none such was ever *made*.

"We find the Apostle Paul declaring that 'there must needs be heresies, that they who are approved may be made manifest;' we find him labouring to repress the irregularities and party spirit which even in his own time had crept into the Church of Corinth; and warning the Elders of Ephesus and Miletus to 'take heed, because after his departure grievous wolves would enter into the fold.' Corruptions in doctrine, disorders, dissension, and insubordination, are evils of which he is continually giving notice to his People as what they must be prepared to encounter.

"And when we look to the ecclesiastical history of subsequent Ages—exhibiting the sad spectacle of contests almost equally dividing the Church, between the Arians, for instance, and the Athanasians, on points of doctrine, and between the Donatists and their opponents, on a question of ecclesiastical Polity,—besides the mutual anathemas of the Eastern and Western Churches, and besides all the cabals, and intrigues, and secular motives and evil passions, which have notoriously found their way into Councils and Conclaves, and ecclesiastical Courts—when we contemplate all this, we see but too well what reason the Apostle had for his warnings.

"But there is no need in the present case to resort to ancient history. The very existence of *Protestants* (to say nothing of the Greek Church) is sufficient to nullify, in respect of the Church of Rome at least, the notion of an exemption from error and from schism being promised to *that* as to the Universal or Catholic Church. For the Church of Rome claims all professing Christians as properly belonging to it; considering Protestants as children, though disobedient children;—subjects though revolted subjects. The very rise, therefore, and continued existence, of Protestantism, proves the non-existence in the Catholic Church (if the Church of Rome be supposed such) of any immunity from heresy and schism. And if it be attempted to avoid this conclusion by allowing that Protestants and members of the Greek Church are *not* to be regarded as in any way belonging to the Church of Rome, then, the pretensions of that Church to be *the Catholic* (*i. e.* Universal) Church, must be given up.

"Whatever plausibility therefore there may appear at first sight in the pretensions *separately* taken, of that Church, on the one hand to perfect purity of doctrine and unity, and on the other hand to Universality, it is evident that both *conjointly* cannot be maintained with even any show of reason. Either the one or the other must be abandoned.[1] If Protestants and members of the Greek, the Armenian, and other Churches, do *not* belong to the Romish Church, it cannot be *Universal;* if (which is what its advocates actually maintain) all Christians do belong to it, then, it manifestly is not exempt from *divisions*, and contrariety of doctrine. It is in vain (as far as the present question is concerned) to urge that the doctrine and procedure of Protestants, &c. are *condemned* by the authorities of the Church of Rome, and by all its *sound* members. For an *exemption* from a certain evil must consist, not, in its being *censured* when it arises, but in its *not arising* at all. Indeed it would be very easy,—and also quite nugatory,—for any Church whatever to set up the boast that its doctrines are received by all,—except those who dissent from them; and that all submit to its authority,—except those who refuse submission.

" The extraordinary Providence therefore which is boasted of as securing the true Church from division and from error, and which Protestants are reproached with not trusting to or claiming, has evidently no existence in the very Church to which those who utter the reproach belong. And one can hardly doubt that they must themselves be aware of this ; and that when they speak, in a tone of exulting confidence, of the miraculous exemption of their Church from the inroads of false doctrine and dissension, they are only seeking to quiet the minds of the unthinking Vulgar with a delusive consolation.

" How far this kind of language may work an opposite effect on the minds of the more educated Classes,—how far the great

---

[1] They are evidently on opposite sides of the Thaumatrope. See *Logic*, B. iii. § 11.

prevalence of infidelity among those Classes on the Continent may be accounted for by their continually hearing (from those who, they will conclude, ought to know what their own Scriptures say) of *promises* having been made to the Church, which, it is evident, as a matter of experience, have *not* been fulfilled, is an inquiry into which I will not now enter. My own conviction is that every kind of pious fraud is as much at variance, ultimately, with sound policy, as it is with christian principle."

Lastly, in addition to the foregoing considerations, another, which ought not to be lost sight of, is, that for any evils which *might* be produced through the fault of Legislators, *those Legislators* would be *responsible:* while for the evils (not, which *may* arise, but which are *actually existing*, notorious, and grievous,) caused by the *want* of a Legislature, every Prelate, every Minister, and every member of the Church is responsible, who has it in his power to do anything—much or little—towards the remedy of that want, and neglects to do his utmost.[1]

NOTE O, p. 225.

IT might be added that, among those who express the greatest dread and detestation of "German Neology,"—"German Philosophy,"—the "daring speculations of the Germans," &c., are to be found some of that class of Anglican Divines, whose doctrines apparently correspond the most closely (as far as we can judge respecting two confessedly mystic schools) with those of that very Neology. The very circumstance itself that both *are* schools of Mysticism,—that both parties have one system for the mass of mankind, and another—whether expressed in different language, or in the same words understood in a totally different sense—for the initiated,—this affords a presumption, when there are some points of coincidence in the doctrine *divulged*, that a still further agreement may be expected in the *reserved* doctrines.

As the advocates of reserve among us speak of not intending to inculcate generally such conclusions as a logical reasoner will correctly deduce by following out their principles, and again,

---

[1] See *Thoughts on Church-government*, in Charges of 1843 and 1844.

speak of an ordinary reader being likely to " miss their real meaning, by not being aware of the *peculiar sense* in which they employ terms," so, those German Transcendentalists whom I allude to,—whose system of Theology—or rather of Atheology—is little else than a new edition of the Pantheism of the ancient Heathen Philosophers, of the Brahmins, and the Buddhists,—use a similar double-meaning language. They profess Christianity, and employ profusely such terms as a " God," " Faith," " Incarnation," " Miracle," " Immortality," &c., attaching to these words, a meaning quite remote from what is commonly understood by them. Their " God" is the God of Pantheism; not a personal agent, but a certain vital principle diffused through the Material Universe, and of which every human soul is a portion; which is at death to be reabsorbed into the infinite Spirit, and become just what it was before birth,[1] exactly according to the ancient system of philosophy described by Virgil : " Mens agitat molem et toto se corpore miscet; Inde hominum pecudumque genus," &c. And the other terms alluded to are understood by them in a sense no less wide from the popular acceptation.

Both parties again, agree in deprecating all employment of reasoning in matters pertaining to religion : both decry the historical evidence of Christianity, and discourage as profane, all appeal to evidence; and both disparage Miracles considered as a proof of the divine origin of Christianity; alleging that *every* event that occurs is equally a miracle; meaning therefore exactly what in ordinary language would be expressed by saying that *nothing* is miraculous.

Other coincidences may be observed; such as the strong desire manifested by both parties to explain away, or soften down the line of demarcation between what ordinary Christians call the *Scriptures,* and everything subsequent;—between what *we* call the christian Revelation, considered as an historical transaction recorded in the New Testament; and any pretended after-revelation, or improvement, or completion, or perfect development, of " the system of true Religion." To Christianity *as a Revelation completed* in our sacred *books,* both parties, more or less openly, according to circumstances, confess their objection.

And it is remarkable that even the vehement censures pro-

---

[1] See *Essay I*. First Series.

nounced by one of these schools on the speculations of the other, is far from being inconsistent with their fundamental agreement in principles. For of the German Neologists themselves, some of the leading writers strongly condemn the rashness, with which some conclusions have been openly stated by others, of the same school, and confessedly proceeding on principles fundamentally the same.[1]

If any one therefore who belongs to a school of mystical reserve, should be suspected, in consequence of a remarkable agreement between some of his acknowledged tenets and the German Neology, of a further degree of secret concurrence, beyond, perhaps, what he is really conscious of, he must not wonder at, or complain of such suspicion; nor expect at once to repel it by the strongest censure of those writers, and professed renunciation of their doctrines; unless he can also make up his mind to renounce likewise the system of a "Double doctrine" altogether, resolving, and proclaiming his resolution to speak henceforth "the truth, the whole truth, and nothing but the truth," respecting his religious tenets, and forswearing totally the practice of employing language "in a peculiar sense" different from what is ordinarily understood by it.

It is worth remarking, in reference to one of the points here touched on, that the peculiar phases of infidelity which are exhibited in the present day, furnish an additional objection (if any could be needed) to the system, advocated by some intelligent men, of making the profession of Christianity,—not of any particular form of it, but of Christianity generally—the indispensable and the sole qualification to entitle a man to the full rights of citizenship in what they call "a christian Country."

Of this system I have treated pretty largely in the Appendix to the first of the foregoing *Essays*, and also in the Appendix to the *Essays on the Dangers*, &c.

But the circumstance to which I am now adverting, is, that in the present day, antichristian and even atheistical writers—unlike their predecessors—generally profess to be Christians; and indeed sometimes obtain, or are proposed for, theological Professorships in christian Universities.

The proposed system, therefore, would admit to civil rights

---

[1] See Dr. West's Discourse on *Reserve*.

some who are much further removed from Christianity than some others whom it would exclude. A Mahometan, for instance, or a Jew, would be excluded, as not *calling* themselves Christians; though the one admits the true Messiahship of Jesus, his divine mission and his miraculous powers; and the other the divine character of the Old Testament; while Christians, so called, would be admitted, who resolve the whole Bible into a series of *Myths*, (or call it "ONE GREAT PARABLE,") and who deny not only the divine mission of Jesus or of Moses, but the very existence of *any* Being who *could* have given them such a mission.—[See *Scr. Revelations concerning Good and Evil Angels*, L. iv.]

INDEX

TO SOME OF THE PRINCIPAL WORDS.

	PAGE
AGREEABLE to Scripture, distinguished from what is based on Scripture, Essay II. § 26	169
Alliance of Church and State, Warburton's, Essay I. § 13	44
Altar, Essay II. § 14	111
American Episcopalian Church, Essay II. § 33, 198; and Note M	264
Angel, or Bishop, of a Church, Essay II. § 20	138
Anglican-Church, principles of, Essay II. §§ 24 and 43	157, 227
Antient, uncertainty in application of the title, Essay II. §§ 17 and 21	124, 142
Antiquity, pretended inspiration to be found in, Essay II. § 24	159
Apostles, no successors to, in apostolic office, Essay II. § 43, 228; and Note B	234
Appeal in behalf of Church-government, referred to, Appendix to Essay I.	49
Arnold, *Christian Life*, Essay I. § 13	46
Articles, authoritative declaration of our Church, Essay II. § 24	157
Augustine, his interpretation of Christ's disclaimer of a temporal kingdom, Essay I. § 10	29
Authority, ambiguity of the term, Essay II. § 22, 144; and Note I	257
Baptism, according to certain principles, ought to be *repeated* again and again, Essay II. § 30, 188; by laymen; questions relative to Note N	266
Bernard, *Abridgment of Vitringa*, Preface, p. v.; and Essay II. §§ 4 and 11	83, 101
Binding and Loosing, power of, what, Essay II. § 5	85
Bishop, each, originally Head of a distinct Church, Essay II. §§ 20 and 37	138, 207
Blasphemy, Jewish notion of, Essay I. § 6	18
Brydone, anecdote related by, Essay I. § 13	45
Bye-Laws [or Rules], Essay II. § 2	79

288 *Index.*

	PAGE
Canon of Scripture, not established by the authority of any one Church or Council, Note I	257
Catholic [or Universal] Church, supposed decisions of, Essay II. § 22	144
Christ, the, not expected by the Jews to be a *divine* person, Essay I. § 6	18
Christs, false; pretensions of, clear, to the Jews, Essay II. § 41	223
Christianity, a social religion, Essay II. § 1	75
Church, authority of, Essay II. § 23	156
— Universal, Essay II. § 22	144
— of England, Essay II. § 43	227
— government, Note N	266
— Principles, pretended, Essay II. § 20	137
Clement, Epistle of, Essay II. § 20; Note	140
Clergy, temptation to exalt unduly their office, Essay II. § 38	212
Coercion, not allowable in behalf of religion, Appendix to Essay I. and Essay II. § 32	194
Community [or Society] *spiritual* and *secular*, Essay I. § 12, 40, and Appendix to Essay I.; ordinary sense of, Essay II. § 2, 78; Jewish, Essay II. § 4	83
Conformable to Scripture. See *Agreeable.*	
Congregation [or Ecclesia], Essay II. § 9	94
Corinthian Church, apparently not under Episcopal government, when Rome was, Essay II. § 20; Note	140
Councils, supposed, Essay II. § 15	117
Creeds, why not found in the New Testament, Essay II. § 9	98
— on what ground received by our Church, Essay II. § 26	169
Croly's *Index to Tracts*, Essay II. § 38	212
D'Aubigné, *History of Reformation*, Note M	264
Dangers to Christianity, Essay on, referred to, Appendix to Essay I.	57
Deacons, supposed first appointment of, Essay II. § 11	102
Deposed Bishops and other Ministers, case of, Essay II. § 39	216
Descent, difficult for each Minister to trace his own, Essay II. § 30	181
Details, directions for, recorded in Scripture only in cases where it was plain they could not be meant to be of perpetual obligation, Essay II. § 11	101
Devout Gentiles, what, Essay II. § 9	95
Dickinson, Bp., Sermon by, Essay II. § 1	77
Dictionary, Theological, Rev. R. Eden's, Essay II. § 11, &c.	101
Divine origin, a phrase used ambiguously, Essay II. § 17	125

	PAGE
Donatists, schism of, Essay II. § 31	189
Double Doctrine, Essay II. § 19, 135; and Note O	285
Edinburgh Review, reference to, Appendix to Essay I.	62
Elders, ordination of Saul and Barnabas by, at Antioch, Essay II. § 15	118
Encyclopædia Metropolitana, extract from, Essay II. § 11	102
Episcopacy might have been retained by all the reformed Churches, Essay II. § 37	209
Erastianism, Note M	265
Essentials, according to our Church, are to be found in Scripture, Essay II. §§ 12 and 20	107, 137
— differences as to, Essay II. § 33	199
Excluded points, from Christianity, importance of, Essay II. § 16	121
Excommunication, not a *punishment* in the strict sense, Note A	232
— power of, inherent in a Society, Essay II. § 3	82
Faith, as described and inculcated by some, answers to the *want of faith* censured in the unbelieving Jews, Essay II. § 42	224
Father, God, the "proper" or "peculiar" (ἴδιος) Father of Jesus, Essay I. § 5	14
Fathers, references to, employed fallaciously, Essay II. § 22	144
Fighting for, religion, what properly so called, Appendix to Essay I.	62
Forgiveness, of offences against *God*, and against a *Community*, distinguished, Essay II. § 6	87
Glory [or Shechinah] of the Lord, Essay I. § 3	8
Gnostics, ancient and modern, Essay II. § 19	130
Goode, Rev. Mr., pamphlet by, Essay II. § 42	226
Government, of a Church, needful, Note N	267
Hampden, Dr., pretended elucidation of his *Bampton Lectures*, Essay II. § 28[1]	174
Hawkins, Dr., Sermon by, Note K	260
Hinds, Dr., *History of the Rise of Christianity*, Essay II. § 33	199
Hoare, Dean, Essay II. § 9	98
Hooker, his opinion of lay-baptism, Essay II. § 39, Note	219

---

[1] See Note to *Essay II.* § 28.

Human good, generally, how far the object of the political community, Essay I. § 12, 39; and Appendix to Essay I. - 51
Humility, false representation of, Essay II. § 42 - - 225

Idols of the Race, Bacon's, Appendix to Essay I. - - - 55
Index, to *Tracts for the Times*, Essay II. § 38, &c. - - - 212
Indistinctness, of statement, an advantage in the inculcation of some doctrines, Essay II. §§ 38 and 40 - - - 211, 219
Infallible guide, on earth, for future Churches in all Ages, would have been pointed out by the Apostles, had there been any, Essay II. § 15 - - - - - - - 119
Inspired men, proximity to, in time and place, no security against error, Note K - - - - - - - 261
Institutions, perpetual obligation of, not to be based on Tradition, Essay II. § 24 - - - - - - - - 160
Interpreter, of *Tradition*, is *Scripture*; not *vice versâ*, Note G 252
Intolerance, naturally the fruit of insincerity, Essay I. § 13 - 46
Irregularly [established] Churches, Essay II. § 32 - - - 191

Jewish Church, Essay II. § 4 - - - - - - - 83

Keys, power of, Essay II. § 7, 89; and Note B - - - - 237
King, in what sense Jesus was, Essay I. § 9 - - - - 24
— in what sense represented, Essay I. § 10 - - - 27
Kingdom of this world disclaimed, Essay I. § 10 - - - 29
— of Heaven announced, Essay II. § 1 - - - - 75

Latitudinarian, naturally intolerant, Essay I. § 13 - - - 45
Laymen, whether obliged to rely implicitly on the guidance of certain learned theologians, Essay II. § 21 - - - 141
Lenient exercise, *at first*, of usurped power, Essay II. § 25 - 165
Lightfoot, Note B - - - - - - - - - 235
Luther, his opinion of Christian Ministry, Note M - - - 264

Magistrate [civil], coercive power of, not to be exercised in behalf of Christianity, Essay I. § 12 - - - - 42
Majority, supposed rights of, Essay II. § 22 - - - - 149
Members, of a community, power of admitting or excluding, Essay II. § 2 - - - - - - - - - 81
Ministers [Christian], Church of England's notion of them, Essay II. § 19 - - - - - - - - - 129
Miraculous [Evidence], when needed, Essay II. § 19 - - - 131

Index. 291

Monopoly, of civil rights, by professors of a certain religion,
    Essay II. §§ 10 and 11 - - - - - - 99, 101
Mysticism, Note O - - - - - - - - 285

Name, peculiar Scriptural use of, Essay II. § 1 - - - - 77
Neology, German, its coincidence with the views of those who
    the most loudly declaim against it,[1] Note O - - 283
Non-jurors, schism of, Essay II. § 31 - - - - - 190

Obedience, distinguished from *deference*, Essay II. § 22 - - 151
Officers, requisite in a Community, Essay II. § 2 - - - 79
Omissions in Scripture, importance of. Essay II. § 8 - - - 93
One-ness [or Unity], not consisting in singleness of Church-
    government, Essay II. § 22 - - - - - - 147
Orders, holy. See *Ordination*.
Ordination, supposed sacramental character of, Essay II. §§ 30
    and 38, 181, 211; valid only when conferred by the power
    of a Community, Essay II. §§ 20 and 39 - - 137, 216

Paper currency, illustration from, Essay II. § 27 - - - 171
Penalties [or Punishments], Essay I. § 10, 31; II. § 6, 88; and
    Note A - - - - - - - - - 231
Peter, how far the chief of the Apostles, Essay II. § 7 - - 90
— Apostle of the devout Gentiles, Essay II. § 9 - - - 95
Pope, has no authority over the Anglican Church, Essay II. § 33 107
Powell, *Tradition unveiled*, Essay II. §§ 21, 40 - - - 141, 219
Power, distinct from *authority*, Note I - - - - - 257
— does not admit of degrees, Essay II. § 22 - - - 149
Preaching, proper meaning of the word, Essay II. § 2 - - 78
Priest, Essay II. § 14 - - - - - - - - 111
Primitive Churches, degree of deference due to, Note E - 247

Rationalists, German, Note O - - - - - - - 283
Reformers, Anglican, principles of, Essay II. §§ 23 and 43 - 153, 226
Religion, sophisms relative to, such as would not be endured, on
    any other subject, Essay II. §§ 32 and 41, 192, 222.
    What is properly fighting *for* our Religion, Appendix
    to Essay I. - - - - - - - - - 62

---

[1] See *Index to Tracts for the Times*, by the Rev. D. Croly, a work which should be in the hands of every theological student, whatever may be his opinion of the *Tracts*.

	PAGE
Remedies of *new* evils, easier, Note N	277
Reserve, system of, Essay II. § 28	173
— impious to attribute to our Lord, Essay I. § 11, 34; Statue, illustration from, Essay II. § 28	174
Right, *legal*, distinguished from *moral*, Essay II. § 37	206
Romish Church, supposed beginning of its apostasy, at the Council of Trent,[1] Essay II. § 34	201
Roman [Governors], motives of, Essay I. § 10	31
Sabbath, power over it claimed by Jesus, Essay I. § 5	14
— distinct from the Lord's Day, Essay II. § 29	177
Sacerdotal Priesthood, excluded from Christian Church, Essay II. § 14	113
Sacramental, ordination, supposed such, Essay II. § 38	211
Sacrifice, Essay II. § 14	111
Sanhedrim, limited power of, Essay I. § 1	4
Scepticism, not implied by absence of a claim to infallibility, Note L	262
Schism, Essay II. § 32	194
Scotch Episcopalian Church, Essay II. § 33, 197, and Note M	265
Scripture, distinction between what is *based* on, and what is merely *conformable* to, Essay II. § 26	169
Separation, a duty, or, a sin, Essay II. § 33	198
— when justifiable, Essay II. § 36	203
Social character of Christianity, Essay II. § 1	75
Society. See *Community*.	
Sojourners of the Dispersion, Essay II. § 9	96
Son of God, distinction between "*a* Son" and "*the* Son," Essay I. § 3	8
Standard [of Faith], the Scriptures so regarded by our Reformers, Essay II. § 23	155
Stanley, Bishop, speech in the House of Lords, referred to, Essay II. § 6	87
State, [or Political Community], proper office of, Appendix to Essay I. 50; common to the German Neologists and the Tractites, Note O	283
Succession, apostolical, distinction between an *individual* and a *class* of men, as to this point, Essay II. § 30, 184; what it really consists in, II. §§ 32 and 43	197, 228
Suppression, equivalent to alteration, Essay II. § 28	174

---

[1] See *Index to the Tracts for the Times*, by Rev. D. Croly.

	PAGE
Supremacy, of the Political Community, what, Appendix to Essay I.	52
Synagogue, origin of Christian Churches from, Essay II. § 9	94
Teaching [human], necessity of, Essay II. § 27	172
Temple, of Christ's body, Essay I. § 4, 12; None, literally, in the Christian Church, Essay II. § 14	111
Timothy ⎰ apparently temporary bishops, Essay II. § 20; Titus ⎱ Note	140
Tracts for the Times, Index to, Essay II. § 38	212
Tradition not to be "blended with Scripture," Essay II. § 25, 165; Scripture the Interpreter of Tradition, Note G	252
Transcendentalists [German], Note O	284
Trials [of our Lord], *two*, Essay I. § 1	4
Truth, in what sense Christ's was a Kingdom of, Essay I. § 9	24
Via media, mistake as to, Essay II. § 25	165
Vitringa, *on the Church and the Synagogue*, Essay II. § 9	96
Voluntary System, Essay II. § 37, 208; and Appendix to Essay I.	60
Warburton, *Alliance of Church and State*, Essay I. § 12	44
West, Dr., Discourse on *Reserve*, Essay II. §§ 19, 28, 135, 173; and Note O	285
Wild-beasts, illustration from the exposure to them of the early Christians, Essay II. § 28, Note	174
Wilson, *on the New Testament*, Essay I. § 6	17
Wisdom, province of, Essay II. § 37	207
— of the Anglican Reformers, Essay II. § 43	226
Worship of Christ, Essay I. § 4	9
Wotton, on the *Mishna*, Essay II. § 4	83
Zillerthal, people of, separatists from the Church of Rome, Essay II. § 36	205

LONDON:
PRINTED BY GEORGE PHIPPS, 13 & 14, TOTHILL STREET,
WESTMINSTER.

39 PATERNOSTER ROW, E.C.
LONDON, *August* 1875.

GENERAL LIST OF WORKS

PUBLISHED BY

MESSRS. LONGMANS, GREEN, AND CO.

	PAGE		PAGE
ARTS, MANUFACTURES, &c.	26	MENTAL & POLITICAL PHILOSOPHY	8
ASTRONOMY & METEOROLOGY	16	MISCELLANEOUS & CRITICAL WORKS	12
BIOGRAPHICAL WORKS	7	NATURAL HISTORY & PHYSICAL SCIENCE	18
CHEMISTRY & PHYSIOLOGY	24	POETRY & the DRAMA	35
DICTIONARIES & other BOOKS of REFERENCE	14	RELIGIOUS & MORAL WORKS	28
FINE ARTS & ILLUSTRATED EDITIONS	24	RURAL SPORTS, HORSE & CATTLE MANAGEMENT, &c.	36
		TRAVELS, VOYAGES, &c.	32
HISTORY, POLITICS, HISTORICAL MEMOIRS, &c.	1	WORKS of FICTION	34
		WORKS of UTILITY & GENERAL INFORMATION	37
INDEX	40 to 43		

HISTORY, POLITICS, HISTORICAL MEMOIRS, &c.

Journal of the Reigns of King George the Fourth and King William the Fourth.

By the late Charles Cavendish Fulke Greville, Esq.

Edited by Henry Reeve, Esq.

Fifth Edition. 3 vols. 8vo. price 36s.

The Life of Napoleon III. derived from State Records, Unpublished Family Correspondence, and Personal Testimony.

By Blanchard Jerrold.

Four Vols. 8vo. with numerous Portraits and Facsimiles. VOLS. I. and II. price 18s. each.

*** Vols. III. and IV. are in preparation.

A

Recollections and Suggestions, 1813–1873. By *John Earl Russell, K.G.*
New Edition, revised and enlarged. 8vo. 16s.

Introductory Lectures on Modern History delivered in Lent Term 1842; *with the Inaugural Lecture delivered in December* 1841. By the late Rev. Thomas Arnold, D.D.
8vo. price 7s. 6d.

On Parliamentary Government in England: its Origin, Development, and Practical Operation. By *Alpheus Todd.*
2 vols. 8vo. £1. 17s.

The Constitutional History of England since the Accession of George III. 1760–1870. By Sir Thomas Erskine May, K.C.B.
Fourth Edition. 3 vols. crown 8vo. 18s.

Democracy in Europe; a History. By Sir Thomas Erskine May, K.C.B.
2 vols. 8vo. [*In the press.*

The History of England from the Fall of Wolsey to the Defeat of the Spanish Armada. By *J. A. Froude, M.A.*
CABINET EDITION, 12 vols. cr. 8vo. £3. 12s.
LIBRARY EDITION, 12 vols. 8vo. £8. 18s.

The English in Ireland in the Eighteenth Century. By *J. A. Froude, M.A.*
3 vols. 8vo. £2. 8s.

The History of England from the Accession of James II. By Lord Macaulay.
STUDENT'S EDITION, 2 vols. cr. 8vo. 12s.
PEOPLE'S EDITION, 4 vols. cr. 8vo. 16s.
CABINET EDITION, 8 vols. post 8vo. 48s.
LIBRARY EDITION, 5 vols. 8vo. £4.

Critical and Historical Essays contributed to the Edinburgh Review. By the Right Hon. Lord Macaulay.
Cheap Edition, authorised and complete, crown 8vo. 3s. 6d.
STUDENT'S EDITION, crown 8vo. 6s.
PEOPLE'S EDITION, 2 vols. crown 8vo. 8s.
CABINET EDITION, 4 vols. 24s.
LIBRARY EDITION, 3 vols. 8vo. 36s.

Lord Macaulay's Works. Complete and uniform Library Edition. Edited by his Sister, Lady Trevelyan.
8 vols. 8vo. with Portrait, £5. 5s.

Lectures on the History of England from the Earliest Times to the Death of King Edward II. By *W. Longman, F.S.A.*
Maps and Illustrations. 8vo. 15s.

The History of the Life and Times of Edward III. By *W. Longman, F.S.A.*
With 9 Maps, 8 Plates, and 16 Woodcuts.
2 vols. 8vo. 28s.

History of England under the Duke of Buckingham and Charles the First, 1624–1628. By S. Rawson Gardiner, late Student of Ch. Ch.
2 vols. 8vo. with two Maps, 24s.

History of Civilization in England and France, Spain and Scotland. By Henry Thomas Buckle.
3 vols. crown 8vo. 24s.

A Student's Manual of the History of India from the Earliest Period to the Present. By Col. Meadows Taylor, M.R.A.S.
Second Thousand. Cr. 8vo. Maps, 7s. 6d.

Studies from Genoese History. By Colonel G. B. Malleson, C.S.I. Guardian to His Highness the Mahárájá of Mysore.
Crown 8vo. 10s. 6d.

The Native States of India in Subsidiary Alliance with the British Government; an Historical Sketch. With a Notice of the Mediatized and Minor States. By Colonel G. B. Malleson, C.S.I. Guardian to His Highness the Mahárájá of Mysore.
With 6 Coloured Maps, 8vo. price 15s.

The History of India from the Earliest Period to the close of Lord Dalhousie's Administration. By John Clark Marshman.
3 vols. crown 8vo. 22s. 6d.

Indian Polity; a View of the System of Administration in India. By Lieut.-Colonel George Chesney.
Second Edition, revised, with Map. 8vo. 21s.

Waterloo Lectures; a Study of the Campaign of 1815. By Colonel Charles C. Chesney, R.E.
Third Edition. 8vo. with Map, 10s. 6d.

Essays in Modern Military Biography. By Colonel Charles C. Chesney, R.E.
8vo. 12s. 6d.

The Imperial and Colonial Constitutions of the Britannic Empire, including Indian Institutions. By Sir E. Creasy, M.A.
With 6 Maps. 8vo. 15s.

The Oxford Reformers—John Colet, Erasmus, and Thomas More; being a History of their Fellow-Work. By Frederic Seebohm.
Second Edition. 8vo. 14s.

The New Reformation, a Narrative of the Old Catholic Movement, from 1870 to the Present Time; with an Historical Introduction.
By Theodorus.
8vo. price 12s.

The Mythology of the Aryan Nations.
By Geo. W. Cox, M.A. late Scholar of Trinity College, Oxford.
2 vols. 8vo. 28s.

A History of Greece.
By the Rev. Geo. W. Cox, M.A. late Scholar of Trinity College, Oxford.
Vols. I. and II. 8vo. Maps, 36s.

A School History of Greece to the Death of Alexander the Great.
By the Rev. George W. Cox, M.A. late Scholar of Trinity College, Oxford; Author of 'The Aryan Mythology' &c.
1 vol. crown 8vo. [In the press.

The History of the Peloponnesian War, by Thucydides.
Translated by Richd. Crawley, Fellow of Worcester College, Oxford.
8vo. 21s.

The Tale of the Great Persian War, from the Histories of Herodotus.
By Rev. G. W. Cox, M.A.
Fcp. 8vo. 3s. 6d.

Greek History from Themistocles to Alexander, in a Series of Lives from Plutarch.
Revised and arranged by A. H. Clough.
Fcp. 8vo. Woodcuts, 6s.

General History of Rome from the Foundation of the City to the Fall of Augustulus, B.C. 753—A.D. 476.
By the Very Rev. C. Merivale, D.D. Dean of Ely.
With 5 Maps, crown 8vo. 7s. 6d.

History of the Romans under the Empire.
By Dean Merivale, D.D.
8 vols. post 8vo. 48s.

The Fall of the Roman Republic; a Short History of the Last Century of the Commonwealth.
By Dean Merivale, D.D.
12mo. 7s. 6d.

The Sixth Oriental Monarchy; or the Geography, History, and Antiquities of Parthia. Collected and Illustrated from Ancient and Modern sources.
By Geo. Rawlinson, M.A.
With Maps and Illustrations. 8vo. 16s.

The Seventh Great Oriental Monarchy; or, a History of the Sassanians: with Notices Geographical and Antiquarian.
By Geo. Rawlinson, M.A.
8vo. with Maps and Illustrations.
[*In the press.*

Encyclopædia of Chronology, Historical and Biographical; comprising the Dates of all the Great Events of History, including Treaties, Alliances, Wars, Battles, &c. Incidents in the Lives of Eminent Men, Scientific and Geographical Discoveries, Mechanical Inventions, and Social, Domestic, and Economical Improvements.
By B. B. Woodward, B.A. and W. L. R. Cates.
8vo. 42s.

The History of Rome.
By Wilhelm Ihne.
Vols. I. and II. 8vo. 30s. Vols. III. and IV. in preparation.

History of European Morals from Augustus to Charlemagne.
By W. E. H. Lecky, M.A.
2 vols. 8vo. 28s.

History of the Rise and Influence of the Spirit of Rationalism in Europe.
By W. E. H. Lecky, M.A.
Cabinet Edition, 2 vols. crown 8vo. 16s.

Introduction to the Science of Religion: Four Lectures delivered at the Royal Institution; with two Essays on False Analogies and the Philosophy of Mythology.
By F. Max Müller, M.A.
Crown 8vo. 10s. 6d.

The Stoics, Epicureans, and Sceptics.
Translated from the German of Dr. E. Zeller, by Oswald J. Reichel, M.A.
Crown 8vo. 14s.

Socrates and the Socratic Schools.
Translated from the German of Dr. E. Zeller, by the Rev. O. J. Reichel, M.A.
Crown 8vo. 8s. 6d.

Sketch of the History of the Church of England to the Revolution of 1688. By T. V. Short, D.D. sometime Bishop of St. Asaph.
New Edition. Crown 8vo. 7s. 6d.

The Historical Geography of Europe. By E. A. Freeman, D.C.L.
8vo. Maps. [In the press.

Essays on the History of the Christian Religion. By John Earl Russell, K.G.
Fcp. 8vo. 3s. 6d.

The Student's Manual of Ancient History: containing the Political History, Geographical Position, and Social State of the Principal Nations of Antiquity. By W. Cooke Taylor, LL.D.
Crown 8vo. 7s. 6d.

The Student's Manual of Modern History: containing the Rise and Progress of the Principal European Nations, their Political History, and the Changes in their Social Condition. By W. Cooke Taylor, LL.D.
Crown 8vo. 7s. 6d.

The History of Philosophy, from Thales to Comte. By George Henry Lewes.
Fourth Edition, 2 vols. 8vo. 32s.

The Crusades. By the Rev. G. W. Cox, M.A.
Fcp. 8vo. with Map, 2s. 6d.

The Era of the Protestant Revolution. By F. Seebohm, Author of 'The Oxford Reformers.'
With 4 Maps and 12 Diagrams. Fcp. 8vo. 2s. 6d.

The Thirty Years' War, 1618–1648. By Samuel Rawson Gardiner.
Fcp. 8vo. with Maps, 2s. 6d.

The Houses of Lancaster and York; with the Conquest and Loss of France. By James Gairdner.
Fcp. 8vo. with Map, 2s. 6d.

Edward the Third. By the Rev. W. Warburton, M.A.
Fcp. 8vo. with Maps, 2s. 6d.

BIOGRAPHICAL WORKS.

Autobiography.
By *John Stuart Mill.*
8vo. 7s. 6d.

The Life and Letters of Lord Macaulay.
By his Nephew, G. Otto Trevelyan, M.P. for the Hawick District of Burghs.
2 vols. 8vo. [*In the press.*

Admiral Sir Edward Codrington, a Memoir of his Life; with Selections from his Private and Official Correspondence. Abridged from the larger work, and edited by his Daughter, Lady Bourchier.
With Portrait, Maps, &c. crown 8vo. price 7s. 6d.

Life and Letters of Gilbert Elliot, First Earl of Minto, from 1751 to 1806, when his Public Life in Europe was closed by his Appointment to the Vice-Royalty of India. Edited by the Countess of Minto.
3 vols. post 8vo. 31s. 6d.

Recollections of Past Life.
By Sir *Henry Holland,* Bart. M.D. F.R.S.
Third Edition. Post 8vo. 10s. 6d.

Isaac Casaubon, 1559-1614.
By Mark Pattison, Rector of Lincoln College, Oxford.
8vo. price 18s.

The Memoirs of Sir John Reresby, of Thrybergh, Bart. M.P. for York, &c. 1634-1689. Written by Himself. Edited from the Original Manuscript by James J. Cartwright, M.A. Cantab. of H.M. Public Record Office.
8vo. price 21s.

Biographical and Critical Essays, reprinted from Reviews, with Additions and Corrections.
By A. Hayward, Q.C.
Second Series, 2 vols. 8vo. 28s. Third Series, 1 vol. 8vo. 14s.

The Life of Isambard Kingdom Brunel, Civil Engineer.
By I. Brunel, B.C.L.
With Portrait, Plates, and Woodcuts. 8vo. 21s.

Lord George Bentinck; a Political Biography.
By the Right Hon. B. Disraeli, M.P.
New Edition. Crown 8vo. 6s.

The Life and Letters of the Rev. Sydney Smith. Edited by his Daughter, Lady Holland, and Mrs. Austin.
Crown 8vo. 2s. 6d. sewed; 3s. 6d. cloth.

Essays in Ecclesiastical Biography. By the Right Hon. Sir J. Stephen, LL.D.
Cabinet Edition. Crown 8vo. 7s. 6d.

Leaders of Public Opinion in Ireland; Swift, Flood, Grattan, O'Connell. By W. E. H. Lecky, M.A.
Crown 8vo. 7s. 6d.

Dictionary of General Biography; containing Concise Memoirs and Notices of the most Eminent Persons of all Ages and Countries. By W. L. R. Cates.
New Edition, 8vo. 25s. Supplement, 4s. 6d.

Life of the Duke of Wellington. By the Rev. G. R. Gleig, M.A.
Crown 8vo. with Portrait, 5s.

Felix Mendelssohn's Letters from Italy and Switzerland, and Letters from 1833 to 1847. Translated by Lady Wallace.
With Portrait. 2 vols. crown 8vo. 5s. each.

The Rise of Great Families; other Essays and Stories. By Sir Bernard Burke, C.B. LL.D.
Crown 8vo. 12s. 6d.

Memoirs of Sir Henry Havelock, K.C.B. By John Clark Marshman.
Crown 8vo. 3s. 6d.

Vicissitudes of Families. By Sir Bernard Burke, C.B.
2 vols. crown 8vo. 21s.

MENTAL and POLITICAL PHILOSOPHY.

Comte's System of Positive Polity, or Treatise upon Sociology.
Translated from the Paris Edition of 1851-1854, and furnished with Analytical Tables of Contents. In Four Volumes, each forming in some degree an independent Treatise:—
Vol. I. *General View of Positivism and Introductory Principles.* Translated by J. H. Bridges, M.B. *formerly Fellow of Oriel College, Oxford.* 8vo. price 21s.

Vol. II. *The Social Statics, or the Abstract Laws of Human Order.* Translated by Frederic Harrison, M.A. [*In Oct.*

Vol. III. *The Social Dynamics, or the General Laws of Human Progress (the Philosophy of History).* Translated by E. S. Beesly, M.A. *Professor of History in University College, London.* 8vo. [*In Dec.*

Vol. IV. *The Synthesis of the Future of Mankind.* Translated by Richard Congreve, M.D., *and an Appendix, containing the Author's Minor Treatises,* translated by H. D. Hutton, M.A. *Barrister-at-Law.* 8vo. [*Early in* 1876.

Order and Progress: Part I. Thoughts on Government; Part II. Studies of Political Crises. By FREDERIC HARRISON, M.A. of Lincoln's Inn. 8vo. 14*s.*

Essays, Political, Social, and Religious. By RICHD. CONGREVE, M.A. 8vo. 18*s.*

Essays, Critical and Biographical, contributed to the Edinburgh Review. By HENRY ROGERS.
New Edition. 2 vols. crown 8vo. 12*s.*

Essays on some Theological Controversies of the Time, contributed chiefly to the Edinburgh Review. By HENRY ROGERS.
New Edition. Crown 8vo. 6*s.*

Democracy in America. By ALEXIS DE TOCQUEVILLE. Translated by HENRY REEVE, Esq.
New Edition. 2 vols. crown 8vo. 16*s.*

On Representative Government. By JOHN STUART MILL.
Fourth Edition, crown 8vo. 2*s.*

On Liberty. By JOHN STUART MILL.
Post 8vo. 7*s.* 6*d.* crown 8vo. 1*s.* 4*d.*

Principles of Political Economy. By JOHN STUART MILL.
2 vols. 8vo. 30*s.* or 1 vol. crown 8vo. 5*s.*

Essays on some Unsettled Questions of Political Economy. By JOHN STUART MILL.
Second Edition. 8vo. 6*s.* 6*d.*

Utilitarianism. By JOHN STUART MILL.
Fourth Edition. 8vo. 5*s.*

A System of Logic, Ratiocinative and Inductive. By JOHN STUART MILL.
Eighth Edition. 2 vols. 8vo. 25*s.*

The Subjection of Women. By JOHN STUART MILL.
New Edition. Post 8vo. 5*s.*

Examination of Sir William Hamilton's Philosophy, and of the principal Philosophical Questions discussed in his Writings. By JOHN STUART MILL.
Fourth Edition. 8vo. 16*s.*

Dissertations and Discussions. By JOHN STUART MILL.
Second Edition. 3 vols. 8vo. 36*s.* VOL. *IV.* (completion) price 10*s.* 6*d.*

B

Analysis of the Phenomena of the Human Mind. By *James Mill.* New Edition, with Notes, Illustrative and Critical.
2 vols. 8vo. 28s.

A Systematic View of the Science of Jurisprudence. By Sheldon Amos, M.A.
8vo. 18s.

A Primer of the English Constitution and Government. By Sheldon Amos, M.A.
Second Edition. Crown 8vo. 6s.

Principles of Economical Philosophy. By H. D. Macleod, M.A. Barrister-at-Law.
Second Edition, in 2 vols. Vol. I. 8vo. 15s. Vol. II. Part I. price 12s.

The Institutes of Justinian; with English Introduction, Translation, and Notes. By T. C. Sandars, M.A.
Fifth Edition. 8vo. 18s.

Lord Bacon's Works, Collected and Edited by R. L. Ellis, M.A. J. Spedding, M.A. and D. D. Heath.
New and Cheaper Edition. 7 vols. 8vo. £3. 13s. 6d.

Letters and Life of Francis Bacon, including all his Occasional Works. Collected and edited, with a Commentary, by *J. Spedding.*
7 vols. 8vo. £4. 4s.

The Nicomachean Ethics of Aristotle. Newly translated into English. By R. Williams, B.A.
8vo. 12s.

The Politics of Aristotle; Greek Text, with English Notes. By Richard Congreve, M.A.
New Edition, revised. 8vo. 18s.

The Ethics of Aristotle; with Essays and Notes. By Sir A. Grant, Bart. M.A. LL.D.
Third Edition. 2 vols. 8vo. price 32s.

Bacon's Essays, with Annotations. By R. Whately, D.D.
New Edition. 8vo. 10s. 6d.

Picture Logic; an Attempt to Popularise the Science of Reasoning by the combination of Humorous Pictures with Examples of Reasoning taken from Daily Life. By A. Swinbourne, B.A.
With Woodcut Illustrations from Drawings by the Author. Fcp. 8vo. price 5s.

Elements of Logic.
By R. Whately, D.D.
New Edition. 8vo. 10s. 6d. cr. 8vo. 4s. 6d.

Elements of Rhetoric.
By R. Whately, D.D.
New Edition. 8vo. 10s. 6d. cr. 8vo. 4s. 6d.

An Outline of the Necessary Laws of Thought: a Treatise on Pure and Applied Logic.
By the Most Rev. W. Thomson, D.D. Archbishop of York.
Ninth Thousand. Crown 8vo. 5s. 6d.

An Introduction to Mental Philosophy, on the Inductive Method.
By J. D. Morell, LL.D.
8vo. 12s.

Elements of Psychology, containing the Analysis of the Intellectual Powers.
By J. D. Morell, LL.D.
Post 8vo. 7s. 6d.

The Secret of Hegel: being the Hegelian System in Origin, Principle, Form, and Matter.
By J. H. Stirling, LL.D.
2 vols. 8vo. 28s.

Sir William Hamilton; being the Philosophy of Perception: an Analysis.
By J. H. Stirling, LL.D.
8vo. 5s.

Ueberweg's System of Logic, and History of Logical Doctrines.
Translated, with Notes and Appendices, by T. M. Lindsay, M.A. F.R.S.E.
8vo. 16s.

The Senses and the Intellect.
By A. Bain, LL.D. Prof. of Logic, Univ. Aberdeen.
8vo. 15s.

Mental and Moral Science; a Compendium of Psychology and Ethics.
By A. Bain, LL.D.
Third Edition. Crown 8vo. 10s. 6d. Or separately: Part I. Mental Science, 6s. 6d. Part II. Moral Science, 4s. 6d.

The Philosophy of Necessity; or, Natural Law as applicable to Mental, Moral, and Social Science.
By Charles Bray.
Second Edition. 8vo. 9s.

Hume's Treatise on Human Nature.
Edited, with Notes, &c. by T. H. Green, M.A. and the Rev. T. H. Grose, M.A.
2 vols. 8vo. 28s.

Hume's Essays Moral, Political, and Literary.
By the same Editors.
2 vols. 8vo. 28s.

*** The above form a complete and uniform Edition of HUME'S Philosophical Works.

MISCELLANEOUS & CRITICAL WORKS.

Miscellaneous and Posthumous Works of the late Henry Thomas Buckle. Edited, with a Biographical Notice, by Helen Taylor.
3 vols. 8vo. £2. 12s. 6d.

Short Studies on Great Subjects.
By J. A. Froude, M.A. formerly Fellow of Exeter College, Oxford.
CABINET EDITION, 2 vols. crown 8vo. 12s.
LIBRARY EDITION, 2 vols. 8vo. 24s.

Lord Macaulay's Miscellaneous Writings.
LIBRARY EDITION, 2 vols. 8vo. Portrait, 21s.
PEOPLE'S EDITION, 1 vol. cr. 8vo. 4s. 6d.

Lord Macaulay's Miscellaneous Writings and Speeches.
Students' Edition. Crown 8vo. 6s.

Speeches of the Right Hon. Lord Macaulay, corrected by Himself.
People's Edition. Crown 8vo. 3s. 6d.

Lord Macaulay's Speeches on Parliamentary Reform in 1831 and 1832.
16mo. 1s.

Manual of English Literature, Historical and Critical.
By Thomas Arnold, M.A.
New Edition. Crown 8vo. 7s. 6d.

The Rev. Sydney Smith's Essays contributed to the Edinburgh Review.
Authorised Edition, complete in One Volume. Crown 8vo. 2s. 6d. sewed, or 3s. 6d. cloth.

The Rev. Sydney Smith's Miscellaneous Works.
Crown 8vo. 6s.

The Wit and Wisdom of the Rev. Sydney Smith.
Crown 8vo. 3s. 6d.

The Miscellaneous Works of Thomas Arnold, D.D. Late Head Master of Rugby School and Regius Professor of Modern History in the Univ. of Oxford.
8vo. 7s. 6d.

Realities of Irish Life.
By W. Steuart Trench.
Cr. 8vo. 2s. 6d. sewed, or 3s. 6d. cloth.

Lectures on the Science of Language.
By F. Max Müller, M.A. &c.
Eighth Edition. 2 vols. crown 8vo. 16s.

Chips from a German Workshop; being Essays on the Science of Religion, and on Mythology, Traditions, and Customs.
By F. Max Müller, M.A. &c.
3 vols. 8vo. £2.

Southey's Doctor, complete in One Volume.
Edited by Rev. J. W. Warter, B.D.
Square crown 8vo. 12s. 6d.

Families of Speech.
Four Lectures delivered at the Royal Institution.
By F. W. Farrar, D.D.
New Edition. Crown 8vo. 3s. 6d.

Chapters on Language.
By F. W. Farrar, D.D. F.R.S.
New Edition. Crown 8vo. 5s.

A Budget of Paradoxes.
By Augustus De Morgan, F.R.A.S.
Reprinted, with Author's Additions, from the Athenæum. 8vo. 15s.

Apparitions; a Narrative of Facts.
By the Rev. B. W. Savile, M.A. Author of 'The Truth of the Bible' &c.
Crown 8vo. price 4s. 6d.

Miscellaneous Writings of John Conington, M.A.
Edited by J. A. Symonds, M.A. With a Memoir by H. J. S. Smith, M.A.
2 vols. 8vo. 28s.

Recreations of a Country Parson.
By A. K. H. B.
Two Series, 3s. 6d. each.

Landscapes, Churches, and Moralities.
By A. K. H. B.
Crown 8vo. 3s. 6d.

Seaside Musings on Sundays and Weekdays.
By A. K. H. B.
Crown 8vo. 3s. 6d.

Changed Aspects of Unchanged Truths.
By A. K. H. B.
Crown 8vo. 3s. 6d.

Counsel and Comfort from a City Pulpit.
By A. K. H. B.
Crown 8vo. 3s. 6d.

Lessons of Middle Age.
By A. K. H. B.
Crown 8vo. 3s. 6d.

Leisure Hours in Town
By A. K. H. B.
Crown 8vo. 3s. 6d.

The Autumn Holidays of a Country Parson.
By A. K. H. B.
Crown 8vo. 3s. 6d.

Sunday Afternoons at the Parish Church of a Scottish University City.
By A. K. H. B.
Crown 8vo. 3s. 6d.

The Commonplace Philosopher in Town and Country.
By A. K. H. B.
Crown 8vo. 3s. 6d.

Present-Day Thoughts.
By A. K. H. B.
Crown 8vo. 3s. 6d.

Critical Essays of a Country Parson.
By A. K. H. B.
Crown 8vo. 3s. 6d.

The Graver Thoughts of a Country Parson.
By A. K. H. B.
Two Series, 3s. 6d. each.

DICTIONARIES and OTHER BOOKS of REFERENCE.

A Dictionary of the English Language.
By R. G. Latham, M.A. M.D. Founded on the Dictionary of Dr. S. Johnson, as edited by the Rev. H. J. Todd, with numerous Emendations and Additions.
4 vols. 4to. £7.

Thesaurus of English Words and Phrases, classified and arranged so as to facilitate the expression of Ideas, and assist in Literary Composition.
By P. M. Roget, M.D.
Crown 8vo. 10s. 6d.

English Synonymes.
By E. J. Whately. Edited by Archbishop Whately.
Fifth Edition. Fcp. 8vo. 3s.

Handbook of the English Language. For the use of Students of the Universities and the Higher Classes in Schools.
By R. G. Latham, M.A. M.D. &c. late Fellow of King's College, Cambridge; late Professor of English in Univ. Coll. Lond.
The Ninth Edition. Crown 8vo. 6s.

A Practical Dictionary of the French and English Languages.
By Léon Contanseau, many years French Examiner for Military and Civil Appointments, &c.
Post 8vo. 10s. 6d.

Contanseau's Pocket Dictionary, French and English, abridged from the Practical Dictionary, by the Author.
Square 18mo. 3s. 6d.

*New Practical Diction-
ary of the German Lan-
guage; German - English
and English-German.*
By Rev. W. L. Blackley,
M.A. and Dr. C. M.
Friedländer.
Post 8vo. 7s. 6d.

*A Dictionary of Roman
and Greek Antiquities.
With 2,000 Woodcuts
from Ancient Originals,
illustrative of the Arts
and Life of the Greeks and
Romans.*
By Anthony Rich, B.A.
Third Edition. Crown 8vo. 7s. 6d.

*The Mastery of Lan-
guages; or, the Art of
Speaking Foreign Tongues
Idiomatically.*
By Thomas Prendergast.
Second Edition. 8vo. 6s.

*A Practical English Dic-
tionary.*
By John T. White, D.D.
Oxon. and T. C. Donkin,
M.A.
1 vol. post 8vo. uniform with Contanseau's
Practical French Dictionary.
[*In the press.*

*A Latin-English Dic-
tionary.*
By John T. White, D.D.
Oxon. and J. E. Riddle,
M.A. Oxon.
Third Edition, revised. 2 vols. 4to. 42s.

*White's College Latin-
English Dictionary;
abridged from the Parent
Work for the use of Uni-
versity Students.*
Medium 8vo. 18s.

*A Latin-English Dic-
tionary adapted for the use
of Middle-Class Schools,*
By John T. White, D.D.
Oxon.
Square fcp. 8vo. 3s.

*White's Junior Student's
Complete Latin - English
and English-Latin Dic-
tionary.*
Square 12mo. 12s.

Separately { ENGLISH-LATIN, 5s. 6d.
            { LATIN-ENGLISH, 7s. 6d.

*A Greek-English Lexi-
con.*
By H. G. Liddell, D.D.
Dean of Christchurch,
and R. Scott, D.D.
Dean of Rochester.
Sixth Edition. Crown 4to. 36s.

*A Lexicon, Greek and
English, abridged for
Schools from Liddell and
Scott's Greek - English
Lexicon.*
Fourteenth Edition. Square 12mo. 7s. 6d.

*An English-Greek Lexi-
con, containing all the Greek
Words used by Writers of
good authority.*
By C. D. Yonge, B.A.
New Edition. 4to. 21s.

C. D. Yonge's New Lexicon, English and Greek, abridged from his larger Lexicon.
Square 12mo. 8s. 6d.

M'Culloch's Dictionary, Practical, Theoretical, and Historical, of Commerce and Commercial Navigation.
Edited by H. G. Reid.
8vo. 63s.

A General Dictionary of Geography, Descriptive, Physical, Statistical, and Historical; forming a complete Gazetteer of the World.
By A. Keith Johnston, F.R.S.E.
New Edition, thoroughly revised.
[*In the press.*

The Public Schools Manual of Modern Geography. Forming a Companion to 'The Public Schools Atlas of Modern Geography'
By Rev. G. Butler, M.A.
[*In the press.*

The Public Schools Atlas of Modern Geography. In 31 Maps, exhibiting clearly the more important Physical Features of the Countries delineated.
Edited, with Introduction, by Rev. G. Butler, M.A.
Imperial quarto, 3s. 6d. sewed; 5s. cloth.

The Public Schools Atlas of Ancient Geography.
Edited, with an Introduction on the Study of Ancient Geography, by the Rev. G. Butler, M.A.
Imperial Quarto. [*In the press.*

ASTRONOMY and METEOROLOGY.

The Universe and the Coming Transits; Researches into and New Views respecting the Constitution of the Heavens.
By R. A. Proctor, B.A.
With 22 Charts and 22 Diagrams. 8vo. 16s.

Saturn and its System.
By R. A. Proctor, B.A.
8vo. with 14 Plates, 14s.

The Transits of Venus;
A Popular Account of Past and Coming Transits, from the first observed by Horrocks A.D. 1639 to the Transit of A.D. 2012.
By R. A. Proctor, B.A.
With 20 Plates (12 Coloured) and 27 Woodcuts. Crown 8vo. 8s. 6d.

Essays on Astronomy.
A Series of Papers on
Planets and Meteors, the
Sun and Sun-surrounding
Space, Stars and Star
Cloudlets.
By R. A. Proctor, B.A.
With 10 Plates and 24 Woodcuts. 8vo. 12s.

The Moon; her Motions,
Aspect, Scenery, and Physical Condition.
By R. A. Proctor, B.A.
With Plates, Charts, Woodcuts, and Lunar Photographs. Crown 8vo. 15s.

The Sun; Ruler, Light,
Fire, and Life of the Planetary System.
By R. A. Proctor, B.A.
Second Edition. Plates and Woodcuts. Cr. 8vo. 14s.

The Orbs Around Us; a
Series of Familiar Essays
on the Moon and Planets,
Meteors and Comets, the
Sun and Coloured Pairs of
Suns.
By R. A. Proctor, B.A.
Second Edition, with Chart and 4 Diagrams. Crown 8vo. 7s. 6d.

Other Worlds than Ours;
The Plurality of Worlds
Studied under the Light
of Recent Scientific Researches.
By R. A. Proctor, B.A.
Third Edition, with 14 Illustrations. Cr. 8vo. 10s. 6d.

Brinkley's Astronomy.
Revised and partly re-written, with Additional Chapters, and an Appendix of
Questions for Examination.
By John W. Stubbs, D.D.
and F. Brünnow, Ph.D.
With 49 Diagrams. Crown 8vo. 6s.

Outlines of Astronomy.
By Sir J. F. W. Herschel,
Bart. M.A.
Latest Edition, with Plates and Diagrams. Square crown 8vo. 12s.

A New Star Atlas, for
the Library, the School, and
the Observatory, in 12 Circular Maps (with 2 Index Plates).
By R. A. Proctor, B.A.
Crown 8vo. 5s.

Celestial Objects for Common Telescopes.
By T. W. Webb, M.A.
F.R.A.S.
New Edition, with Map of the Moon and Woodcuts. Crown 8vo. 7s. 6d.

Larger Star Atlas, for the
Library, in Twelve Circular Maps, photolithographed by A. Brothers,
F.R.A.S. With 2 Index
Plates and a Letterpress
Introduction.
By R. A. Proctor, BA.
Second Edition. Small folio, 25s.

C

Dove's Law of Storms, considered in connexion with the ordinary Movements of the Atmosphere.
Translated by R. H. Scott, M.A.
8vo. 10s. 6d.

Air and Rain; the Beginnings of a Chemical Climatology.
By R. A. Smith, F.R.S.
8vo. 24s.

Air and its Relations to Life, 1774–1874. Being, with some Additions, a Course of Lectures delivered at the Royal Institution of Great Britain in the Summer of 1874.
By Walter Noel Hartley, F.C.S. Demonstrator of Chemistry at King's College, London.
1 vol. small 8vo. with Illustratrations.
[Nearly ready.

Magnetism and Deviation of the Compass. For the use of Students in Navigation and Science Schools.
By J. Merrifield, LL.D.
18mo. 1s. 6d.

Nautical Surveying, an Introduction to the Practical and Theoretical Study of.
By J. K. Laughton, M.A.
Small 8vo. 6s.

Schellen's Spectrum Analysis, in its Application to Terrestrial Substances and the Physical Constitution of the Heavenly Bodies.
Translated by Jane and C. Lassell; edited, with Notes, by W. Huggins, LL.D. F.R.S.
With 13 Plates and 223 Woodcuts. 8vo. 28s.

NATURAL HISTORY and PHYSICAL SCIENCE.

The Correlation of Physical Forces.
By the Hon. Sir W. R. Grove, F.R.S. &c.
Sixth Edition, with other Contributions to Science. 8vo. 15s.

Professor Helmholtz' Popular Lectures on Scientific Subjects.
Translated by E. Atkinson, F.C.S.
With many Illustrative Wood Engravings. 8vo. 12s. 6d.

Ganot's Natural Philosophy for General Readers and Young Persons; a Course of Physics divested of Mathematical Formulæ and expressed in the language of daily life. Translated by E. Atkinson, F.C.S.
Second Edition, with 2 Plates and 429 Woodcuts. Crown 8vo. 7s. 6d.

Ganot's Elementary Treatise on Physics, Experimental and Applied, for the use of Colleges and Schools. Translated and edited by E. Atkinson, F.C.S.
New Edition, with a Coloured Plate and 726 Woodcuts. Post 8vo. 15s.

Weinhold's Introduction to Experimental Physics, Theoretical and Practical; including Directions for Constructing Physical Apparatus and for Making Experiments. Translated by B. Loewy, F.R.A.S. With a Preface by G. C. Foster, F.R.S.
With 3 Coloured Plates and 404 Woodcuts. 8vo. price 31s. 6d.

Principles of Animal Mechanics. By the Rev. S. Haughton, F.R.S.
Second Edition. 8vo. 21s.

Text-Books of Science, Mechanical and Physical, adapted for the use of Artisans and of Students in Public and other Schools. (The first Ten edited by T. M. Goodeve, M.A. Lecturer on Applied Science at the Royal School of Mines; the remainder edited by C. W. Merrifield, F.R.S. an Examiner in the Department of Public Education.)
Small 8vo. Woodcuts.

Edited by T. M. Goodeve, M.A.
Anderson's *Strength of Materials*, 3s. 6d.
Bloxam's *Metals*, 3s. 6d.
Goodeve's *Mechanics*, 3s. 6d.
———— *Mechanism*, 3s. 6d.
Griffin's *Algebra & Trigonometry*, 3s. 6d.
Notes on the same, with Solutions, 3s. 6d.
Jenkin's *Electricity & Magnetism*, 3s. 6d.
Maxwell's *Theory of Heat*, 3s. 6d.
Merrifield's *Technical Arithmetic*, 3s. 6d. Key, 3s. 6d.
Miller's *Inorganic Chemistry*, 3s. 6d.
Shelley's *Workshop Appliances*, 3s. 6d.
Watson's *Plane & Solid Geometry*, 3s. 6d.

Edited by C. W. Merrifield, F.R.S.
Armstrong's *Organic Chemistry*, 3s. 6d.
Thorpe's *Quantitative Analysis*, 4s. 6d.
Thorpe and Muir's *Qualitative Analysis*, 3s. 6d.

Fragments of Science. By John Tyndall, F.R.S.
New Edition, in the press.

Address delivered before the British Association assembled at Belfast. By John Tyndall, F.R.S. President.
8th Thousand, with New Preface and the Manchester Address. 8vo. price 4s. 6d.

Heat a Mode of Motion.
By John Tyndall, F.R.S.
Fifth Edition, Plate and Woodcuts. Crown 8vo. 10s. 6d.

Sound.
By John Tyndall, F.R.S.
Third Edition, including Recent Researches on Fog-Signalling; Portrait and Woodcuts. Crown 8vo. 10s. 6d.

Researches on Diamagnetism and Magne-Crystallic Action; including Diamagnetic Polarity.
By John Tyndall, F.R.S.
With 6 Plates and many Woodcuts. 8vo. 14s.

Contributions to Molecular Physics in the domain of Radiant Heat.
By John Tyndall, F.R.S.
With 2 Plates and 31 Woodcuts. 8vo. 16s.

Six Lectures on Light, delivered in America in 1872 and 1873.
By John Tyndall, F.R.S.
Second Edition, with Portrait, Plate, and 59 Diagrams. Crown 8vo. 7s. 6d.

Notes of a Course of Nine Lectures on Light, delivered at the Royal Institution.
By John Tyndall, F.R.S.
Crown 8vo. 1s. sewed, or 1s. 6d. cloth.

Notes of a Course of Seven Lectures on Electrical Phenomena and Theories, delivered at the Royal Institution.
By John Tyndall, F.R.S.
Crown 8vo. 1s. sewed, or 1s. 6d. cloth.

A Treatise on Magnetism, General and Terrestrial.
By H. Lloyd, D.D. D.C.L.
8vo. price 10s. 6d.

Elementary Treatise on the Wave-Theory of Light.
By H. Lloyd, D.D. D.C.L.
Third Edition. 8vo. 10s. 6d.

An Elementary Exposition of the Doctrine of Energy.
By D. D. Heath, M.A.
Post 8vo. 4s. 6d.

The Comparative Anatomy and Physiology of the Vertebrate Animals.
By Richard Owen, F.R.S.
With 1,472 Woodcuts. 3 vols. 8vo. £3. 13s. 6d.

Sir H. Holland's Fragmentary Papers on Science and other subjects.
Edited by the Rev. J. Holland.
8vo. price 14s.

Light Science for Leisure Hours; Familiar Essays on Scientific Subjects, Natural Phenomena, &c.
By R. A. Proctor, B.A.
First and Second Series. 2 vols. crown 8vo. 7s. 6d. each.

Kirby and Spence's Introduction to Entomology, or Elements of the Natural History of Insects.
Crown 8vo. 5s.

Strange Dwellings; a Description of the Habitations of Animals, abridged from 'Homes without Hands.'
By Rev. J. G. Wood, M.A.
With Frontispiece and 60 Woodcuts. Crown 8vo. 7s. 6d.

Homes without Hands; a Description of the Habitations of Animals, classed according to their Principle of Construction.
By Rev. J. G. Wood, M.A.
With about 140 Vignettes on Wood. 8vo. 14s.

Out of Doors; a Selection of Original Articles on Practical Natural History.
By Rev. J. G. Wood, M.A.
With 6 Illustrations from Original Designs engraved on Wood. Crown 8vo. 7s. 6d.

The Polar World: a Popular Description of Man and Nature in the Arctic and Antarctic Regions of the Globe.
By Dr. G. Hartwig.
With Chromoxylographs, Maps, and Woodcuts. 8vo. 10s. 6d.

The Sea and its Living Wonders.
By Dr. G. Hartwig.
Fourth Edition, enlarged. 8vo. with many Illustrations, 10s. 6d.

The Tropical World.
By Dr. G. Hartwig.
With about 200 Illustrations. 8vo. 10s. 6d.

The Subterranean World.
By Dr. G. Hartwig.
With Maps and Woodcuts. 8vo. 10s. 6d.

The Aerial World; a Popular Account of the Phenomena and Life of the Atmosphere.
By Dr. George Hartwig.
With Map, 8 Chromoxylographs, and 60 Woodcuts. 8vo. price 21s.

Game Preservers and Bird Preservers, or 'Which are our Friends?'
By George Francis Morant, late Captain 12th Royal Lancers & Major Cape Mounted Riflemen.
Crown 8vo. price 5s.

A Familiar History of Birds.
By E. Stanley, D.D. late Ld. Bishop of Norwich.
Fcp. 8vo. with Woodcuts, 3s. 6d.

Insects at Home; a Popular Account of British Insects, their Structure Habits, and Transformations.
By Rev. J. G. Wood, M.A.
With upwards of 700 Woodcuts. 8vo. 21s.

Insects Abroad; being a Popular Account of Foreign Insects, their Structure, Habits, and Transformations.
By Rev. J. G. Wood, M.A.
With upwards of 700 Woodcuts. 8vo. 21s.

Rocks Classified and Described.
By B. Von Cotta.
English Edition, by P. H. LAWRENCE (with English, German, and French Synonymes), revised by the Author. Post 8vo. 14s.

Heer's Primæval World of Switzerland.
Translated by W. S. Dallas, F.L.S. and edited by James Heywood, M.A. F.R.S.
2 vols. 8vo. with numerous Illustrations. [In the press.

The Origin of Civilisation, and the Primitive Condition of Man; Mental and Social Condition of Savages.
By Sir J. Lubbock, Bart. M.P. F.R.S.
Third Edition, with 25 Woodcuts. 8vo. 18s

The Native Races of the Pacific States of North America.
By Hubert Howe Bancroft.
Vol. I. Wild Tribes, their Manners and Customs; with 6 Maps. 8vo. 25s.
Vol. II. Native Races of the Pacific States. 25s.
*** To be completed early in the year 1876, in Three more Volumes—
Vol. III. Mythology and Languages of both Savage and Civilized Nations.
Vol. IV. Antiquities and Architectural Remains.
Vol. V. Aboriginal History and Migrations; Index to the Entire Work.

The Ancient Stone Implements, Weapons, and Ornaments of Great Britain.
By John Evans, F.R.S.
With 2 Plates and 476 Woodcuts. 8vo. 28s.

The Elements of Botany for Families and Schools.
Eleventh Edition, revised by Thomas Moore, F.L.S.
Fcp. 8vo. with 154 Woodcuts, 2s. 6d.

Bible Animals; a Description of every Living Creature mentioned in the Scriptures, from the Ape to the Coral.
By Rev. J. G. Wood, M.A.
With about 100 Vignettes on Wood. 8vo. 21s.

The Rose Amateur's Guide.
By Thomas Rivers.
Tenth Edition. Fcp. 8vo. 4s.

A Dictionary of Science, Literature, and Art.
Re-edited by the late W. T. Brande (the Author) and Rev. G. W. Cox, M.A.
New Edition, revised. 3 vols. medium 8vo. 63s.

On the Sensations of Tone, as a Physiological Basis for the Theory of Music.
By H. Helmholtz, Professor of Physiology in the University of Berlin. Translated by A. J. Ellis, F.R.S.
8vo. 36s.

The History of Modern Music, a Course of Lectures delivered at the Royal Institution of Great Britain.
By John Hullah, Professor of Vocal Music in Queen's College and Bedford College, and Organist of Charterhouse.
New Edition, 1 vol. post 8vo. [*In the press.*

The Treasury of Botany, or Popular Dictionary of the Vegetable Kingdom; with which is incorporated a Glossary of Botanical Terms.
Edited by J. Lindley, F.R.S. and T. Moore, F.L.S.
With 274 Woodcuts and 20 Steel Plates. Two Parts, fcp. 8vo. 12s.

A General System of Descriptive and Analytical Botany.
Translated from the French of Le Maout and Decaisne, by Mrs. Hooker. Edited and arranged according to the English Botanical System, by J. D. Hooker, M.D. &c. Director of the Royal Botanic Gardens, Kew.
With 5,500 Woodcuts. Imperial 8vo. 52s. 6d.

Loudon's Encyclopædia of Plants; comprising the Specific Character, Description, Culture, History, &c. of all the Plants found in Great Britain.
With upwards of 12,000 Woodcuts. 8vo. 42s.

Handbook of Hardy Trees, Shrubs, and Herbaceous Plants; containing Descriptions &c. of the Best Species in Cultivation; with Cultural Details, Comparative Hardiness, suitability for particular positions, &c. Based on the French Work of Decaisne and Naudin, and including the 720 Original Woodcut Illustrations.
By W. B. Hemsley.
Medium 8vo. 21s.

Forest Trees and Woodland Scenery, as described in Ancient and Modern Poets.
By William Menzies, Deputy Surveyor of Windsor Forest and Parks, &c.
In One Volume, imperial 4to. with Twenty Plates, Coloured in facsimile of the original drawings, price £5. 5s.
[*Preparing for publication.*

CHEMISTRY and PHYSIOLOGY.

Miller's Elements of Chemistry, Theoretical and Practical.
Re-edited, with Additions, by H. Macleod, F.C.S.
3 vols. 8vo. £3.
PART I. CHEMICAL PHYSICS, 15s.
PART II. INORGANIC CHEMISTRY, 21s.
PART III. ORGANIC CHEMISTRY, New Edition in the press.

A Dictionary of Chemistry and the Allied Branches of other Sciences.
By Henry Watts, F.C.S. assisted by eminent Scientific and Practical Chemists.
6 vols. medium 8vo. £8. 14s. 6d.

Second Supplement to Watts's Dictionary of Chemistry, completing the Record of Discovery to the year 1873.
8vo. price 42s.

Select Methods in Chemical Analysis, chiefly Inorganic.
By Wm. Crookes, F.R.S.
With 22 Woodcuts. Crown 8vo. 12s. 6d.

Todd and Bowman's Physiological Anatomy, and Physiology of Man.
Vol. II. with numerous Illustrations, 25s.
Vol. I. New Edition by Dr. LIONEL S. BEALE, F.R.S. Parts I. and II. in 8vo. price 7s. 6d. each.

Health in the House, Twenty-five Lectures on Elementary Physiology in its Application to the Daily Wants of Man and Animals.
By Mrs. C. M. Buckton.
Crown 8vo. Woodcuts, 5s.

Outlines of Physiology, Human and Comparative.
By J. Marshall, F.R.C.S. Surgeon to the University College Hospital.
2 vols. cr. 8vo. with 122 Woodcuts, 32s.

The FINE ARTS and ILLUSTRATED EDITIONS.

Poems.
By William B. Scott.
I. Ballads and Tales. II. Studies from Nature. III. Sonnets &c.
Illustrated by Seventeen Etchings by L. Alma Tadema and William B. Scott.
Crown 8vo. 15s.

Half-hour Lectures on the History and Practice of the Fine and Ornamental Arts.
By W. B. Scott.
Third Edition, with 50 Woodcuts. Crown 8vo. 8s. 6d.

In Fairyland; Pictures from the Elf-World. By Richard Doyle. With a Poem by W. Allingham.

With 16 coloured Plates, containing 36 Designs. Second Edition, folio, 15s.

A Dictionary of Artists of the English School: Painters, Sculptors, Architects, Engravers, and Ornamentists; with Notices of their Lives and Works. By Samuel Redgrave.

8vo. 16s.

The New Testament, illustrated with Wood Engravings after the Early Masters, chiefly of the Italian School.

Crown 4to. 63s.

Lord Macaulay's Lays of Ancient Rome. With 90 *Illustrations on Wood from Drawings by G. Scharf.*

Fcp. 4to. 21s.

Miniature Edition, with Scharf's 90 *Illustrations reduced in Lithography.*

Imp. 16mo. 10s. 6d.

Moore's Lalla Rookh, Tenniel's Edition, with 68 Wood Engravings.

Fcp. 4to. 21s.

Moore's Irish Melodies, Maclise's Edition, with 161 Steel Plates.

Super royal 8vo. 31s. 6d.

Sacred and Legendary Art. By Mrs. Jameson.

6 vols. square crown 8vo. price £5. 15s. 6d. as follows:—

Legends of the Saints and Martyrs.

New Edition, with 19 Etchings and 187 Woodcuts. 2 vols. 31s. 6d.

Legends of the Monastic Orders.

New Edition, with 11 Etchings and 88 Woodcuts. 1 vol. 21s.

Legends of the Madonna.

New Edition, with 27 Etchings and 165 Woodcuts. 1 vol. 21s.

The History of Our Lord, with that of his Types and Precursors. Completed by Lady Eastlake.

Revised Edition, with 13 Etchings and 281 Woodcuts. 2 vols. 42s.

D

The USEFUL ARTS, MANUFACTURES, &c.

Industrial Chemistry; a Manual for Manufacturers and for Colleges or Technical Schools. Being a Translation of Professors Stohmann and Engler's German Edition of Payen's 'Précis de Chimie Industrielle,' by Dr. J. D. Barry. Edited, and supplemented with Chapters on the Chemistry of the Metals, by B. H. Paul, Ph.D.
8vo. with Plates and Woodcuts.
[*In the press.*

Gwilt's Encyclopædia of Architecture, with above 1,600 Woodcuts.
Fifth Edition, with Alterations and Additions, by Wyatt Papworth.
8vo. 52s. 6d.

The Three Cathedrals dedicated to St. Paul in London; their History from the Foundation of the First Building in the Sixth Century to the Proposals for the Adornment of the Present Cathedral. By W. Longman, F.S.A.
With numerous Illustrations. Square crown 8vo. 21s.

Lathes and Turning, Simple, Mechanical, and Ornamental.
By W. Henry Northcott.
With 240 Illustrations. 8vo. 18s.

Hints on Household Taste in Furniture, Upholstery, and other Details.
By Charles L. Eastlake, Architect.
New Edition, with about 90 Illustrations. Square crown 8vo. 14s.

Handbook of Practical Telegraphy.
By R. S. Culley, Memb. Inst. C.E. Engineer-in-Chief of Telegraphs to the Post-Office.
Sixth Edition, Plates & Woodcuts. 8vo. 16s.

Principles of Mechanism, for the use of Students in the Universities, and for Engineering Students.
By R. Willis, M.A. F.R.S. Professor in the University of Cambridge.
Second Edition, with 374 Woodcuts. 8vo. 18s.

Perspective; or, the Art of Drawing what one Sees: for the Use of those Sketching from Nature.
By Lieut. W. H. Collins, R.E. F.R.A.S.
With 37 Woodcuts. Crown 8vo. 5s.

Encyclopædia of Civil Engineering, Historical, Theoretical, and Practical.
By E. Cresy, C.E.
With above 3,000 Woodcuts. 8vo. 42s.

A Treatise on the Steam Engine, in its various applications to Mines, Mills, Steam Navigation, Railways and Agriculture.
By J. Bourne, C.E.
With Portrait, 37 Plates, and 546 Woodcuts. 4to. 42s.

Catechism of the Steam Engine, in its various Applications.
By John Bourne, C.E.
New Edition, with 89 Woodcuts. Fcp. 8vo. 6s.

Handbook of the Steam Engine.
By J. Bourne, C.E. forming a KEY to the Author's Catechism of the Steam Engine.
With 67 Woodcuts. Fcp. 8vo. 9s.

Recent Improvements in the Steam Engine.
By J. Bourne, C.E.
With 124 Woodcuts. Fcp. 8vo. 6s.

Lowndes's Engineer's Handbook; explaining the Principles which should guide the Young Engineer in the Construction of Machinery.
Post 8vo. 5s.

Ure's Dictionary of Arts, Manufactures, and Mines. Seventh Edition, re-written and greatly enlarged by R. Hunt, F.R.S. assisted by numerous Contributors.
With 2,100 Woodcuts. 3 vols. medium 8vo. price £5. 5s.

Practical Treatise on Metallurgy, Adapted from the last German Edition of Professor Kerl's Metallurgy by W. Crookes, F.R.S. &c. and E. Röhrig, Ph.D.
3 vols. 8vo. with 625 Woodcuts. £4. 19s.

Treatise on Mills and Millwork.
By Sir W. Fairbairn, Bt.
With 18 Plates and 322 Woodcuts. 2 vols. 8vo. 32s.

Useful Information for Engineers.
By Sir W. Fairbairn, Bt.
With many Plates and Woodcuts. 3 vols. crown 8vo. 31s. 6d.

The Application of Cast and Wrought Iron to Building Purposes.
By Sir W. Fairbairn, Bt.
With 6 Plates and 118 Woodcuts. 8vo. 16s.

Practical Handbook of Dyeing and Calico-Printing.
By W. Crookes, F.R.S. &c.
With numerous Illustrations and Specimen of Dyed Textile Fabrics. 8vo. 42s.

Occasional Papers on Subjects connected with Civil Engineering, Gunnery, and Naval Architecture.
By Michael Scott, Memb. Inst. C.E. & of Inst. N.A.
2 vols. 8vo. with Plates, 42s.

Mitchell's Manual of Practical Assaying.
Fourth Edition, revised, with the Recent Discoveries incorporated, by W. Crookes, F.R.S.
8vo. Woodcuts, 31s. 6d.

Loudon's Encyclopædia of Gardening; comprising the Theory and Practice of Horticulture, Floriculture, Arboriculture, and Landscape Gardening.
With 1,000 Woodcuts. 8vo. 21s.

Loudon's Encyclopædia of Agriculture; comprising the Laying-out, Improvement, and Management of Landed Property, and the Cultivation and Economy of the Productions of Agriculture.
With 1,100 Woodcuts. 8vo. 21s.

RELIGIOUS and MORAL WORKS.

An Exposition of the 39 Articles, Historical and Doctrinal.
By E. H. Browne, D.D. Bishop of Winchester.
New Edition. 8vo. 16s.

Historical Lectures on the Life of Our Lord Jesus Christ.
By C. J. Ellicott, D.D.
Fifth Edition. 8vo. 12s.

An Introduction to the Theology of the Church of England, in an Exposition of the 39 Articles. By Rev. T. P. Boultbee, LL.D.
Fcp. 8vo. 6s.

Three Essays on Religion: Nature; the Utility of Religion; Theism.
By John Stuart Mill.
Second Edition. 8vo. price 10s. 6d.

Sermons Chiefly on the Interpretation of Scripture.
By the late Rev. Thomas Arnold, D.D.
8vo. price 7s. 6d.

Sermons preached in the Chapel of Rugby School; with an Address before Confirmation.
By the late Rev. Thomas Arnold, D.D.
Fcp. 8vo. price 3s. 6d.

Christian Life, its Course, its Hindrances, and its Helps; Sermons preached mostly in the Chapel of Rugby School.
By the late Rev. Thomas Arnold, D.D.
8vo. 7s. 6d.

Christian Life, its Hopes, its Fears, and its Close; Sermons preached mostly in the Chapel of Rugby School.
By the late Rev. Thomas Arnold, D.D.
8vo. 7s. 6d.

Synonyms of the Old Testament, their Bearing on Christian Faith and Practice.
By Rev. R. B. Girdlestone.
8vo. 15s.

The Primitive and Catholic Faith in Relation to the Church of England.
By the Rev. B. W. Savile, M.A. Rector of Shillingford, Exeter; Author of 'The Truth of the Bible' &c.
8vo. price 7s.

Reasons of Faith; or, the Order of the Christian Argument Developed and Explained.
By Rev. G. S. Drew, M.A.
Second Edition Fcp. 8vo. 6s.

The Eclipse of Faith; or a Visit to a Religious Sceptic.
By Henry Rogers.
Latest Edition. Fcp. 8vo. 5s.

Defence of the Eclipse of Faith.
By Henry Rogers.
Latest Edition. Fcp. 8vo. 3s. 6d.

A Critical and Grammatical Commentary on St. Paul's Epistles.
By C. J. Ellicott, D.D.
8vo. Galatians, 8s. 6d. Ephesians, 8s. 6d. Pastoral Epistles, 10s. 6d. Philippians, Colossians, & Philemon, 10s. 6d. Thessalonians, 7s. 6d.

The Life and Epistles of St. Paul.
By Rev. W. J. Conybeare, M.A. and Very Rev. J. S. Howson, D.D.

LIBRARY EDITION, *with all the Original Illustrations, Maps, Landscapes on Steel, Woodcuts, &c.* 2 vols. 4to. 42s.

INTERMEDIATE EDITION, *with a Selection of Maps, Plates, and Woodcuts.* 2 vols. square crown 8vo. 21s.

STUDENT'S EDITION, *revised and condensed, with 46 Illustrations and Maps.* 1 vol. crown 8vo. 9s.

An Examination into the Doctrine and Practice of Confession.
By the Rev. W. E. Jelf, B.D.
8vo. price 7s. 6d.

Fasting Communion, how Binding in England by the Canons. With the testimony of the Early Fathers. An Historical Essay.

By the Rev. H. T. Kingdon, M.A.

Second Edition. 8vo. 10s. 6d.

Evidence of the Truth of the Christian Religion derived from the Literal Fulfilment of Prophecy.

By Alexander Keith, D.D.

40th Edition, with numerous Plates. Square 8vo. 12s. 6d. or in post 8vo. with 5 Plates, 6s.

Historical and Critical Commentary on the Old Testament; with a New Translation.

By M. M. Kalisch, Ph.D.

Vol. I. Genesis, 8vo. 18s. or adapted for the General Reader, 12s. Vol. II. Exodus, 15s. or adapted for the General Reader, 12s. Vol. III. Leviticus, Part I. 15s. or adapted for the General Reader, 8s. Vol. IV. Leviticus, Part II. 15s. or adapted for the General Reader, 8s.

The History and Literature of the Israelites, according to the Old Testament and the Apocrypha.

By C. De Rothschild and A. De Rothschild.

Second Edition. 2 vols. crown 8vo. 12s. 6d. Abridged Edition, in 1 vol. fcp. 8vo. 3s. 6d.

Ewald's History of Israel.
Translated from the German by J. E. Carpenter, M.A. with Preface by R. Martineau, M.A.

5 vols. 8vo. 63s.

The Types of Genesis, briefly considered as revealing the Development of Human Nature.
By Andrew Jukes.

Third Edition. Crown 8vo. 7s. 6d.

The Second Death and the Restitution of all Things; with some Preliminary Remarks on the Nature and Inspiration of Holy Scripture. (A Letter to a Friend.)
By Andrew Jukes.

Fourth Edition. Crown 8vo. 3s. 6d.

Commentary on Epistle to the Romans.
By Rev. W. A. O'Conor.

Crown 8vo. 3s. 6d.

A Commentary on the Gospel of St. John.
By Rev. W. A. O'Conor.

Crown 8vo. 10s. 6d.

The Epistle to the Hebrews; with Analytical Introduction and Notes.
By Rev. W. A. O'Conor.

Crown 8vo. 4s. 6d.

Thoughts for the Age.
By Elizabeth M. Sewell.
New Edition. Fcp. 8vo. 3s. 6d.

Passing Thoughts on Religion.
By Elizabeth M. Sewell.
Fcp. 8vo. 3s. 6d.

Preparation for the Holy Communion; the Devotions chiefly from the works of Jeremy Taylor.
By Elizabeth M. Sewell.
32mo. 3s.

Bishop Jeremy Taylor's Entire Works; with Life by Bishop Heber.
Revised and corrected by the Rev. C. P. Eden.
10 vols. £5. 5s.

Hymns of Praise and Prayer.
Collected and edited by Rev. J. Martineau, LL.D.
Crown 8vo. 4s. 6d. 32mo. 1s. 6d.

Spiritual Songs for the Sundays and Holidays throughout the Year.
By J. S. B. Monsell, LL.D.
9th Thousand. Fcp. 8vo. 5s 18mo. 2s.

Lyra Germanica; Hymns translated from the German by Miss C. Winkworth.
Fcp. 8vo. 5s.

Endeavours after the Christian Life; Discourses.
By Rev. J. Martineau, LL.D.
Fifth Edition. Crown 8vo. 7s. 6d.

Lectures on the Pentateuch & the Moabite Stone; with Appendices.
By J. W. Colenso, D.D. Bishop of Natal.
8vo. 12s.

Supernatural Religion; an Inquiry into the Reality of Divine Revelation.
Fifth Edition. 2 vols. 8vo. 24s.

The Pentateuch and Book of Joshua Critically Examined.
By J. W. Colenso, D.D. Bishop of Natal.
Crown 8vo. 6s.

The New Bible Commentary, by Bishops and other Clergy of the Anglican Church, critically examined by the Rt. Rev. J. W. Colenso, D.D. Bishop of Natal.
8vo. 25s.

TRAVELS, VOYAGES, &c.

Italian Alps; Sketches in the Mountains of Ticino, Lombardy, the Trentino, and Venetia.
By Douglas W. Freshfield, Editor of 'The Alpine Journal.'
Square crown 8vo. Illustrations. 15s.

Here and There in the Alps.
By the Hon. Frederica Plunket.
With Vignette-title. Post 8vo. 6s. 6d.

The Valleys of Tirol; their Traditions and Customs, and How to Visit them.
By Miss R. H. Busk.
With Frontispiece and 3 Maps. Crown 8vo. 12s. 6d.

Two Years in Fiji, a Descriptive Narrative of a Residence in the Fijian Group of Islands; with some Account of the Fortunes of Foreign Settlers and Colonists up to the time of British Annexation.
By Litton Forbes, M.D. L.R.C.P. F.R.G.S. late Medical Officer to the German Consulate, Apia, Navigator Islands.
Crown 8vo. 8s. 6d.

Eight Years in Ceylon.
By Sir Samuel W. Baker, M.A. F.R.G.S.
New Edition, with Illustrations engraved on Wood by G. Pearson. Crown 8vo. Price 7s. 6d.

The Rifle and the Hound in Ceylon.
By Sir Samuel W. Baker, M.A. F.R.G.S.
New Edition, with Illustrations engraved on Wood by G. Pearson. Crown 8vo. Price 7s. 6d.

Meeting the Sun; a Journey all round the World through Egypt, China, Japan, and California.
By William Simpson, F.R.G.S.
With Heliotypes and Woodcuts. 8vo. 24s.

The Dolomite Mountains. Excursions through Tyrol, Carinthia, Carniola, and Friuli.
By J. Gilbert and G. C. Churchill, F.R.G.S.
With Illustrations. Sq. cr. 8vo. 21s.

The Alpine Club Map of the Chain of Mont Blanc, from an actual Survey in 1863-1864.
By A. Adams-Reilly, F.R.G.S. M.A.C.
In Chromolithography, on extra stout drawing paper 10s. or mounted on canvas in a folding case, 12s. 6d.

The Alpine Club Map of the Valpelline, the Val Tournanche, and the Southern Valleys of the Chain of Monte Rosa, from actual Survey.
By A. Adams-Reilly, F.R.G.S. M.A.C.

Price 6s. on extra Stout Drawing Paper, or 7s. 6d. mounted in a Folding Case.

Untrodden Peaks and Unfrequented Valleys; a Midsummer Ramble among the Dolomites.
By Amelia B. Edwards.

With numerous Illustrations. 8vo. 21s.

The Alpine Club Map of Switzerland, with parts of the Neighbouring Countries, on the scale of Four Miles to an Inch.
Edited by R. C. Nichols, F.S.A. F.R.G.S.

In Four Sheets, in Portfolio, price 42s. coloured, or 34s. uncoloured.

The Alpine Guide.
By John Ball, M.R.I.A. late President of the Alpine Club.

Post 8vo. with Maps and other Illustrations.

Eastern Alps.

Price 10s. 6d.

Central Alps, including all the Oberland District.

Price 7s. 6d.

Western Alps, including Mont Blanc, Monte Rosa, Zermatt, &c.

Price 6s. 6d.

Introduction on Alpine Travelling in general, and on the Geology of the Alps.

Price 1s. Either of the Three Volumes or Parts of the 'Alpine Guide' may be had with this Introduction prefixed, 1s. extra. The 'Alpine Guide' may also be had in Ten separate Parts, or districts, price 2s. 6d. each.

Guide to the Pyrenees, for the use of Mountaineers.
By Charles Packe.

Second Edition, with Maps &c. and Appendix. Crown 8vo. 7s. 6d.

How to See Norway; embodying the Experience of Six Summer Tours in that Country.
By J. R. Campbell.

With Map and 5 Woodcuts, fcp. 8vo. 5s.

Visits to Remarkable Places, and Scenes illustrative of striking Passages in English History and Poetry.
By William Howitt.

2 vols. 8vo. Woodcuts, 25s.

E

WORKS of FICTION.

Whispers from Fairyland.
By the Rt. Hon. E. H. Knatchbull - Hugessen, M.P. Author of 'Stories for my Children,' &c.

With 9 Illustrations from Original Designs engraved on Wood by G. Pearson. Crown 8vo. price 6s.

Lady Willoughby's Diary during the Reign of Charles the First, the Protectorate, and the Restoration.

Crown 8vo. 7s. 6d.

The Folk-Lore of Rome, collected by Word of Mouth from the People.
By Miss R. H. Busk.

Crown 8vo. 12s. 6d.

Becker's Gallus; or Roman Scenes of the Time of Augustus.

Post 8vo. 7s. 6d.

Becker's Charicles: Illustrative of Private Life of the Ancient Greeks.

Post 8vo. 7s. 6d.

Tales of the Teutonic Lands.
By Rev. G. W. Cox, M.A. and E. H. Jones.

Crown 8vo. 10s. 6d.

Tales of Ancient Greece.
By the Rev. G. W. Cox, M.A.

Crown 8vo. 6s. 6d.

The Modern Novelist's Library.
Atherstone Priory, 2s. boards; 2s. 6d. cloth.
Mlle. Mori, 2s. boards; 2s. 6d. cloth.
The Burgomaster's Family, 2s. and 2s. 6d.
MELVILLE'S Digby Grand, 2s. and 2s. 6d.
—————— Gladiators, 2s. and 2s.6d.
—————— Good for Nothing, 2s. & 2s. 6d.
—————— Holmby House, 2s. and 2s. 6d.
—————— Interpreter, 2s. and 2s. 6d.
—————— Kate Coventry, 2s. and 2s. 6d.
—————— Queen's Maries, 2s. and 2s. 6d.
—————— General Bounce, 2s. and 2s. 6d.
TROLLOPE'S Warden, 1s. 6d. and 2s.
—————— Barchester Towers, 2s. & 2s.6d.
BRAMLEY-MOORE'S Six Sisters of the Valleys, 2s. boards; 2s. 6d. cloth.

Novels and Tales.
By the Right Hon. Benjamin Disraeli, M.P.
Cabinet Editions, complete in Ten Volumes, crown 8vo. 6s. each, as follows :—

Lothair, 6s.	Venetia, 6s.
Coningsby, 6s.	Alroy, Ixion, &c. 6s.
Sybil, 6s.	Young Duke, &c. 6s.
Tancred, 6s.	Vivian Grey, 6s.

Henrietta Temple, 6s.
Contarini Fleming, &c. 6s.

Stories and Tales.
By Elizabeth M. Sewell, Author of 'The Child's First History of Rome,' 'Principles of Education,' &c. Cabinet Edition, in Ten Volumes :—

Amy Herbert, 2s. 6d.	Ivors, 2s. 6d.
Gertrude, 2s. 6d.	Katharine Ashton, 2s. 6d.
Earl's Daughter, 2s. 6d.	Margaret Percival, 3s. 6d.
Experience of Life, 2s. 6d.	Laneton Parsonage, 3s. 6d.
Cleve Hall, 2s. 6d.	Ursula, 3s. 6d.

POETRY and THE DRAMA.

Ballads and Lyrics of Old France; with other Poems.
By A. Lang.
Square fcp. 8vo. 5s.

Moore's Lalla Rookh, Tenniel's Edition, with 68 Wood Engravings.
Fcp. 4to. 21s.

Moore's Irish Melodies, Maclise's Edition, with 161 Steel Plates.
Super-royal 8vo. 31s. 6d.

Miniature Edition of Moore's Irish Melodies, with Maclise's 161 Illustrations reduced in Lithography.
Imp. 16mo. 10s. 6d.

Milton's Lycidas and Epitaphium Damonis. Edited, with Notes and Introduction, by C. S. Jerram, M.A.
Crown 8vo. 2s. 6d.

Lays of Ancient Rome; with Ivry and the Armada.
By the Right Hon. Lord Macaulay.
16mo. 3s. 6d.

Lord Macaulay's Lays of Ancient Rome. With 90 Illustrations on Wood from Drawings by G. Scharf.
Fcp. 4to. 21s.

Miniature Edition of Lord Macaulay's Lays of Ancient Rome, with Scharf's 90 Illustrations reduced in Lithography.
Imp. 16mo. 10s. 6d.

Horatii Opera, Library Edition, with English Notes, Marginal References and various Readings. Edited by Rev. J. E. Yonge.
8vo. 21s.

Southey's Poetical Works with the Author's last Corrections and Additions.
Medium 8vo. with Portrait, 14s.

Poems by Jean Ingelow.
2 vols. Fcp. 8vo. 10s.
FIRST SERIES, containing 'Divided,' 'The Star's Monument,' &c. 16th Thousand.
Fcp. 8vo. 5s.
SECOND SERIES, 'A Story of Doom,' 'Gladys and her Island,' &c. 5th Thousand.
Fcp. 8vo. 5s.

Poems by Jean Ingelow. First Series, with nearly 100 Woodcut Illustrations.
Fcp. 4to. 21s.

Bowdler's Family Shakspeare, cheaper Genuine Edition.
Complete in 1 vol. medium 8vo. large type, with 36 Woodcut Illustrations, 14s. or in 6 vols. fcp. 8vo. price 21s.

The Æneid of Virgil Translated into English Verse.
By J. Conington, M.A.
Crown 8vo. 9s.

RURAL SPORTS, HORSE and CATTLE MANAGEMENT, &c.

Down the Road; or, Reminiscences of a Gentleman Coachman.
By C. T. S. Birch Reynardson.
Second Edition, with 12 Coloured Illustrations from Paintings by H. Alken. Medium 8vo. price 21s.

Blaine's Encyclopædia of Rural Sports; Complete Accounts, Historical, Practical, and Descriptive, of Hunting, Shooting, Fishing, Racing, &c.
With above 600 Woodcuts (20 from Designs by JOHN LEECH). 8vo. 21s.

A Book on Angling: a Treatise on the Art of Angling in every branch, including full Illustrated Lists of Salmon Flies.
By Francis Francis.
Post 8vo. Portrait and Plates, 15s.

Wilcocks's Sea-Fisherman: comprising the Chief Methods of Hook and Line Fishing, a glance at Nets, and remarks on Boats and Boating.
New Edition, with 80 Woodcuts. Post 8vo. 12s. 6d.

The Ox, his Diseases and their Treatment; with an Essay on Parturition in the Cow.
By J. R. Dobson, Memb. R.C.V.S.
Crown 8vo. with Illustrations 7s. 6d.

Youatt on the Horse.
Revised and enlarged by W. Watson, M.R.C.V.S.
8vo. Woodcuts, 12s. 6d.

Youatt's Work on the Dog, revised and enlarged.
8vo. Woodcuts, 6s.

Horses and Stables.
By Colonel F. Fitzwygram, XV. the King's Hussars.
With 24 Plates of Illustrations. 8vo. 10s. 6d.

The Dog in Health and Disease.
By Stonehenge.
With 73 Wood Engravings. Square crown 8vo. 7s. 6d.

The Greyhound.
By Stonehenge.
Revised Edition, with 25 Portraits of Greyhounds, &c. Square crown 8vo. 15s.

NEW WORKS published by LONGMANS & CO. 37

Stables and Stable Fittings.
By W. Miles, Esq.
Imp. 8vo. with 13 Plates, 15s.

The Horse's Foot, and how to keep it Sound.
By W. Miles, Esq.
Ninth Edition. Imp. 8vo. Woodcuts, 12s. 6d.

A Plain Treatise on Horse-shoeing.
By W. Miles, Esq.
Sixth Edition. Post 8vo. Woodcuts, 2s. 6d.

Remarks on Horses' Teeth, addressed to Purchasers.
By W. Miles, Esq.
Post 8vo. 1s. 6d.

The Fly-Fisher's Entomology.
By Alfred Ronalds.
With 20 coloured Plates. 8vo. 14s.

The Dead Shot, or Sportsman's Complete Guide.
By Marksman.
Fcp. 8vo. with Plates, 5s.

WORKS of UTILITY and GENERAL INFORMATION.

Maunder's Treasury of Knowledge and Library of Reference; comprising an English Dictionary and Grammar, Universal Gazetteer, Classical Dictionary, Chronology, Law Dictionary, Synopsis of the Peerage, Useful Tables, &c.
Fcp. 8vo. 6s.

Maunder's Biographical Treasury.
Latest Edition, reconstructed and partly rewritten, with about 1,000 additional Memoirs, by W. L. R. Cates.
Fcp. 8vo. 6s.

Maunder's Scientific and Literary Treasury; a Popular Encyclopædia of Science, Literature, and Art.
New Edition, in part rewritten, with above 1,000 new articles, by J. Y. Johnson.
Fcp. 8vo. 6s.

Maunder's Treasury of Geography, Physical, Historical, Descriptive, and Political.
Edited by W. Hughes, F.R.G.S.
With 7 Maps and 16 Plates. Fcp. 8vo. 6s.

Maunder's Historical Treasury; General Introductory Outlines of Universal History, and a Series of Separate Histories.
Revised by the Rev. G. W. Cox, M.A.
Fcp. 8vo. 6s.

Maunder's Treasury of Natural History; or Popular Dictionary of Zoology.
Revised and corrected Edition. Fcp. 8vo. with 900 Woodcuts, 6s.

The Treasury of Bible Knowledge; being a Dictionary of the Books, Persons, Places, Events, and other Matters of which mention is made in Holy Scripture.
By Rev. J. Ayre, M.A.
With Maps, 15 Plates, and numerous Woodcuts. Fcp. 8vo. 6s.

Collieries and Colliers: a Handbook of the Law and Leading Cases relating thereto.
By J. C. Fowler.
Third Edition. Fcp. 8vo. 7s. 6d.

The Theory and Practice of Banking.
By H. D. Macleod, M.A.
Second Edition. 2 vols. 8vo. 30s.

Modern Cookery for Private Families, reduced to a System of Easy Practice in a Series of carefully-tested Receipts.
By Eliza Acton.
With 8 Plates & 150 Woodcuts. Fcp. 8vo. 6s.

A Practical Treatise on Brewing; with Formulæ for Public Brewers, and Instructions for Private Families.
By W. Black.
Fifth Edition. 8vo. 10s. 6d.

Three Hundred Original Chess Problems and Studies.
By Jas. Pierce, M.A. and W. T. Pierce.
With many Diagrams. Sq. fcp. 8vo. 7s. 6d.
Supplement, price 3s.

The Theory of the Modern Scientific Game of Whist.
By W. Pole, F.R.S.
Seventh Edition. Fcp. 8vo. 2s. 6d.

The Cabinet Lawyer; a Popular Digest of the Laws of England, Civil, Criminal, and Constitutional.
Twenty-fourth Edition, corrected and extended. Fcp. 8vo. 9s.

Pewtner's Comprehensive Specifier; a Guide to the Practical Specification of every kind of Building-Artificer's Work. Edited by W. Young.
Crown 8vo. 6s.

Protection from Fire and Thieves. Including the Construction of Locks, Safes, Strong-Room, and Fire-proof Buildings; Burglary, and the Means of Preventing it; Fire, its Detection, Prevention, and Extinction; &c. By G. H. Chubb, Assoc. Inst. C.E.
With 32 Woodcuts. Cr. 8vo. 5s.

Chess Openings. By F. W. Longman, Balliol College, Oxford.
Second Edition, revised. Fcp. 8vo. 2s. 6d.

Hints to Mothers on the Management of their Health during the Period of Pregnancy and in the Lying-in Room. By Thomas Bull, M.D.
Fcp. 8vo. 5s.

The Maternal Management of Children in Health and Disease. By Thomas Bull, M.D.
Fcp. 8vo. 5s.

INDEX.

Acton's Modern Cookery	38
Aird's Blackstone Economised	39
Alpine Club Map of Switzerland	33
Alpine Guide (The)	33
Amos's Jurisprudence	10
—— Primer of the Constitution	10
Anderson's Strength of Materials	19
Armstrong's Organic Chemistry	19
Arnold's (Dr.) Christian Life	29
—————— Lectures on Modern History	2
—————— Miscellaneous Works	12
—————— School Sermons	28
—————— (T.) Manual of English Literature	12
Atherstone Priory	34
Autumn Holidays of a Country Parson	13
Ayre's Treasury of Bible Knowledge	38
Bacon's Essays, by *Whately*	10
—— Life and Letters, by *Spedding*	10
—— Works	10
Bain's Mental and Moral Science	11
—— on the Senses and Intellect	11
Baker's Two Works on Ceylon	33
Ball's Guide to the Central Alps	33
—— Guide to the Western Alps	33
—— Guide to the Eastern Alps	33
Bancroft's Native Races of the Pacific	22
Becker's Charicles and Gallus	34
Black's Treatise on Brewing	38
Blackley's German-English Dictionary	15
Blaine's Rural Sports	36
Bloxam's Metals	19
Boultbee on 39 Articles	28
Bourne's Catechism of the Steam Engine	27
—— Handbook of Steam Engine	27
—— Treatise on the Steam Engine	27
—— Improvements in the same	27
Bowdler's Family *Shakspeare*	36
Bramley-Moore's Six Sisters of the Valley	36
Brande's Dictionary of Science, Literature, and Art	22
Bray's Philosophy of Necessity	11
Brinkley's Astronomy	18
Browne's Exposition of the 39 Articles	28
Brunel's Life of *Brunel*	7
Buckle's History of Civilisation	3
—— Posthumous Remains	12
Buckton's Health in the House	24
Bull's Hints to Mothers	39
—— Maternal Management of Children	39
Burgomaster's Family (The)	34
Burke's Rise of Great Families	8
Burke's Vicissitudes of Families	8
Busk's Folk-lore of Rome	34
—— Valleys of Tirol	32
Cabinet Lawyer	38
Campbell's Norway	33
Cates's Biographical Dictionary	8
—— and *Woodward's* Encyclopædia	5
Changed Aspects of Unchanged Truths	13
Chesney's Indian Polity	3
—— Modern Military Biography	3
—— Waterloo Campaign	3
Chubb on Protection	39
Clough's Lives from Plutarch	4
Codrington's Life and Letters	7
Colenso on Moabite Stone &c.	31
——'s Pentateuch and Book of Joshua	31
—— Speaker's Bible Commentary	31
Collins's Perspective	26
Commonplace Philosopher in Town and Country, by A. K. H. B.	14
Comte's Positive Polity	8
Congreve's Essays	9
—— Politics of Aristotle	10
Conington's Translation of Virgil's Æneid	36
—— Miscellaneous Writings	13
Contanseau's Two French Dictionaries	14
Conybeare and *Howson's* Life and Epistles of St. Paul	29
Counsel and Comfort from a City Pulpit	13
Cox's (G. W.) Aryan Mythology	4
—— Crusades	6
—— History of Greece	4
—— School ditto	4
—— Tale of the Great Persian War	4
—— Tales of Ancient Greece	34
—— and *Jones's* Teutonic Tales	34
Crawley's Thucydides	4
Creasy on British Constitution	3
Cresy's Encyclopædia of Civil Engineering	26
Critical Essays of a Country Parson	14
Crookes's Chemical Analysis	24
—— Dyeing and Calico-printing	27
Culley's Handbook of Telegraphy	26
Dead Shot (The), by *Marksman*	37
De Caisne and *Le Maout's* Botany	23
De Morgan's Paradoxes	13
De Tocqueville's Democracy in America	9
Disraeli's Lord George Bentinck	7

Disraeli's Novels and Tales	34
Dobson on the Ox	36
Dove's Law of Storms	18
Doyle's Fairyland	25
Drew's Reasons of Faith	29
Eastlake's Hints on Household Taste	26
Edwards's Rambles among the Dolomites	33
Elements of Botany	22
Ellicott's Commentary on Ephesians	29
———————— Galatians	29
———————— Pastoral Epist.	29
———————— Philippians, &c.	29
———————— Thessalonians	29
———— Lectures on Life of Christ	28
Evans's Ancient Stone Implements	22
Ewald's History of Israel	30
Fairbairn's Application of Cast and Wrought Iron to Building	27
———— Information for Engineers	27
———— Treatise on Mills and Millwork	27
Farrar's Chapters on Language	13
———— Families of Speech	13
Fitzwygram on Horses and Stables	36
Forbes's Two Years in Fiji	32
Fowler's Collieries and Colliers	38
Francis's Fishing Book	36
Freeman's Historical Geography of Europe	6
Freshfield's Italian Alps	32
Froude's English in Ireland	2
———— History of England	2
———— Short Studies	12
Gairdner's Houses of Lancaster and York	6
Ganot's Elementary Physics	19
———— Natural Philosophy	19
Gardiner's Buckingham and Charles	3
———— Thirty Years' War	6
Gilbert and Churchill's Dolomites	32
Girdlestone's Bible Synonyms	29
Goodeve's Mechanics	19
———— Mechanism	19
Grant's Ethics of Aristotle	10
Graver Thoughts of a Country Parson	14
Greville's Journal	1
Griffin's Algebra and Trigonometry	20
Grove on Correlation of Physical Forces	18
Gwilt's Encyclopædia of Architecture	26
Harrison's Order and Progress	9
Hartley on the Air	18
Hartwig's Aerial World	21
———— Polar World	21
———— Sea and its Living Wonders	21
———— Subterranean World	21
———— Tropical World	21
Haughton's Animal Mechanics	19
Hayward's Biographical and Critical Essays	7
Heath on Energy	20
Heer's Switzerland	22
Helmholtz on Tone	22

Helmholtz's Scientific Lectures	18
Helmsley's Trees, Shrubs, and Herbaceous Plants	23
Herschel's Outlines of Astronomy	18
Holland's Fragmentary Papers	20
———— Recollections	7
Howitt's Visits to Remarkable Places	32
Hullah's History of Modern Music	23
Hume's Essays	11
———— Treatise on Human Nature	11
Ihne's History of Rome	5
Ingelow's Poems	35
Jameson's Legends of Saints and Martyrs	25
———— Legends of the Madonna	25
———— Legends of the Monastic Orders	25
———— Legends of the Saviour	25
Jelf on Confession	29
Jenkin's Electricity and Magnetism	19
Jerram's Lycidas of Milton	35
Jerrold's Life of Napoleon	1
Johnston's Geographical Dictionary	16
Jukes's Types of Genesis	30
———— on Second Death	30
Kalisch's Commentary on the Bible	30
Keith's Evidence of Prophecy	30
Kerl's Metallurgy, by Crookes and Röhrig	27
Kingdon on Communion	30
Kirby and Spence's Entomology	20
Knatchbull-Hugessen's Whispers from Fairy-Land	34
Landscapes, Churches, &c. by A. K. H. B.	13
Lang's Ballads and Lyrics	35
Latham's English Dictionary	14
———— Handbook of the English Language	14
Laughton's Nautical Surveying	18
Lawrence on Rocks	22
Lecky's History of European Morals	5
———— Rationalism	5
———— Leaders of Public Opinion	8
Leisure Hours in Town, by A. K. H. B.	13
Lessons of Middle Age, by A. K. H. B.	13
Lewes's Biographical History of Philosophy	6
Liddell and Scott's Greek-English Lexicons	15
Lindley and Moore's Treasury of Botany	23
Lloyd's Magnetism	20
———— Wave-Theory of Light	20
Longman's Chess Openings	39
———— Edward the Third	2
———— Lectures on History of England	2
———— Old and New St. Paul's	26
Loudon's Encyclopædia of Agriculture	28
———— Gardening	28
———— Plants	23
Lowndes's Engineer's Handbook	27
Lubbock's Origin of Civilisation	22
Lyra Germanica	31

F

NEW WORKS PUBLISHED BY LONGMANS & CO.

Macaulay's (Lord) Essays	2
——— History of England	2
——— Lays of Ancient Rome	25, 35
——— Life and Letters	7
——— Miscellaneous Writings	12
——— Speeches	12
——— Works	2
McCulloch's Dictionary of Commerce	16
Macleod's Principles of Economical Philosophy	10
——— Theory and Practice of Banking	38
Mademoiselle Mori	34
Malleson's Genoese Studies	3
——— Native States of India	3
Marshall's Physiology	24
Marshman's History of India	3
——— Life of Havelock	8
Martineau's Christian Life	31
——— Hymns	31
Maunder's Biographical Treasury	37
——— Geographical Treasury	37
——— Historical Treasury	38
——— Scientific and Literary Treasury	37
——— Treasury of Knowledge	37
——— Treasury of Natural History	38
Maxwell's Theory of Heat	19
May's History of Democracy	2
——— History of England	2
Melville's Digby Grand	34
——— General Bounce	34
——— Gladiators	34
——— Good for Nothing	34
——— Holmby House	34
——— Interpreter	34
——— Kate Coventry	34
——— Queen's Maries	34
Mendelssohn's Letters	8
Menzies' Forest Trees and Woodland Scenery	23
Merivale's Fall of the Roman Republic	4
——— General History of Rome	4
——— Romans under the Empire	4
Merrifield's Arithmetic and Mensuration	19
——— Magnetism	18
Miles on Horse's Foot and Horse Shoeing	37
——— on Horse's Teeth and Stables	37
Mill (J.) on the Mind	10
——— (J. S.) on Liberty	9
——— Subjection of Women	9
——— on Representative Government	9
——— Utilitarianism	9
——'s Autobiography	7
——— Dissertations and Discussions	9
——— Essays on Religion &c.	28
——— Hamilton's Philosophy	9
——— System of Logic	9
——— Political Economy	9
——— Unsettled Questions	9
Miller's Elements of Chemistry	24
——— Inorganic Chemistry	19
Minto's (Lord) Life and Letters	7
Mitchell's Manual of Assaying	28
Modern Novelist's Library	34
Monsell's 'Spiritual Songs'	31
Moore's Irish Melodies, illustrated	25, 35
——— Lalla Rookh, illustrated	25, 35
Morant's Game Preservers	21
Morell's Elements of Psychology	11
——— Mental Philosophy	11
Müller's Chips from a German Workshop	12
Müller's Science of Language	12
——— Science of Religion	5
New Reformation, by *Theodorus*	4
New Testament, Illustrated Edition	25
Northcott's Lathes and Turning	26
O'Conor's Commentary on Hebrews	30
——— Romans	30
——— St. John	30
Owen's Comparative Anatomy and Physiology of Vertebrate Animals	20
Packe's Guide to the Pyrenees	33
Pattison's Casaubon	7
Payen's Industrial Chemistry	26
Pewtner's Comprehensive Specifier	39
Pierce's Chess Problems	38
Plunket's Travels in the Alps	32
Pole's Game of Whist	38
Prendergast's Mastery of Languages	15
Present-Day Thoughts, by A. K. H. B.	14
Proctor's Astronomical Essays	17
——— Moon	17
——— Orbs around Us	17
——— Other Worlds than Ours	17
——— Saturn	17
——— Scientific Essays (New Series)	20
——— Sun	17
——— Transits of Venus	16
——— Two Star Atlases	17
——— Universe	16
Public Schools Atlas	16
——— Modern Geography	16
——— Ancient Geography	16
Rawlinson's Parthia	5
——— Sassanians	5
Recreations of a Country Parson	13
Redgrave's Dictionary of Artists	25
Reilly's Map of Mont Blanc	32
——— Monte Rosa	33
Reresby's Memoirs	7
Reynardson's Down the Road	36
Rich's Dictionary of Antiquities	15
River's Rose Amateur's Guide	22
Rogers's Eclipse of Faith	29
——— Defence of Eclipse of Faith	29
——— Essays	9
Roget's Thesaurus of English Words and Phrases	14
Ronald's Fly-Fisher's Entomology	37
Rothschild's Israelites	30
Russell on the Christian Religion	6
——'s Recollections and Suggestions	2
Sandars's Justinian's Institutes	10
Savile on Apparitions	13
——— on Primitive Faith	29

Schellen's Spectrum Analysis	18
Scott's Lectures on the Fine Arts	24
—— Poems	24
—— Papers on Civil Engineering	28
Seaside Musing, by A. K. H. B.	13
Seebohm's Oxford Reformers of 1498	3
—— Protestant Revolution	6
Sewell's Passing Thoughts on Religion	31
—— Preparation for Communion	31
—— Stories and Tales	34
—— Thoughts for the Age	31
Shelley's Workshop Appliances	19
Short's Church History	6
Simpson's Meeting the Sun	32
Smith's (Sydney) Essays	12
—— Life and Letters	8
—— Miscellaneous Works	12
—— Wit and Wisdom	12
—— (Dr. R. A.) Air and Rain	18
Southey's Doctor	13
—— Poetical Works	35
Stanley's History of British Birds	26
Stephen's Ecclesiastical Biography	8
Stirling's Secret of Hegel	11
—— Sir *William Hamilton*	11
Stonehenge on the Dog	36
—— on the Greyhound	36
Sunday Afternoons at the Parish Church of a University City, by A. K. H. B.	13
Supernatural Religion	31
Swinbourne's Picture Logic	10
Taylor's History of India	3
—— Manual of Ancient History	6
—— Manual of Modern History	6
—— *(Jeremy)* Works, edited by *Eden*	31
Text-Books of Science	20
Thomson's Laws of Thought	11
Thorpe's Quantitative Analysis	19
—— and *Muir's* Qualitative Analysis	19
Todd (A.) on Parliamentary Government	2
—— and *Bowman's* Anatomy and Physiology of Man	24
Trench's Realities of Irish Life	12
Trollope's Barchester Towers	36
—— Warden	36
Tyndall's American Lectures on Light	20
—— Belfast Address	19
—— Diamagnetism	20
—— Fragments of Science	19
—— Lectures on Electricity	20
—— Lectures on Light	20
—— Lectures on Sound	20
—— Heat a Mode of Motion	20
—— Molecular Physics	20
Ueberweg's System of Logic	11
Ure's Dictionary of Arts, Manufactures, and Mines	27
Warburton's Edward the Third	6
Watson's Geometry	19
Watts's Dictionary of Chemistry	24
Webb's Objects for Common Telescopes	18
Weinhold's Experimental Physics	19
Wellington's Life, by *Gleig*	8
Whately's English Synonymes	14
—— Logic	11
—— Rhetoric	11
White and *Donkin's* English Dictionary	15
—— and *Riddle's* Latin Dictionaries	15
Wilcocks's Sea-Fisherman	36
Williams's Aristotle's Ethics	10
Willis's Principles of Mechanism	26
Willoughby's (Lady) Diary	34
Wood's Bible Animals	22
—— Homes without Hands	21
—— Insects at Home	21
—— Insects Abroad	21
—— Out of Doors	21
—— Strange Dwellings	21
Yonge's English-Greek Lexicons	15, 16
—— Horace	35
Youatt on the Dog	36
—— on the Horse	36
Zeller's Socrates	5
—— Stoics, Epicureans, and Sceptics	5

Spottiswoode & Co., Printers, New-street Square, London.